ALL NEW!

SQUARE FOOT GARDENING

~4TH EDITION~

Quarto.com

© 2025 Quarto Publishing Group USA Inc.

First Published in 2025 by Cool Springs Press,
an imprint of The Quarto Group,
100 Cummings Center, Suite 265-D, Beverly, MA 01915, USA.
T (978) 282-9590 F (978) 283-2742

29 28 27 26 25   1 2 3 4 5

ISBN: 978-0-7603-8893-8

Digital edition published in 2025
eISBN: 978-0-7603-8894-5

Library of Congress Cataloging-in-Publication Data available.

Contributing editor: Lisa Munniksma

Book development: Vanessa Gotthainer and Kateryna Horbach
Build manager: Dan Brennan
Project photographer: Angelo Merendino
Design: Landers Miller Design, LLC
Cover Image: Angelo Merendino
Page Layout: Sylvia McArdle
Photography: Angelo Merendino, except those courtesy of Square Foot Gardening Foundation (pages 8–14, 19, 21, 23–32, 33 [top], 35, 36 [top], 37–43, 47, 48, 51, 52, 57 [top], 58, 59, 61, 62, 64–67, 75, 78, 84, 91–93, 99, 102, 108, 110, 111 [bottom], 112, 113, 124, 138, 139, 142, 144, 145 [top], 147, 149 [bottom], 150 [bottom], 152 [top], 153, 154, 162–169, 174, 176, 179, 180, 182, 190, 195–199, 204, 205 [top], 208, 210 [left], 211–216, 217 [top], 218, 222, 224, 225 [top], 226 [top], 227 [right], 229–233, 236 [right], 238, 240, 242, 243); JLY Gardens (pages 6, 20, 205 [bottom], 206, 217 [bottom], 219 [bottom], 234 [bottom], 235, 236 [left], 237, 241); Shutterstock (pages 140, 145 [bottom], 185, 186, 188, 189, 219 [top], 220, 234 [top])
Illustration: Zoe Naylor
Models: Sarah Beasley, Grayson Brennan, Samuel Jordan, Shareen Jordan, Shawn Kenney, Avelyn Klug, Richelle Klug, Brayden Leasure, Tamiya Martin, James McDaid, Shayla McGee, Jason Mileto, Jason Morris, Nikole Newberry, Joseph Watkins

Printed in China

ALL NEW!

SQUARE FOOT GARDENING

—4TH EDITION—

The World's Most Popular Growing Method to Harvest More Food from Less Space

SQUARE FOOT GARDENING FOUNDATION

COOL SPRINGS PRESS

Contents

Dedication

The delight of growing your own fresh food is something that can be enjoyed by all. At the Square Foot Gardening Foundation, we want to make gardening an easy, successful, and accessible activity that is shared throughout the world.

This fourth edition of *All New Square Foot Gardening* is dedicated to all of the passionate Square Foot Gardening enthusiasts who've made this work their own. It's also a nod of sincere gratitude to the Foundation's dedicated volunteers who spread the SFG principles far and wide.

As Mel would say, "Happy gardening, friends."

Foreword

In my early twenties, I was lost and confused with no clue where to take my life. I spent most of my time playing competitive video games, in which I sadly wasn't very competitive. Nonetheless, it took up inordinate amounts of my time and only contributed to a further sense of desperation and lack of direction in my life.

As a self-professed nerd, I was always into computers—having tinkered with building little websites in my teenage years.

To generate some income later on in my life, I started back building websites again, and one day I responded to an advertisement looking for "someone to help with a gardening non-profit website." I wasn't a gardener at the time, and I was barely a competent web designer, but I threw my hat in the ring all the same.

As luck would have it, a man named Mel Bartholomew responded to my email and asked if I could meet him. Nervously, I arrived at his home and met Mel, then in his late seventies, sitting at a small wooden desk, sipping on tea with honey and eating from a plate of small cookies. He explained

he was the author of a book called *Square Foot Gardening* that had helped many millions learn to garden, and he needed help spreading that mission further with his non-profit, the Square Foot Gardening Foundation.

I worked directly with Mel for about a year, and in that time I myself became captivated by the wondrous craft of gardening, specifically growing your own food at home. The approach Mel took in demystifying gardening in his book was perfect for me, a non-gardener who didn't grow up learning from anyone with any expertise. In many ways, that book and Mel's tutelage changed my life forever.

You see, over ten years later, I now run a company called Epic Gardening, with a similar goal to Mel's—to teach the world to grow. Over the years, we have become one of the largest voices in gardening education in the world. The lessons I learned over that year working with Mel taught me not only how to grow delicious produce at home, but how to think about life and business. How to communicate so that you're

understood. How to create works that people connect to, that inspire them, and that change their lives for the better.

So, as you thumb through this fourth edition of Mel's seminal work, I hope it does for you what it did for me: unlock a lifelong passion for growing your own food, reconnecting to nature, and the multitude of other benefits that becoming a gardener bestows upon your life. Trust me when I say that you have no idea the richness gardening can bring to your life.

Good luck in the garden and keep on growing.

Kevin Espiritu
Founder, Epic Gardening

Memoriam

This book would be incomplete without honoring Mel Bartholomew himself. The Square Foot Gardening Method would not be available to home gardeners if not for his forward-thinking approach to growing more food in less space.

An engineer by training, Mel was a novice gardener. After his retirement in the early 1970s, he was excited about growing nutritious fresh vegetables for his family. At his local community garden Mel became frustrated with the wasted space, resources, and energy involved in traditional row gardening. By mid-summer, few gardeners showed up to maintain their unkempt, overgrown plots, and he knew there had to be a better way. Mel's engineering mind led him first to design a 12-foot-by-12-foot garden plot and then to divide that further into 4-foot-by-4-foot raised beds with 1-foot grid squares, giving us the efficient system used by millions of gardeners today.

As Mel's enthusiasm for his Square Foot Gardening Method grew, the technique caught on and led to his original instructional book, *Square Foot Gardening: A New Way to Garden in Less Space with Less Work*, in 1981, and then a nationally syndicated television series on PBS and the Discovery Channel. Since then, three more editions of the original book have been published, as well as related books on cooking, growing for profit, and Square Foot Gardening with kids.

Mel Bartholomew passed away in 2016, and his legacy continues to shape our gardening endeavors, serving as inspiration for us all.

1

An Introduction to Square Foot Gardening

For more than four decades, millions of people have looked to Square Foot Gardening (SFG) as a simple, common-sense, and fun approach to gardening. In backyards and front yards, on patios and rooftops, at community centers and schools, SFG beds produce abundant fruits, vegetables, herbs, and flowers.

Growing food in long rows works for large-scale vegetable operations because they use tractors and other farming equipment. For anyone interested in growing food for themselves and their families as a hobby or a pursuit in sustainability, the SFG Method shows another way—a more efficient means of growing more food in less space with more enjoyment and success. By giving plants the space they need to grow—no more, no less—and providing them with a rich growing medium and the right amount of moisture, they'll offer up the harvest you've always hoped for.

About the Fourth Edition

The fourth edition of *All New Square Foot Gardening* is being released more than forty years after the SFG Method was established. In it, you will learn, step-by-step how to grow a great garden using this time-tested technique. This book incorporates important feedback and addresses many of the questions that the SFG Foundation has received from SFG users over the years, and it brings in tips, techniques, and thinking from recent decades of gardening innovation—making it the most complete and accessible edition yet. The focus of this book is on being flexible and making your garden your own while staying rooted in the principles of the SFG Method.

The information here is backed by research and experience. You'll find examples of how the SFG Method is used in various situations, get ideas for your own SFG crop plans, move step-by-step through DIY building plans for SFG beds and accessories that are easily customized to fit your growing space, learn how to plant in and harvest from a SFG bed, and more. Throughout are glossary terms, photos depicting SFG beds in use, and options for how you can make the SFG Method work in your situation.

Follow the SFG principles and you'll have a productive and beautiful edible garden.

The SFG Method takes gardening to a new level of efficiency by:

- Reducing space requirements, doing away with in-garden, weed-filled walkways, and producing more in several square feet than you would in the same area of a row garden.
- Conserving water, delivering water directly to the plants that need it and not to the unused areas in between rows and planting areas.
- Using fewer seeds, planting only what you need and requiring minimum plant thinning.
- Doing away with food waste, growing only what you want to eat in the quantity you want to eat it.
- Consuming fewer resources, eliminating costly and unnecessary fertilizers.
- Saving time and energy, getting rid of the endless to-do list of weeding, tilling, watering large areas, and more.

For beginning gardeners, the SFG Method is a great place to start without becoming overwhelmed by the effort that can go into growing food. For seasoned gardeners, a switch to the SFG Method means more flexibility in how and what you grow, giving you more food in less time and space. And for anyone who wants a beautiful landscape, the SFG Method adds to a yard's aesthetic appeal with a lovely raised-bed box, trellises, and "top hat" stacked boxes that enhance visual interest. (It goes without saying that the range of colors, shapes, and textures of leaves, flowers, and fruits contained in a garden box is a landscaping element unto itself.)

The SFG Method was developed over years of trial and error. Throughout that time, 10 principles have remained true. These form the backbone of the garden that you're about to create:

SFG Principles

Plant in squares. Using 1-square-foot grid squares is the most efficient way to plant, and the grid is essential to the SFG Method. Plant for abundance with the basic and most used 1-, 4-, 9-, and 16-plant spacing strategy SFG is known for—and occasionally with one plant per two or more squares for very large vegetables.

Plant densely. You can grow a lot of produce in less space than you might think. The size of the plant at maturity guides how many plants you can fit into one square-foot space. You don't want empty space between plants. That space is wasted in a SFG bed.

Be sparing with seeds. The SFG Method uses simple plant-spacing guidelines and doesn't ask you to overseed your garden. Use the seeds you need, and thin out very few plants when multiple seeds germinate.

Rotate crops. Crop rotation happens almost without thought in a SFG bed. Thanks to your gardening plan, you'll know what plants were growing in each square each season, and you can change that up when it comes time to replant those squares.

Grow up. Vining plants take up too much space if left to sprawl across a SFG bed. Growing up a trellis or other supports, vining plants can grow and produce as they are meant to without requiring so much space. You have lots of options for building your own or purchasing a trellis to support your beans, tomatoes, melons, and more.

Use Mel's Mix, not garden soil. The Mel's Mix growing medium recipe is a result of years of formulation to achieve optimum plant nutrition, soil friability, and water retention. As opposed to garden soil, which contains weed seeds, tends to be heavy, and may have only marginal nutritional value, Mel's Mix offers plants the conditions they need to thrive—and you know exactly what your plants are growing in.

Grow shallow. Raised beds that are more than about 6 to 8 inches deep are unnecessary for growing most garden crops. Growing in a shallower bed conserves the resources that go into Mel's Mix and the water needed to keep it moist.

Stop using fertilizer. The combination of composts in Mel's Mix provides all the nutrients your plants need. Each time you replant a grid square, you add a little compost to replenish those nutrients, and that's it.

Garden where it's most convenient. A garden that you look at every day is one that you'll pay the most attention to. Putting a SFG bed outside your door is ideal but certainly not always possible. Look for the spot that's most convenient, receives adequate sun, and makes the most sense to you.

Maintain narrow aisles. Between your SFG boxes, a 3-foot aisle gives you room to work and gives your plants room to grow over the sides. Anything wider than 3 feet is unnecessary empty space; anything narrower will be difficult to work in.

Throughout this book, you'll learn about how these ten principles are put into practice in the SFG Method. The next chapter offers a quick-start summary of the eight steps that will lead you from thinking about growing in a SFG bed to harvesting and enjoying fresh vegetables and herbs from one. Each subsequent chapter then dives deeper into each of these eight steps, offering you a wealth of insight for successful growing using the SFG Method.

Place your SFG next to your patio or somewhere that's convenient and be sure you have access to the beds from at least three sides.

2

Your Square Foot Garden Quick-Start Guide

Now that you understand the principles behind the Square Foot Gardening Method, you have the background needed to simplify and amplify your gardening journey. The following eight steps outline how to use the SFG Method in your own garden. Taking this step-by-step will put the principles into practice and springboard your SFG bed into life.

What's covered in this chapter is an overview of what you can expect to find in-depth in each chapter following. If you're left with questions here, don't worry—you'll get your answers as you continue working your way through the book.

Step 1: Lay Out Your Square Foot Garden

Getting started is often the hardest part of gardening. The first step in the SFG Method asks you to envision what your garden will look like. Here, you're creating not just a place to grow food but also something beautiful for your yard, patio, balcony, or even a rooftop.

The most convenient location for any garden is close to your home, as you're more likely to pay the most attention to it there. The most convenient location isn't always the most practical, though. Ideally, your garden will have at least 6 to 8 hours of sunlight and good drainage—not too much shade or pooling water. In laying out your garden, also consider the microclimates created by walls, high spots, and wind tunnels and how these will boost or challenge your growing efforts.

Get out paper and a pencil, and draw a map of your yard, including buildings, fences, and other structures. Mark north, south, east, and west on the paper. Mark the shady spots and the spots where water pools, and then sketch your SFG bed in the place that makes the most sense for your situation. This same exercise is useful when working with a patio, balcony, or rooftop as your growing space.

If you're new to gardening, begin with a traditional SFG design: 4 foot x 4 foot, divided into a grid of 16 total growing squares. Once you're more confident in using this system, you won't be held to the traditional box configuration. One of the joys of the SFG Method is that, while you're given clear principles and steps to follow, the simple design allows you to use your creativity in laying out a growing space you'll love. Add to your growing space and change up the design. Just be sure to keep the grid, and don't make your bed wider than 4 feet for ease of reaching the middle squares. Having access to the box from all sides via a 3-foot-wide pathway is helpful, too.

Chapter 3 dives into this topic more extensively.

Microclimate

A microclimate is the distinct climate of a small area, such as that on the west side of a wall, in the shade of a shrub, or behind a windbreak.

Step 2: Plan Your Square Foot Garden

A companion step to laying out your garden is planning what to put in it. Planning is a great activity for the off season, while you're in garden-dreaming mode.

You may find planning a SFG bed is less intimidating than planning a traditional garden that's laid out in straight rows. On a piece of paper, draw your garden grid. Starting out your SFG experience with one 16-square-foot bed, you'll draw a 4-square by 4-square garden grid, for a total of sixteen planting squares. This grid will act as your garden roadmap.

Decide what crop you'd like to plant in each square. The number of plants in each square depends on the size of the plant. The math has already been done for you, so you know how many of each type of plant to put in each square. Some squares will hold just one large plant, such as cabbage or broccoli; four medium plants, including parsley and lettuce; nine small plants, such as beets or bush beans; or as many as sixteen extra-small plants, like carrots or radishes. There are also some extra-large plants that spread over two or more squares. See page 54 for an illustrated listing of which vegetable plants fit into each of these size and spacing categories.

Depending on the crop's growing preferences, you may plant and harvest early, and then plant a different crop in that same square again later in the same season. Radishes (a spring crop) followed by bush beans (a summer crop) is a good example of this succession planting. Other plants— like oregano, a perennial—might take up that same square for the entire year or for several years. By the time you're finished with this planning step, you'll understand how many and what kind of seeds or transplants you will need for each square, and at what time you should plant and harvest your crops.

See chapter 4 for complete details on planning your SFG.

> "
>
> **Succession Planting**
> *Succession planting is a strategy of staggering the planting of crops or planting crop varieties that mature at different times to have a continuous harvest.*

Step 3: Build Your SFG Box and Grid

This is the first of two construction steps in the SFG Method. Before you can grow anything, you need to build your SFG box. This raised bed is integral to the SFG Method for a few reasons. Constructed in square-foot dimensions—4 feet by 4 feet is the traditional size you may want to start with—the SFG box supports the grid in which you'll grow your plants and contains the Mel's Mix growing medium.

A basic SFG box sits flat and level on the ground. You can also elevate the box to allow easier access for gardeners with limited mobility and those who use mobility devices such as walkers or wheelchairs, to match your landscaping aesthetic, or to meet the needs of your outdoor space.

A SFG box doesn't need to be deep. Most vegetables, herbs, and flowers can grow in about 6 to 8 inches of growing medium, as long as their roots can spread wide. You can make a bed deeper than this, though you'll be spending more money than necessary to fill it with Mel's Mix.

In addition to building your SFG box in this step, you also need to build your grid. Without this structure to guide your plant spacing, you could end up with overcrowded plants or wasted space—think of a parking lot with no spaces marked.

Options for building beds and grids range from those requiring a power drill to those that need no tools at all. Some boxes can be built indoors and moved to the garden site, while others—the elevated beds, in particular—are best built in place. Whichever way you build your box and grid, have this work done before it's time to put your seeds and transplants into the garden so you don't waste a moment of the growing season. Chapter 5 offers building plans and ideas for constructing your bed and grid.

Step 4: Build Your SFG Box Accessories

While you can grow a nice garden in a SFG box on its own, smart and often-simple accessories can yield healthier plants with more productivity. Assembling these garden add-ons is the second of two construction steps in the SFG Method. There are several different types of accessories you can use to make growing easier in your SFG box.

Protective covers serve a range of purposes, from insect and animal exclusion to season extension. As birds, rodents, and insect pests discover the treasures growing in your SFG bed, add-on cages can keep your crops safe. These accessories can also help create a beneficial microclimate, get the spring growing season started a few weeks early, provide shade for cool-weather crops, and extend the harvest of fresh vegetables into the late fall.

Trellises and various other stakes and supports provide space and structure for vining crops to grow vertically.

Top hat boxes add depth to the Mel's Mix in individual squares to give root crops the ability to grow deeper.

Both trellis and top hat accessories bring depth to your landscape, as well. This book discusses these accessories and many others, along with how to properly use them.

The many possible add-ons for a SFG bed is one area where the flexibility of the SFG Method is evident. You can use the accessories you want and leave behind those that don't meet your needs or your style. Look at your SFG plans for the year, and consider which box add-ons will most benefit those plans.

Assemble your accessories in the off season—before you need them. This level of preparation means you get a jump on the growing season and allows you to stay ahead of the insects and animals that want to share your garden. Plus, you'll want to install your trellis and growing supports before your plants get too big.

Chapters 5 and 6 offer extensive plans and information on building SFG beds and accessories.

Friable Soil

Friable soil is loose, crumbly, workable soil. Friability makes it easy for plant roots, air, and water to move through the growing medium, promoting healthy plant growth and maintaining good moisture content throughout.

Step 5: Fill Your SFG Box

The growing medium you use in your SFG box makes all the difference. Mel's Mix is not just some bagged raised-bed potting mix. This growing medium is specially formulated to support plant health and productivity. It's a nice growing medium to work with as a gardener, too, because it doesn't require heavy digging, turning, or tilling. Plus, there are no synthetic additives or fertilizers in Mel's Mix.

Mel's Mix consists of one-third compost, one-third peat moss, and one-third coarse vermiculite. To make this mix, you need a measuring vessel—a 5-gallon bucket is a good choice—a wheelbarrow or tarp for combining ingredients, and a source of water. From here, you fill your SFG box, put the grid on top, keep the mix hydrated, and start planting.

Each ingredient can be sourced from home-improvement and garden-supply stores or from online sources. The compost component can also come from your very own food and garden scraps. In fact, the most valuable compost is the compost you make at home. Compost provides plants with the nutrition they need for growth and productivity.

The peat moss ingredient lightens the Mel's Mix, improves friability, and boosts water-holding and water-draining ability. Coarse vermiculite is similar, boosting aeration and excess-water drainage.

Mel's Mix ingredient sourcing and mixing takes some effort and intention, but you don't have to do it each season. It's only necessary to fill your SFG box with Mel's Mix once. As you harvest crops from your grid squares, you'll add back compost to replace the nutrients that plants used. Every few years, you'll top up the Mel's Mix to bring it back to its original depth.

Reference chapter 7 for more details on creating Mel's Mix and calculating how much you'll need to fill your bed.

Step 6: Plant According to Your SFG Plan

With your SFG plan in one hand and a trowel in the other, your SFG bed is on the cusp of producing fresh food throughout the seasons, and you are mere weeks away from your first harvest.

In the planning step, you get to select the right varieties for your taste and climate. Start some of your own seeds indoors ahead of the garden season, source your transplants locally, and/or direct seed crops when appropriate. The readily available

nutrition in, and the friability of, the Mel's Mix, plus the sun-soaked warmth of Mel's Mix in the raised bed, will set up plants for quick growth early in the season.

It's in this step that the purpose of the grid becomes most evident. While the grid structure sitting atop the Mel's Mix looks like empty boxes on a garden bed to start out, once you populate it with your plants and seeds, the whole plan comes to life. Go back to your SFG plan to divide your squares into 1, 4, 9, or 16 spaces (or, occasionally, spacing 1 extra-large veggie per multiple squares) based on the seeds and plants you've chosen. Follow the spacing guidelines found on page 54 to draw lines in the Mel's Mix to easily see how this spacing

works out, and put in your plants and seeds accordingly.

Because crops mature faster in a SFG bed and you've already prepared your garden for the change of seasons with season-extension add-ons, you'll rotate crops through your succession-planting plan like a pro in no time. Out comes the lettuce, in go the peppers, and in a few months, you'll have radishes in that grid square—growing more food in less space than you ever have before.

Visit chapter 8 for deeper insight into SFG planting and spacing techniques.

Step 7: Maintain Your SFG Bed

The SFG Method is a less labor-intensive means of growing food and flowers than traditional row gardening. Some maintenance tasks that you won't ever have to deal with are tilling and weeding. The occasional weed can be easily plucked out. You do still have a basic to-do list: watering, season extension, pollinator support, general tidying, and pest and disease control, among the tasks.

Watering a garden the size of a SFG box doesn't take much time or water. Mel's Mix is formulated to retain moisture, and when you deliver water directly to the plants' root zones—by hose, watering can, or drip irrigation—you're making the most efficient use of water resources.

Thanks to the nutrition and root support provided by Mel's Mix, your plants are set up for strong, healthy growth. When insect pests and signs of plant disease show up, your SFG bed is small enough that you can deal with them quickly and with little effort. Chemical control is a last-resort means of doing away with pests and disease in a SFG bed. Rely instead on optimum plant health, pruning out disease issues before they get out of hand, and removing pest insects as soon as you notice them.

Another maintenance task comes with the change of seasons in setting up and managing season-extension accessories.

Mulch, shade cloth, cold frames, row cover, and greenhouse plastic are tools that can allow you to enjoy a harvest from your SFG bed throughout the year.

And your garden will be better off with a strong pollinator population. As you get to know the pollinators that visit your space, you'll also get to know how to keep them coming back. When your pollinator population isn't able to do its job, it's possible for you to step in and pollinate some flowers by hand (see page 205).

Maintaining your SFG is covered in detail in chapter 9. You'll find troubleshooting advice in chapter 11.

Step 8: Harvest from Your SFG Bed

Each step in the SFG Method leads you on a journey toward your harvest. Because you planned for maximum crop production with your garden planning in Step 2, you'll have crops to harvest throughout most of the year. The design of the SFG box—no more than 4 feet across—allows you to easily reach your crops for harvest.

In this last step, you come to recognize that leafy greens can be picked at any stage of growth, but beans, eggplant, and peppers require patience. The time it takes between planting and harvesting varies not just by crop—radishes are ready in a few weeks, whereas broccoli takes a few months—but by variety, weather conditions, climate, length of daylight, and more.

The care you take in handling your produce during and after harvesting is as important as the care you took in tending it throughout its growth. Harvesting early in the day, before the heat or sun can cause wilting, and immediate cooling leads to the longest storage life. Storage conditions vary for each type of crop you grow, with leafy greens preferring cold, moist refrigeration; tomatoes wanting to sit on the countertop; and winter squash needing warmth for curing and then cool conditions for long-term keeping. Getting the storage conditions right allows you to keep and enjoy your fresh food longer.

When you've grown enough food to preserve for future use, you can process it by pickling, fermenting, canning, dehydrating, or freezing. These methods mean you can have a taste of spring asparagus in the fall, a cup of calendula tea in the dead of winter, and a crisp dill pickle any time of year.

For the full scoop on harvesting, please visit chapter 10.

With the eight steps outlined in mind, it's now time to get your SFG journey started.

3

Choosing a Site for Your Square Foot Garden

Choosing the right location for your Square Foot Garden bed is the first step in the Square Foot Gardening process. Whether you're growing in the city, the country, or somewhere in between, there's an ideal location for your SFG. Once your SFG box is filled with Mel's Mix, it will be too heavy to move, so this first step is an important one.

In this chapter, you'll learn the characteristics of a good garden spot, learn how to map your space and its sunlight and shadows, learn about microclimates, learn to dig into your region's weather conditions, and learn about SFGs beyond the boundaries of a typical yard.

The Right Site

The right location can make or break your gardening plans. So often, people want to rush to put in a garden so they can start growing plants. In the long run, it pays to be intentional about where you locate your SFG bed.

The ideal SFG location has several characteristics:

- It is close to your house.
- It is sunny, with at least 6 to 8 hours of sunlight each day.
- It doesn't compete for space with trees and large shrubs.
- It is on level ground.
- It has good water drainage and movement away from the area.
- It is near a water source.
- Its microclimate works in your garden's favor.

Proximity to your house

Placing your garden close to your home—ideally close to the door you most often use to come and go—keeps your garden front of mind. Not that you'll forget about the beautiful flowers and delicious foods you're growing, but you can appreciate them more when you see them all the time. Witnessing your garden as it changes every day teaches you a lot about different types of plants, how they grow, and what they need from you. Passing by the SFG bed regularly makes it easy to pick a few peppers on your way inside to make dinner or to help a cucumber plant find its bearings on a trellis on your way out for a walk. A garden closer to the home is less likely to attract wildlife and neighborhood animals, as well.

Of course, if your only option for a SFG bed is in the back corner of your yard, at a friend's house, in a community garden, or in another location away from where you live, installing it there is better than not installing it at all. Regardless of how near or far your SFG bed is from your door, you'll be visiting it often for regular tending and harvesting.

Full sun is essential for most vegetables so choose your SFG's location carefully.

A spot close to the house affords easier access to a water source and makes harvesting from your SFG a snap.

The shade spectrum

Sunny patches can be hard to come by in urban, suburban, and wooded places, yet sunlight is essential for crop production. Through photosynthesis, plants absorb light, carbon dioxide, and water to create energy for themselves—not to mention releasing oxygen for the rest of us.

Some plants do better than others with limited sun. (See Sample Garden Plan 1: Shade Garden on page 69 for an example of a vegetable-and-herb garden located in partial sun.) Edible plants that fare better with less sun are mostly leafy greens, which are also cool-season vegetables. In fact, partial sun can allow you to grow cool-season crops during the hotter times of year. It's the warm-season plants that produce fruits—tomatoes, peppers, cucumbers, etc.—that really need at least 6 to 8 hours a day of direct sunlight.

Not all sunlight is created equal. Morning sunlight, while the sun is still low, is less harsh than afternoon sunlight, when the sun is high in the sky. In the mid- to late afternoon, the sun's rays can cause sunscald on fruits like tomatoes and peppers, just like they can sunburn your skin. If you have the option of choosing between morning shade and afternoon shade, go for the afternoon shade.

Exposure to direct sun changes throughout the seasons. The sun is lower in the sky in early spring and late fall, but there are fewer leaves on the trees in most places. The sun is higher in the sky during the summer, but heavy leaf cover can block it from reaching garden spaces. As the sun's track changes, the shadows cast by trees and structures change, as well. Pay attention to the sun and shade locations in your available area for several months before installing your SFG bed, if possible. You will collect valuable information about sun and shade through the seasons that will help with your garden positioning and planning.

Many gardens may be in the shade for a certain part of the day, but as long as they receive 6 to 8 hours of full sun during other parts of the day, most veggies will grow well.

Measuring Sun Exposure

The terms used to describe sun exposure sound similar and can be confusing. These are actual measures of sunlight used in the gardening industry:

Full sun: 6 hours or more of direct sunlight per day. This is not necessarily 6 consecutive hours of direct sunlight, but 6 total hours.

Partial sun: 4 to 6 hours of direct sunlight per day

Partial shade: 2 to 4 hours of direct sunlight per day

Full shade: Less than 2 hours of direct sunlight per day

Tree and shrub competition

There is one obvious reason why trees and shrubs don't make great garden companions—and a couple of less obvious reasons.

Trees and large shrubs cast shade. If most of your available space gets a blazing hot ten hours per day of direct sunlight in the summertime, a bit of tree shade could be welcome to block a few hours of intense afternoon rays. Many SFG growers will have the opposite problem, needing more sunlight.

While a small amount of shade could be a good thing, you can't bank on this filtered light over time. Trees and shrubs keep growing (and growing). Soon, what was a nice couple of hours of shade late in the day can turn into only a few scant hours of sunlight. Locating your SFG bed at the edge of a tree's shade footprint is a time-limited opportunity.

Trees and shrubs can take water and nutrients from your garden plants. As you water your SFG, some of the water will drain through the Mel's Mix, filtering through the landscape fabric barrier beneath it, and travel out into the ground surrounding the box. Deep tree roots and shallow shrub roots will grow toward the box in search of this water and could grow up through the landscape fabric lining the bottom of the box. If an area near trees and shrubs is your only location option, you can counter this root infiltration with a plywood box bottom (drilled with a few drainage holes) or by building an elevated SFG bed.

Trees can seed themselves into your SFG bed. Those maple whirligigs and papery elm seedpods are fun to watch in the breeze, but they can create chaos in the

Be mindful of competition from nearby trees for sunlight and soil moisture. This Square Foot Gardener will make the most of a shady situation by planting a lot of shade-tolerant greens.

garden. Seeds from trees near your SFG box are just waiting to land in soil as penetrable as Mel's Mix, which is easy for them to set root in. If this is the case you may have a lot of little tree seedlings popping up in your garden squares.

Level ground

Your SFG box should be as level as possible. A slope will cause water to drain toward the lower end of the bed by the simple rule of gravity. The Mel's Mix on the high side will dry out faster, and the Mel's Mix on the low side will retain water for longer. Finding a level spot may require soil moving—which could be anything from an easy leveling-out of a sloping yard to an actual digging out of a terrace along a hillside.

Square Foot Gardening on a Hillside

In many parts of the world, the majority of land available for growing vegetables is on hillsides.

This terrain poses drainage and erosion issues for in-ground gardens. On hillsides that are sloped but not steep—where you can still access your garden safely—a terraced SFG bed solves those problems. Terracing shortens a long slope into a series of shorter, more even steps.

You can create a flat area that's large enough for your SFG bed and a walkway on at least three sides in a few hours. This is one case where a traditional 4-foot-by-4-foot SFG box may not be ideal, depending on how much earth it would require you to move.

Create a simple terrace on a shallow slope using the cut-and-fill method:

Step 1. Locate utility lines.
Contact your region's call-before-you-dig telephone number or website to identify the location of any buried utility lines. In the United States, call 811. If your region doesn't have this service, check with your local utilities.

Step 2. Mark your project.
Measure and mark the area you want to make level.

Step 3. Remove the slope.
Using a sharp-edged shovel, cut into the hillside, leaving a 90-degree angle, to level out space along the edge of the hillside.

Step 4. Fill in the base.
Use the soil that you dug away from the hillside to fill in the foot of the slope and elongate the flat area.

Step 5. Secure the area.
To keep the fresh soil in place and make it stable enough to place a SFG box on top, reinforce the bottom side with rebar and boards or use a retaining wall if you're working with a significant slope.

Building a terraced SFG is one way to deal with a site that isn't level.

Water movement

Mel's Mix is formulated to act like a sponge, holding and retaining moisture for your plants while still allowing excess water to drain away.

Just as you don't like to have wet feet, your plants don't like to have wet roots. Plant roots need oxygen as well as water, and overwatering is as much a danger to them as underwatering. Allowing your box to sit in pooling water is also bad for wooden construction materials, decreasing the lifespan of this organic material. Plus, you're less likely to enjoy tending your SFG bed if you're sloshing in mud while walking around it.

Take the time to observe your available growing space after a heavy rain. Place your SFG bed in an area that doesn't see standing water or acts as a water channel after a heavy rain. In other words, avoid low-lying areas. If your only available growing space is in a low-lying or water-prone area, consider an elevated SFG bed.

Water sources

When seeds are germinating and transplants' roots are first becoming established in your SFG bed, "watering in" your plants to settle them in the Mel's Mix is essential. As your garden grows, plants need 1 inch of water per week for optimal production. Water isn't only for hydration. The plant roots take in certain nutrients with the water and use water as part of the process of photosynthesis.

It is nearly impossible to have a successful garden without doing some watering. Rainfall may take care of a portion of, or even most of, your watering needs, depending on the season and your local conditions. For the times when rainfall isn't enough, you need another plan. Chapter 9 covers watering techniques. What you need to think about during the planning stage is how to get the water from its source to your garden. The closer your SFG bed is to a water spigot or other potable water source, the easier it will be to keep your plants from getting thirsty.

Nearby access to water is key to successfully establishing seedlings and growing maturing plants throughout the season. You don't want to have to endlessly drag a hose in order to water your garden.

Watering In
Giving a newly planted transplant a good watering is called watering in. *It's meant to settle the plant and the roots into the soil around it.*

Microclimates

A microclimate is just as it sounds: a small area with a climate that differs from surrounding conditions. Microclimates can be as small as a few square feet and as large as a whole county. You may have heard of the urban heat island effect. That's an example of a microclimate. The generally sparse tree cover, combined with the concrete and pavement of buildings and driving surfaces, makes cities and towns hotter than their rural surrounds.

As a gardener, you can take advantage of microclimates within your growing area, allowing you to extend your garden growth further into fall, get your garden started earlier in the spring, and grow a cool-season plant in the summer or a warm-season plant in a cooler season.

Consider these common examples of microclimates and whether your available space offers any:

- **Temperature change in relation to structures.** In the northern hemisphere, the southwest side of a structure tends to be the warmest spot with heat from the sun being trapped there.
- **Elevation effects on temperature and humidity.** Lower and north-facing areas are more humid and less breezy. Cool air hangs in low spots. These are also the first areas to see frost and the last to heat up throughout the day. Higher elevations—even just at the top versus the bottom of a suburban driveway—see more wind and less humidity. South-facing slopes tend to be drier and get more sunlight in the northern hemisphere.
- **Snow creating a temporary microclimate—until it melts.** Snow insulates the soil like a blanket, protecting what's underneath from the harshest temperatures. Regular snowpack could mean a perennial plant might be able to overwinter in an area you wouldn't expect.
- **Wind tunnels between structures placed close together.** Wind can whip between a shed and a house or a shed and a tall fence, which is not ideal for plants. Windbreaks come in the form of fences and densely planted trees and shrubs interrupting the wind's direct path. When windbreaks are set back from your SFG box, these structures and plants can protect delicate seedlings and prevent your Mel's Mix from drying out.
- **Walls, boulders, and rock formations absorb heat during the day and release it at night, creating a warmer microclimate.** Heat radiating from walls, boulders, or rocks can work to your advantage but also to your disadvantage. These areas can become too warm for some plants and can also cause your Mel's Mix to dry out faster.
- **Note: Mel's Mix in a raised SFG bed warms up faster in the springtime than garden soil in the ground.** Just by using a SFG box, you're creating a microclimate to get a jump on the growing season.

You can work with your microclimates just as you do with your overall weather, using season-extension techniques, which you'll read about in chapter 9, and appropriate plant-variety choices, covered in chapter 8.

Fences, sheds, houses, walls, and other structures can create microclimates that can be very helpful to gardens, shielding them from wind or by absorbing heat during the day and releasing it at night.

Get to Know Your Climate

While this chapter focuses on the best spot to locate your SFG bed, it's important to understand the bigger picture affecting your plants—your climate.

The more you know about what to expect from your growing season, the more successful you can be in choosing your plants and setting up your SFG.

Frost Dates

The date of the average *last* frost in the spring is nearly a holiday for gardeners. While there are no guarantees as to what the weather will do, it's generally safe to start planting frost-sensitive plants (also called warm-season plants) in the garden after this date. On the flip side, the date of the average *first* frost in the fall is the day you can generally expect those warm-season crops to end their production.

The National Gardening Association offers an easy way to find frost dates by zip code at Garden.org/apps/frost-dates.

USDA Plant Hardiness Zones

The United States Department of Agriculture divides the United States into twenty-six plant hardiness zones based on the average annual extreme low temperature each region typically sees. The map is updated every ten years or so. This is useful information because many plants are described as being "perennial in Zones X and above," for plants that can survive the winter when temperatures plunge to a certain temperature.

In chapter 4, you'll learn more about the annual, perennial, and biennial life cycle of plants. This life cycle also depends partly on the particular climate the plant is growing in. Rosemary is an example of an herb that is a perennial in its native Mediterranean climate, where it can grow to 4 to 6 feet tall. The lowest temperature rosemary can tolerate depends on the variety, but most varieties will not survive long stretches of winter colder than 20°F. This means rosemary, with exceptions, is grown as a perennial in Zone 9, where temperatures generally stay above that mark, and as an annual in Zones 8 and below. (Tip: You can grow rosemary as a perennial in colder zones by digging it up and bringing it inside each winter.)

Visit PlantHardiness.ARS.USDA.gov to see the USDA Plant Hardiness Zone Map. Enter your zip code to pinpoint your USDA Plant Hardiness Zone. Other countries may have their own growing zone maps, so if you live outside of the United States, be sure to consult the hardiness zone map for your part of the world.

United States Climate Atlas

The National Centers for Environmental Information compiles daily temperature and precipitation data and turns out maps that show expected minimum temperature, maximum temperature, and precipitation by year and by month. You can even compare an area's data between different years and months. A caveat to using these maps is that it's difficult to pinpoint your exact location on the map.

Find the NCEI's climate observations at www.ncei.noaa.gov/access/climateatlas.

Other countries have similar information available. Look into the data from your department of agriculture and meteorological sources.

Regardless of what the maps say, all of this information is only a starting point. The details that matter most are those you're gathering at your own SFG bed. Your details may not always match the data, given the microclimate of your neighborhood and garden space. As you gain experience, you'll come to know your location better than any map can describe.

Gardeners who live in cold climates may have to get creative about protecting their plants. You'll learn all about season extension in chapter 9.

Map Your Space

Fitted with the knowledge of what makes an ideal SFG location, turn your attention to the space you have to work with. For simplicity's sake, this section will refer to this space as your "yard"—whether it is actually the yard around your house, a spot at a friend's house, a plot in a community garden, or somewhere else entirely. Graph paper and colored pencils are useful tools for this exercise. If you're handy with drawing software, that's a good option, too.

Draw all of the permanent and semi-permanent fixtures: your house, shed, fence, trees, shrubs, children's play equipment, driveway, sidewalk, etc. This sketch doesn't need to be perfectly to scale, but make a reasonable effort.

Observe the shadows as the sun moves throughout the day. Ideally, you will be able to do this exercise a few times throughout the year to get the full picture of how the sunlight changes across the seasons. Mark the shade on the map and whether it's morning shade, afternoon shade, or permanent shade. Different colored pencils are handy here.

Mark areas that have a slope, low-lying areas and areas of water movement, microclimates, and potable water sources.

Take everything you learned so far in this chapter and apply it to this map. If there's an area that stands out as ideal for your SFG bed, great! It's more likely that you'll have to make concessions for the ideal placement. Look at all of your options for SFG bed placement, look at the things you can change—removing a shrub you didn't like anyway, moving the kids' sandbox, adding a water spigot outside—and see if there's a compromise.

A wonderful thing about plants is that they want to grow. You will have the most success in your garden if you can put your garden in a spot that checks all of the boxes. Yet you will still have some success in less-than-perfect circumstances. Future chapters covering planning and variety selection can help with this. The important thing here is that you get started.

Before you sow a single seed, it's important to understand your climate and your space. This clever Southern, hot-climate gardener is using an arch trellis covered in a vining squash plant to help shade the plants beneath from strong sun in the summertime. In a cooler climate, this technique might result in too much shade for the plants beneath.

Before building your garden, be sure there's plenty of room to access it from at least three sides and make sure it doesn't have competition from nearby trees or shrubs.

Draw a rough map of your property, marking out the shade during different times of the day. Also indicate any slopes, areas of poor drainage, microclimates, and the location of water sources. This helps you determine where to place your SFG bed(s).

Prepare Your Space

When you've chosen your garden spot, get it ready for the SFG box. Here are a couple of tasks:

Prepare the ground. The ground beneath the SFG box doesn't need to be perfectly level, but the box needs to be stable and not too sloped. Depending on how your box is built, it's possible that uneven ground could even prevent the sides from coming together properly. Your SFG bed will be more stable if all four corners and sides are in contact with the ground.

Prepare the area around the bed. Think about how you will access your SFG bed and maintain the area around it. Consider the mobility needs of all the gardeners using this space.

Setting your SFG bed in the yard and mowing and string trimming around it is one option. Weeds can creep in from the edges, so you'll want to stay on top of keeping this area maintained.

Creating a pathway around the bed is another means of maintaining the space. An easy aisle around the bed can be made with a thick layer of wood chips. If you'd like, you can add a layer of newspaper or plain cardboard beneath the mulch to further suppress weeds. The wood chips provide an attractive, mud-free walkway. Don't allow grass or weed seedlings to take root there. You may need to pull weeds—they should be shallow rooted and easy to pull—and add new wood chips once a year.

It's possible to create an entire landscape around your SFG box, too, with brick pavers or stone pathways. There's no limit to the ways you can work your SFG bed into your vision for your dream yard.

Year 2 and Beyond

It's so important that you start small in your first year with a SFG bed. One 16-square-foot SFG box is a great introduction to this method of growing plants. When you gain confidence with the SFG Method, you may want to put in another box. The same location requirements and mapping exercise will be useful to you here.

Aisles

Adding a second bed brings in the need for planned aisles between the beds. Assuming your SFG beds are located nearby one another, you need enough space to maneuver and work around them. Give yourself 3 feet between beds.

If you have a small area to work in, you will be tempted to put them closer together. Less than 3 feet makes it difficult to squat down, lay out your plantings, harvest items, and move around the larger plants that may have overflowed into the aisle space. You will be more comfortable working in your SFG bed—and therefore more likely to work in your SFG bed—with the appropriate space to maneuver around it comfortably.

Having nice, wide aisles (but not too wide!) between multiple beds provides easy access. 3-foot wide aisles make maneuvering around the garden easy and efficient.

SFG beds can be made in any size, as long as it can be divided into square feet. They can be at ground level or elevated for easy accessibility. Don't be afraid to get creative.

Bed size and shape

The ideal SFG box for the beginning SFG user is 4 feet by 4 feet square, and the advice in this book reflects this configuration. After mapping your available space, you might find a 16-square-foot box isn't going to fit—or that it worked for your first SFG box but you want to try a new shape for future boxes.

It is possible to make a SFG bed that's three squares, two squares, or even one square across to fit your area. Just don't make a bed larger than 4 feet in either its length or its width. Anything larger than that and the center becomes hard to reach. In the case of a box along a wall or fence line, which you can only access from one side, the bed should not be wider than 2 feet.

Your future SFG boxes might look like a series of single SFG boxes along porch steps, which you can build as simple boxes with plywood bottoms, or an 8-foot-by-2-foot box along a fence line. An L-shaped SFG box framing a sidewalk path or nested into the corner of a patio is lovely. For an L-shaped box, make the building process easy on yourself by constructing two separate beds and butting them up against one another. Think about the bed width needed

A basic SFG bed is 4 feet by 4 feet, a perfect width for most kids and adults to reach across to plant, tend, and harvest their garden.

to access those corner boxes if you can only reach them from one side.

A 3-foot-by-3-foot box may be more suitable for very young gardeners or those with mobility issues.

The smaller the area a SFG box covers, the less moisture-holding capacity it has. You'll likely find that a long, narrow box needs more frequent watering than a larger square or rectangular box.

Bed placement

Adding a SFG bed and the tall plants that come with it has the potential to add more shade to your yard. Consider the amount of shade the plants and trellis of an additional SFG box will cast on your original box. Place the beds next to one another running east to west, if possible, for the best sun exposure.

SFG Beyond the Yard

A lot of would-be gardeners don't have access to whole yards, which is one reason why the SFG Method works so well. People can grow crops in a variety of circumstances with a little creative thinking.

Community gardens

Community gardens are plots of land available to residents of a community to grow their own crops. These spaces are typically organized by municipalities and non-profit organizations that see their benefits, including food access for neighborhoods lacking fresh-food choices, public spaces that encourage physical exercise and social connection, and the wider potential as outdoor classrooms. They're a great option for people without their own space to garden.

Each community garden is managed in its own way. Some offer plots for free; others for a fee. Some have strict rules about what can and cannot be grown there and the production methods used—for example, no perennial plants or only organic growing practices. You'll find community gardens that offer classes and community workdays as well as those that let each gardener work on their own. Plots come in all shapes, sizes, and locations.

Community gardens that offer long-term plot rentals may allow a gardener to build a SFG box there. There are even some community gardens already set up using SFG boxes. The SFG Method is great for community gardens because it has fewer weeds and requires less upkeep. SFG boxes also add to the attractiveness of an area.

Communal-living and gathering centers

Substance-use recovery centers, senior-living communities, health care facilities, residential academies, and other places where people live and gather together sometimes have gardens. SFG is a great tool for learning and for physical activity in these locations.

A small and easy-to-manage 3' x 3' elevated raised bed is perfect for a senior-living community or health care facility.

As people age, and in the case of injuries and impairments, it becomes harder to perform certain activities required for traditional gardening. A SFG bed's compact size makes it easy to reach into garden beds to plant and harvest. For people with limited mobility, elevated SFG boxes are ideal. The SFG Method doesn't require heavy lifting or digging, allowing gardening to remain accessible to people from a range of populations.

Annabel's Victory Garden

In 2013, Annabel O'Neill planted a seed to advance food access in Philmont, New York. Annabel, then 14 years old, built four small SFG beds and led workshops to teach kids how to grow and cook vegetables for her Girl Scouts Gold Award project that summer.

Fast forward to 2020 with communities facing mounting challenges as a result of the COVID-19 pandemic, the time was right for the non-profit Philmont Beautification, Inc. (PBI), to carry forth Annabel's vision by designing and creating a permanent Annabel's Victory Garden.

Garden-design professional Taylor Kurtz came on as lead gardener to construct and manage the 1,800-square-foot garden space with 10 4-foot-by-8-foot SFG beds and 10 2-foot-by-8-foot SFG beds. Critter control considerations had to be made, as Philmont, New York, has wildlife of all kinds roaming through the village. Under the SFG beds, metal hardware cloth keeps the burrowing pests at bay. Above ground, an attractive perimeter fence with wire mesh fencing keeps out smaller wildlife and the deer, too.

"The garden employs the Square Foot Gardening Method to maximize the yield for harvesting to supply PBI's local food programs with seasonal vegetables, herbs, and flowers. The garden additionally functions as a teaching garden for kids and families interested in learning and experiencing the benefits of the Square Foot Gardening Method and vertical growing," explains PBI executive director Sally Baker.

Taylor, who is now a SFG Certified Instructor, wasn't familiar with the SFG Method before working on Annabel's Victory Garden but now recommends it to his clients. "It's a great method for people who are beginners and for people who want to make the most out of their space," Taylor says.

Annabel's Victory Garden

Because the goal of Annabel's Victory Garden is to provide food for village residents who are food insecure, Taylor chooses crops that a lot of people like and that grow well in this USDA Zone 6a space. These include leafy greens, carrots, tomatoes, brussels sprouts, and—over beautiful arched trellises—cucumbers, squash, and an abundance of Northeaster heirloom pole beans. The garden is mostly dormant from November until May.

"Local and healthy foods for all must be a right, not a privilege, in order to ensure vibrant, healthy, and diverse communities achieve a strengthening of health equity and local resiliency," says Sally.

The organization partners with the Sylvia Center for free online cooking classes and a teen internship in the Philmont Cooperative Commercial Kitchen; the Philmont Public Library for educational programs and to host the free cooler where people can help themselves to the garden harvest; and

Tomato plants climb up trellis structures in Annabel's Victory Garden, providing fresh tomatoes to residents who are food insecure.

the Philmont Cooperative to co-create a local food system with local farmers, chefs, producers, and customer member-owners.

The Anchor Center for Blind Children

At the Anchor Center for Blind Children, in Denver, Colorado, SFG beds full of vegetables and herbs accompany sensory, pollinator, and perennial edible gardens to create an outdoor oasis and experiential space for 150 children and their families.

Horticultural therapies coordinator Kelly Mitchell explains, "Preschool, toddler, and infant groups participate in structured gardening centers where children complete a garden task that incorporates the physical, cognitive, or social/emotional goals each child is working on. We also have community gardening days where children across programs and their families have opportunities to gather, get to know one another, and work together in the garden."

In the Anchor Center greenhouse, they start seedlings in the spring, and the kids get to choose what they want to plant in their squares. Tomatoes, squash, cucumbers, beans, peas, and radishes top the favorites list.

The children get to taste the harvest, which is shared at lunch. Some of the harvest—especially flowers and herbs—is used in sensory bins so kids can explore different textures and smells. Staff and students take home the extra produce.

The Anchor Center worked with Earth Love Gardens to plan and design the garden, and both Earth Love Gardens and volunteers worked on the installation.

"We love to share the Square Foot Gardening Method with our clients to make the best utilization of the space in the garden beds we build for them," says Earth Love Gardens founder Aaron Michael.

Two 8-foot-by-3-foot SFG beds give them a total of 48 square feet for growing vegetables and flowers. Earth Love Gardens custom-designed an elevated SFG bed to allow young children who use wheelchairs to work with and experience the garden.

Kelly explains that the SFG Method is ideal for the students because many have difficulty visually assessing a whole garden bed. "Breaking it down into smaller sections and providing a physical boundary to each section gives our students the opportunity to plant our garden beds with more independence and autonomy, which often leads to more buy-in and care throughout the growing season," she says.

"It is truly incredible how much interacting with the natural world becomes a channel to help our students make immense progress toward their goals," says Kelly, who's worked with the Anchor Center since 2014 and directed their horticultural therapy program since 2021.

She has many stories of how kids have benefited from the garden program. One student, struggling socially and emotionally, came out of his shell when his sunflower seed sprouted and grew. "This experience helped him to engage socially, have something to cultivate and care for, and just have fun at school and have a reason to look forward to coming to school," Kelly says.

The gardens at The Anchor Center for Blind Children are accessible to all and provide a sense of autonomy and independence to participants.

Onalaska School Gardens

Students in Onalaska, Wisconsin, are getting a different kind of education thanks to Master Gardener Jodie Visker. She has brought the SFG Method to three elementary schools—as well as a church garden and a community garden—and she's on a mission to keep going.

Jodie says, "Square Foot Gardening gave me such a desire to garden. I was reading all these complicated books, and the Square Foot Gardening Method just turned it all around for me."

Thousands of kids have passed through the Onalaska elementary schools' gardens since the garden started in 2011. Each school garden has six 4-foot-by-4-foot SFG boxes that were built by the high school and middle school students. Jodie matched up the first-grade and third-grade curriculum with garden activities. The students experience their subject matter in a tangible way via lettuce, radishes, and spinach. They start their own seeds and then plant, care for, and harvest—and eat from—their SFG beds. Jodie, a cadre of high school student volunteers, and the Family Garden Club grow warm-weather crops in the summer and maintain the gardens all year.

One essential hurdle in school gardening in much of the United States is that the typical garden calendar runs counter to the typical school calendar. This is especially true for this school garden in USDA Zone 4 Wisconsin. Jodie thought creatively and asked the high school students to build multi-purpose cold frame structures that can be converted into crop-protection cages as the weather warms and also modi-fied to make room for a trellis for climbing plants.

Jodie also figured out how to employ the power of community to literally grow the gardens. Compost is a vital ingredient in the Mel's Mix growing medium and a science lesson unto itself. Jodie built 4-foot-by-8-foot compost bins at the schools. In the fall, a "leaf drive" brings parents to the school with bags and bins of raked-up leaves, turning the community's "waste" into the SFG beds' life source.

The children at the Onalaska School Gardens take part in numerous gardening activities.

The Court-Yard Garden

Rick Bickling's garden in Austin, Texas is proof that you don't need soil under your feet to have an abundant harvest using the SFG Method. In 2011, Rick decided he wanted to take control of his family's food choices.

With his two sons grown and their 1,000-square-foot backyard basketball court sitting unused, he turned this paved space into his garden. Today, Rick's "court-yard garden" features a greenhouse, a gazebo, and 12 SFG boxes.

"Austin is in USDA Zone 8b. One of the terrific benefits of Square Foot Gardening is that in many areas, it allows you to grow something pretty much year-round," Rick explains. He rotates crops each season, ranging from tomatoes and potatoes in spring to peppers and okra in summer, then broccoli and cabbage in the cool season. He grows a lot of the produce that his household eats, plus enough peppers and green beans to freeze; black-eyed peas and herbs to dry; and potatoes, sweet potatoes, and winter squash to eat through the winter.

"I always grow all of my own herbs and have a full bed dedicated to asparagus that, once planted, will produce for the next 30 years or so," Rick says.

He maximizes use of this SFG space with trellises for vertical growing and perimeter crop cages to protect his harvest from birds and squirrels. (Find building plans for these SFG bed add-ons in chapter 6.)

Rick is also a Square Foot Gardening Certified Instructor, and you can find his instructional videos on the SFG website (https://squarefootgardening .org/).

A former backyard basketball court is now a thriving Square Foot Garden, thanks to a little ingenuity and elbow grease.

School gardens

Farm-to-school efforts are gaining momentum, taking the form of connecting students with fresh food from local farmers and giving students their own opportunity to garden. In gardening, students can learn science, math, engineering, health, art, and mindfulness. Rarely do students realize they're being taught lessons like this because gardening is also fun. SFG beds make sense in school gardens because they're easy to maintain, the grid system is set up for mathematics, and crops grow quickly, capturing students' attention from week to week. Worldwide, school garden programs have shown gains in students' grade point average—specifically in math and science—and expansion of students' curiosity, flexibility, open-mindedness, informed skepticism, creativity, and critical thinking.

Paved space

The SFG box is a container that holds your growing medium, meaning you don't need to have soil below your feet to grow food in a SFG. If your yard is shaded but your driveway is not, or if you live in a townhome and have a driveway but no yard, put a SFG box in your driveway. Same goes for one on a sidewalk space or a patio.

SFG boxes can add beauty to outdoor spaces. While you can—and should—plant flowers and vegetables, herbs are also beautiful in their own right. Many of these plants produce flowers, and herbs, especially, add lovely fragrance to an area.

Balconies, decks, and porches

Where suburban and urban dwellers may lack a yard, their balconies, decks, and porches can fit a SFG box's location requirements. You may have to adjust the SFG box measurements to be able to put both yourself and your SFG bed on the balcony at the same time.

These structures are located above ground, so be sure the base can handle the weight of a SFG box full of wet Mel's Mix. You're looking at more than 300 pounds of wet growing medium, plus the weight of the bed's building materials. That's a lot of mass for a 16-square-foot area. Also be sure to follow any necessary rules from your community or homeowner association before beginning your garden.

Rooftops

Rooftops abound in cities and towns around the world. In New York City alone, rooftops cover about 40,000 acres. There's room for a few thousand SFG boxes up there.

If this sounds like a great idea, there are a few things you should know before sneaking a SFG bed onto the roof of your apartment building. First, check with your planning and zoning ordinances to be sure a rooftop garden is legal. Second, get permission from the building owner. Third, get confirmation that the roof has the load-bearing capacity to handle the weight of a SFG box full of wet Mel's Mix. Fourth, ensure you will have regular—and safe—access to the roof to tend your SFG bed.

There are a few downsides to rooftop gardening. You have to carry the lumber and growing medium up there to build and fill your SFG box. You have to sort out a water source, which might involve carrying a bucket up the stairs. And you probably have to contend with a lot of direct sunlight on a potentially hot rooftop surface. If these are inconveniences you think you can work around, a rooftop is a great spot for a SFG.

Balconies, decks, porches, and patios make great spaces for SFG adventures.

If all you have is a small apartment terrace, don't fret! You still have room for a SFG.

The Rooftop Gardens of Sheikh Zayed City

In cities, backyards are hard to come by. Backyards with good sun exposure are harder still.

In Sheikh Zayed City, Egypt, Square Foot Gardening Certified Instructor Mustafa Sayed decided to put his garden where there's plenty of sun exposure—on the roof. "Square Foot Gardening is suitable for urban farming because it's very space efficient. Most of my work and my projects are at houses where you don't get very much space," Mustafa says.

On some rooftops, Mustafa can install multiple SFG beds to grow all kinds of vegetables and herbs. In Sheikh Zayed City, the weather is very hot in summer, and the crops they can grow during that time are limited. The rest of the year, the temperatures are mild—they never get frost—and plants grow bountifully.

Mustafa opened his Foodscape edible landscaping business in 2020 and his GrowPro garden center in 2023. Both businesses give him the chance to host workshops and educate people about Square Foot Gardening, among other topics that aren't widely taught in Egypt. At the garden center, Mustafa has SFG demonstration gardens consisting of beds of all sizes, and he's been asked to install more SFG beds around other areas of the shopping center because they're beautiful.

He was already working as a professional gardener before he learned about the SFG Method. "I saw the change that happened in our business, and to

The rooftop gardens of Sheikh Zayed City in Egypt are a marvel of Square Foot Gardening.

me personally, as well. I never had the confidence to teach and educate others about gardening before SFG. It gave me the push to start teaching. Now I have a different method to offer to people," Mustafa says.

Mustafa has had such success with SFG that he even uses Mel's Mix in the container gardens that he designs.

While he doesn't yet make all of the compost that he needs to keep up with his SFG beds, Mustafa has a few compost bins and does vermicomposting, as well. (You'll read about compost and vermicompost in chapter 7.)

Congratulate yourself for having finished the first step in the SFG Method. You've chosen the ideal location for your SFG box, learned about climates and microclimates, and gotten inspiration from others using the SFG Method. The next step is an exciting one: You get to plan what you want to grow in your SFG box.

4

Planning Your Squares

Each season, your Square Foot Garden bed offers a new canvas for you to grow food, herbs, and flowers. This second phase of the SFG Method—planning your garden—is the next step in your journey toward home-grown harvests.

Planning a SFG involves a few elements. To begin, you have to know what you want to grow. This is typically what you and your family want to eat. Then, you have to understand the conditions those plants require to grow, from ideal temperatures to the amount of space. Taking your wants and your plants' wants into account, you can then apply the SFG principles—specifically planting in the grid, planting densely, using vertical space, and rotating crops. If you're new to gardening, or new to the SFG Method, this chapter will break down these ideas and get you excited about turning your garden dreams into reality.

Taking the time to carefully plan what to plant in each square allows you to grow your favorites and provide for a succession of harvests.

What to Plant

Open a seed catalog or visit an online catalog, and prepare to be amazed by the variety of seeds available to you as a home gardener. A gardener browsing seed options is akin to a book lover browsing a library. You have 16 squares in a typical 4-foot-by-4-foot SFG bed to start. Choosing only 16 crops—or fewer—may seem like an impossible task. Here are a few thoughts that can ease your mind:

- Not all crops grow during the same time of year. For example, tomatoes need warm weather to grow but arugula prefers cool temperatures. So, unless you live in a climate with the exact same weather conditions during all four seasons, you can choose different crops for spring, summer, fall, and winter, giving your SFG a rotation of harvests throughout the growing season.

- As you become proficient with one SFG box, you can add another box next season. The idea that you should start small cannot be emphasized enough. Once you get the hang of Square Foot Gardening and understand how simple and easy it is, you may find you have the capacity to build a second box and then a third, giving you all the growing space you could want.

- If you don't like a particular vegetable, you don't have to plant it. Too often gardeners think they're *supposed to* grow green beans because every summer garden has green beans. There's no room for peer pressure in the SFG. You get to choose the plants you want to put in your squares. Only choose the ones you want to eat or share with friends in your community.

Skip the Spreading Plants

While you can technically grow anything in a SFG, there are some plants that are best left out. These are primarily quickly spreading or otherwise aggressive plants. Some plants are overly enthusiastic in their growth and reproduction. In this category are bramble berries (raspberries and blackberries) and some perennial herbs in the mint family (especially nettle, lemon balm, and mint).

If you must have some of these plants in your garden, consider growing them in their own container, separate from your SFG bed, where they can't take over. Otherwise, you may find the spreading plants have become weeds, creeping into all the squares around them.

How Much to Plant

You will find your SFG bed is more productive than a typical garden area of the same size. It's possible that one pepper plant is all your family will need, even if people in your home really love peppers.

With the SFG Method, you are guided by the number of plants you can put in each square which is based on the size of the plant at maturity. This guideline isn't meant to limit the number of plants you grow; rather it's meant to allow those plants to produce to their fullest potential.

The grid as your guide

Look at the spacing guidelines provided in the Quick Reference Plant Spacing Guide on page 50. For each crop you want to grow, ask yourself whether the number of plants called for in that square is enough for you. With 16 squares to work with, you have the option of planting a different crop in each square so you can harvest a variety of produce throughout the year. Alternatively, you can choose to fill two or three squares with the same crop. You might choose to grow more of something if your family loves eating it—kale in your morning smoothies or cilantro as a culturally important ingredient—or if you plan to preserve it— fermented cabbage sauerkraut or canned tomato sauce.

By following SFG spacing guidelines and planting the crops your family enjoys most, it's easy to see success.

It may take a season or two for you to perfect your planting plan, but you'll get the hang of it quickly.

Crop yield

It's difficult to predict exactly how much of each crop you should grow. There are a lot of variables that go into what one plant can produce. These variables include:

- **Variety.** Consider cucumbers. You have pickling cucumbers, which are smaller, and slicing cucumbers, which are larger. A plant from a pickling variety is likely to produce a larger number of cucumbers than a plant from a slicing variety. This is true for different varieties of most crops. Some are known for high production, some for a specific flavor, others for a unique color.
- **Sun exposure.** If your SFG receives 8 hours of direct sun and your neighbor's garden receives 6 hours of direct sun, plants in your bed have an extra two hours each day to grow. All crops need some sun. Plants that set fruit—tomatoes, winter squash, cantaloupe, etc.—are likely to produce more with more exposure to direct sun. In chapter 9, we address what to do if you live at a latitude closer to the equator where your garden may receive *too much sun* and benefit from the protection of light shade.

- **Temperature.** When the temperature unexpectedly dips into the 50s at night in August, your tomato plants are going to know it. Likewise, when you have an unusually hot day in April, your greens will react by turning bitter or going to flower. As the regular weather patterns we have come to know—and the plants that have been bred and hybridized to—are shifting, so have our crops' behaviors. A period of hot or cool weather can cause your plants to produce more or less, depending on that crop's preferences.
- **Water.** Consistent water is a friend to your garden plants. If you forget to water your bed and you're not getting enough rain, plants will not produce as well. If a rainstorm brings 2 inches of water every few days for a week, plants, again, will not produce as well. The SFG Method is designed to absorb many water inconsistencies. Mel's Mix has great water retention and filtration, but it can only do so much to maintain an ideal moisture level when you're working with large rain events or no rain at all. As mentioned in chapter 3, be sure to avoid locating your SFG in a place where rain puddles or drainage is naturally poor.

- **Spacing.** The spacing guidelines outlined in the SFG Method (see page 54) are meant to maximize harvest. Within these guidelines, you have some wiggle room. If you want to harvest kale as baby leaves, for example, and you choose to plant them closer together, you will have a different harvest than if you grew just one large kale plant.
- **Harvesting schedule.** Maybe you want to go on vacation in the peak of summer harvest season, and your green beans don't get picked for ten days. You're going to come home to very large, probably tough green beans. During this time, your plants will slow down production of new beans. Regular harvesting yields more from your crops.

Go into your SFG gardening experience with an open mind, knowing you'll learn something new all the time. After your first season or two, you'll have a better idea of the size of harvest you can expect from your SFG box.

Plant Spacing

The main goal of the *square-foot* concept in the SFG Method is to standardize and achieve proper plant spacing. This is why the grid is essential. Plants, including vegetables, come in all shapes and sizes. Extra-large plants need an extra-large amount of space, just as very small plants need a very small amount of space. The grid and the spacing guidelines ensure each plant gets what it needs.

Let the grid be your guide when it comes to spacing requirements for each different plant you plan to grow.

Quick Reference Plant Spacing Guide

The following chart and the illustrated list on pages 54 and 55 don't include every type of plant you can possibly grow, but just because a certain crop isn't listed in this book doesn't mean you can't grow it in a SFG. You'll most commonly space plants at 1, 4, 9, or 16 plants per square, with extra-large plants requiring multiple squares for each plant. The Planning & Planting Chart on page 244 further details the amount of space each specific crop needs.

Maintain proper plant spacing for any crop or variety with this guide:

Size		Examples	Mature Spacing	Number Per Square
Extra large		Zucchini, pumpkin, Watermelon, lemongrass	18"+	1 per 2 or more squares, depending on the variety
Large		Cauliflower, indeterminate tomato, cabbage	12"	1
Medium		Lettuce, bok choy, parsley, Swiss chard	6"	4
Small		Leeks, bush beans, garlic, beets	4"	9
Very small		Carrots, radish, green onions	2"–4"	16

Special Note about Extra-large Plants

Extra-large plants, with a prescribed spacing of 18 inches or more, can be planted in your SFG bed, if you're willing to give up the space they require. Plan for one plant per two or more squares. Keep in mind that each grid square is 12-square inches. So, a plant with 24-inch spacing at maturity should do fine in 2 squares at the outer edge of the bed, where it can also grow off the side.

For plants with more than 24-inch spacing requirements, this process becomes somewhat subjective. A vining plant with a final spacing of 30 or 36 inches could still get away with two squares if it can grow vertically on a trellis. A bushy plant that prefers a 30- to 36-inch spacing might need four or more squares at the edge of the bed, if you consider that plant will grow in a shrub-like way, not in a straight line.

If you start the growing season and realize you put a plant that is too large into a too-small space, you have the option of removing a plant from an adjacent square to give the affronting plant more room. This isn't an ideal situation, but know that not all is lost if you make a plant-spacing mistake.

Special Note about "Baby" vs. Mature Plant Spacing

Another important note to remember is that spacing is also dependent on the stage at which you plan to harvest the plant. This comes into play primarily with greens and certain root crops, such as beets and turnips, that can be harvested as immature leaves or roots. This is known as harvesting at the "baby" stage. We've all seen baby spinach or baby arugula in those plastic packages at the grocery store. In most cases, they are not a special variety, but rather they are leaves harvested from an immature plant. Greens and root crops intended to be harvested at the baby stage can be spaced much closer together than those left to grow to their full maturity. The illustration on pages 54 and 55 features ideal spacing for both baby-sized harvests and mature-sized harvests of the most popular crops grown for baby harvesting.

This gardener may find they've run out of room mid-season. By planting large summer squash in single squares, the plants will likely outgrow their space. Give extra-large plants like summer squash multiple squares and locate them on the outer edge of the box.

When it Comes to Tomatoes

This popular crop has a special set of considerations that those with a SFG will want to consider.

Tomato plants can be either determinate or indeterminate in their growth habit. It's very important to know the difference when it comes to planning and planting these plants in your SFG.

- **Determinate varieties**, grow to a genetically pre-determined height. Most max out between 3 and 5 feet in height and they grow quite bushy. All the fruit on a determinate tomato variety ripen within a tight timeframe. When growing determinate tomatoes in a SFG, a single plant can take up as many as 4 squares because the plants grow so wide. You can plant fast-maturing spring crops, like radish or green onions, in the squares surrounding a determinate tomato plant as they'll be harvested before the tomato plant requires the additional space. Micro dwarf tomatoes are a very compact type of determinate tomato, with some only reaching a height of 8 to 10 inches. Micro dwarf tomatoes are another terrific option for a SFG and are planted 1 per square.

- **Indeterminate varieties** do not have a genetically pre-determined height. Instead, the branches and vines of these varieties continue to grow until the plant is killed by frost. Fruit on indeterminate tomato plants ripen throughout a longer period of time. Indeterminate tomato plants grow long vines and require frequent pruning (see page 220) to keep their growth habit restricted, especially if you grow them in a SFG. Most cherry tomatoes are indeterminate varieties (with the exception of dwarf cherry types), as are many beefsteak tomatoes. Indeterminate tomatoes require only 1 square per plant, as long as the plants are pruned regularly to only 1 or 2 vines. Special care needs to be taken to manage the size of indeterminate tomatoes in your SFG which is something you should prepare for in advance of planting. You also should plan to have a trellis in place for indeterminate varieties to climb.

It's important to know what type of tomato you're growing before you decide where to plant it.

Stick to the plan

You may be tempted, as you plug in transplants and drop in seeds, to want to put more plants per square than is recommended. Early in the season, the plants are small and the garden looks sparse. These plants will grow, and they likely will grow quickly. The recommended spacing allows the plants to fill your bed in no time. Just wait and see.

Giving plants the space they need to grow is important for a few reasons:

Nutrient and water uptake. Garden plants are more shallow rooted than, say, trees. While trees can send their roots deep into the soil for dozens of feet or more, vegetable and herb plants compete with one another for nutrients and water closer to the surface. The spacing guidelines account for the room the plants need below the ground as well as above.

Disease prevention. Space around plants allows air to circulate which keeps foliage drier and helps prevent pathogens from settling on the leaves. Some plants, such as tomatoes, are pruned to open up airflow and prevent fungal infections.

Photosynthesis. Plants need to absorb light as part of the photosynthesis process. Overcrowding reduces the opportunity for photosynthesis, decreasing plants' ability to grow and produce.

Yield. A crowded cabbage plant will produce a smaller cabbage head. Beets and potatoes do the same, as well as a host of other garden vegetables. There are cases when you want to harvest a smaller size or smaller amount, and then you can use tighter spacing to your advantage.

Sticking to your spacing plan means each plant will have ample space to grow.

Crop-by-Crop Spacing Guide

VERY SMALL (16 plants per square)

Arugula
(baby)

Carrots
(in a top hat)

**Green onions/
scallions**

Komatsuna
(baby)

Radish
(salad types)

Radish
(winter types)

Turnips
(baby)

SMALL (9 plants per square)

Arugula
(mature)

**Beans, bush
types**

Beets

Broccoli rabe

**Daikon
radishes**

Garlic

Leeks (in a
top hat)

Lettuce
(baby)

Mizuna
(baby)

Onions
(mature)

Parsnips
(in top hat)

Peas
(shelling),
bush types

Peas (snap),
bush types

Peas (snow),
bush types

Spinach
(baby)

Turnips
(mature)

MEDIUM (4 plants per square)

**Beans,
pole type**
(on trellis)

Basil
(compact
types)

**Bok choy/
pak choy**
(mini varieties)

Celery

Chives

**Cilantro/
coriander**

Corn

Ginger

Kale
(baby)

Kohlrabi

Komatsuna
(mature)

Lettuce
(mature)

Mizuna
(mature)

**Mustard
greens**

Parsley

Peas
(shelling),
climbing types

Peas (snap),
climbing types

Peas (snow),
climbing types

Rutabaga

Spinach
(mature)

Strawberries

Swiss chard

Turmeric

LARGE (1 plant per square)

Asparagus

Basil (sweet and other large types)

Bok choy/pak choy (full-sized types)

Broccoli

Brussels sprouts

Cabbage

Callaloo/ amaranth

Cantaloupe muskmelon (on trellis)

Cauliflower

Chamomile

Collard greens

Cucamelon (on trellis)

Cucumber (on trellis)

Dill

Eggplant

Fennel, bulb types

Fennel, leaf types

Kale (mature)

Lavender

Luffa gourd (on trellis)

Malabar spinach (on trellis)

Napa cabbage

Okra (dwarf only)

Oregano

Pepper

Potatoes (late-season types in a top hat)

Recao/ culantro Vietnamese coriander

Rosemary (trellis)

Sage

Sorrel

Summer savory

Sweet potato (in top hat)

Thyme

Tomatillos

Tomato (indeterminate, pruned and trellised)

Watermelon (smaller or bush type; in outer square)

Winter squash (compact bush type; in outer square)

Summer squash (compact bush type; in outer square)

EXTRA LARGE (1 plant per 2 or more square)

Gourds (on trellis)

Ground cherry

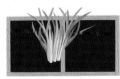
Lemongrass

Pumpkin (in outer squares)

Summer squash zucchini (large vining type; in outer squares)

Tomato (determinate types; staked or caged)

Watermelon (large type; on trellis; in outer squares)

Winter squash (large type; on trellis; in outer squares)

How to Read a Seed Packet

Seed packets are a wealth of information about the plants you're about to grow. On most commercial seed packets, you will find certain valuable details, including:

Botanical name. Knowing a plant's botanical, or scientific, name is important because while a plant's common name may change, its botanical name is always the same. This is especially true with flowers. What you call bachelor buttons, your neighbor may call cornflower. You're both talking about the plant with the botanical name *Centaurea cyanus*. The botanical name ensures you know which plant you're growing.

The botanical name always has two words and sometimes has three: the first is the plant's genus name, the second is the plant's species, and if it has a third, that is the plant's variety or cultivar which should be in a set of single quotation marks. Look at the botanical name of onions (*Allium cepa*) and of leeks (*Allium ampeloprasum*). It's easy to see that onions and leeks are in the same genus, *Allium*—and from there, you can determine they're both in the wider Amaryllidaceae family—of plants. This knowledge is helpful in grouping crops together for planting and in understanding their growth habits.

Days to germination. The anticipation of a seed's germination is akin to waiting for summer break from school as a kid. The days to germination listed on the seed packet give you a timeframe for knowing when you should start looking for the tiny green stem to emerge, though factors like soil moisture and temperature also influence germination times. Some seeds germinate

rapidly. Radishes germinate in a few days. Other seeds seem to take forever. Many herbs and some flowers emerge in a few weeks. Parsley and black-eyed Susan are among those that take their time. If it's well past the projected germination time on the seed packet and the seed hasn't sprouted yet, this is a signal that you may need to try again. Read more about seed starting in chapter 8.

Days to maturity. This number gives you an idea of when your crop can be harvested. Like everything else related to gardening, there are many variables that factor into actual days to maturity. The time listed on the seed packet is a good starting point. Harvest readiness is covered in chapter 10.

Sun exposure. Does this plant prefer full sun or partial shade? The seed packet will tell you. You'll most often see this designation on packets of flower seeds, as it's generally assumed that vegetables grow best in 6 to 8 hours of full sun.

Planting depth. The planting depth suggested on the packet guides you in how deep to place the seed. The smaller the seed, the shallower the planting depth.

Final spacing. This is an especially important number in the SFG Method. As you've learned in this chapter, plant spacing in your SFG box is based on the recommended final spacing for the crop. If the plant you're growing isn't listed in the Planning & Planting Chart

The back of a seed packet is a wealth of information about growing the little treasures inside.

on page 244 or found in the Crop-by-Crop Spacing Guide on page 54, look at the spacing on the seed packet. Use this and the rules in the Quick Reference Plant Spacing Guide on page 50 to guide you in planning that square.

If your seed packets don't have the information you're seeking listed, check the seed catalog or website.

Plant Seasons

When a cousin from Fairbanks, Alaska, visits you in Bangkok, Thailand, in April, they won't know how to act in that heat. When you visit them in December, you won't want to leave the house. The plants growing in home gardens originated from all over the world. When we take a plant from one climate and force it to grow in another, it feels the same way you and your cousin would away from home. But instead of staying indoors or carrying around a fan, the plants express their displeasure about a season's conditions by wilting, bolting, or dying. Your plants will grow and thrive when allowed to grow in the season they're best adapted to.

Annuals, biennials, and perennials

A major differentiator in the way plants grow is their life cycle—whether they are annual, biennial, or perennial.

Most of the plants you'll grow in a SFG bed are annual plants. Annuals are plants gardeners grow anew from seed or from transplant each year. These are melons, peas, zinnias, zucchini, tomatoes, and more.

Perennials survive season after season. You plant them once and continue to enjoy

Some vegetable plants, like this lettuce, are annuals that complete their life cycle in one year or one growing season. Others, like the onions, are biennials that require two years to complete their life cycle. And a third group, known as perennials, live for many years.

them for many years. Some popular herbs—oregano, thyme, sage, etc.—are perennials, as are many fruits—strawberries, tree fruits, bramble berries, etc. Perennial vegetables, besides asparagus and artichokes, are not as common.

Where you live partially dictates whether a particular crop is an annual or a perennial. Echinacea is considered a perennial flower, but in the northern reaches of Vermont, most varieties of echinacea won't survive the winter, making them essentially annuals if you want to grow them. Refer back to Chapter 3 for more about how your garden's location can dictate what you grow there.

Biennial plants are usually lumped in with annuals as far as vegetable garden planning is concerned. Biennials go through two growing seasons before they set seed and die. A biennial plant's life cycle is longer than an annual plant but not as long as a perennial plant. Kale, Swiss chard, carrots, beets, cabbage, and onions are a few examples of biennials. The plants that are capable of overwintering in the garden—if not perennials—are often biennials.

The Planning & Planting Chart on page 244 refers to plants as annuals, biennials, or perennials. This detail is important so you know whether you should plan for the crop you put in a specific square to remain in that square for one season or more.

Annuals

An annual is a plant that goes through its entire life cycle—from seed to plant to flower to seed again—in one growing season.

Many SFGs contain at least a few perennial herbs. This gardener has planted perennial thyme on the corner so it can grow out over the edge of the box.

Bolting

Also referred to as flowering or going to seed, bolting is the start of a non-fruiting plant's reproductive process, when a plant sends up a flower stalk. This typically happens when the plant is under stress, such as a turnip left in the garden too long during hot and dry conditions, or when the plant has lived its normal life cycle, such as kale after it overwinters in the garden.

Perennials

Perennial plants survive more than one season— some for just two years and others for many years. Perennials may die back in the fall and regrow from the ground in the spring.

Cool-season and warm-season crops

Gardening can be a nearly year-round activity for most SFG users in most places, given the right crop choices and the use of season-extension methods. In thinking about your garden's seasons, crops can be divided into cool season and warm season.

Cool-season crops are those that can survive a frost but don't do well in hot weather. These include most crops in the brassica family (radishes, kale, collard greens, brussels sprouts, broccoli, cauliflower, bok choy, etc.), many of the chenopodiums (beets, Swiss chard, etc.), a small handful of legumes (shell, snow, and snap peas), and some umbellifer crops (carrots, parsley, celery, fennel, etc.). Calendula and bachelor buttons, both in the aster family, are two flowers that can handle a light frost, but not a freeze.

Warm-season crops are those that thrive in hot weather but won't survive a frost. In this category are most nightshades (tomatoes, peppers, eggplants, tomatillos, etc.) and cucurbits (melons, squash, cucumbers, pumpkins, etc.). Beans, corn, okra, and most flowers are also warm season crops.

Strawberries are one of a handful of perennial crops you can grow in your SFG.

You'll notice that most cool-season crops are leafy greens and root vegetables, and most warm-season crops are fruiting plants. Knowing this, as you plan your SFG bed, you can be sure to pencil in a tomato for summer and broccoli for fall but not vice versa. The Planning & Planting Chart on page 244 offers a warm season/cool season designation for crops to aid your planning.

Biennials

A biennial plant survives a whole growing season plus a dormant season, then bolts and ends its life cycle in the following growing season.

Each vegetable plant has a preferred growing season. Some are cool season and some are warm season. Knowing which season each variety prefers is essential for success. Case in point: These radishes are a cool-season crop that will not form good roots if the weather is too hot.

Look at the sample succession garden plans on pages 73 and 74 for a four-season succession example. Here, once you're finished harvesting your spring beets, you'll put in a dwarf cherry tomato for the summer. Come late summer, the cherry tomato comes out and lettuce plants are put in that square for a fall and winter harvest.

Plant different varieties. Say you love carrots but don't need sixteen carrots to be ready to harvest all at once. Different varieties of the same crop have different maturation times. You can find carrot varieties that are ready to harvest in 50 days all the way up to varieties ready to harvest in 75 days. You have the option of planting your whole square at one time using half for early maturing carrots and half for late-maturing carrots so you can harvest them over time.

Stagger your plantings. Using the same example of wanting to harvest carrots over time, you can stick with one variety of carrots—the 50-day carrots, for example—and seed one-quarter of your carrot square every week for 4 weeks. This method of succession sowing requires

more planning—you have to remember to seed the carrots each week— but this staggered planting method gives you carrots to harvest throughout the month.

Harvest only what you need. A driver behind the SFG Method is to have less food waste. Succession plan to harvesting only what you need from plants and let them continue producing. For example, when harvesting kale you don't have to cut the whole plant. You can take just the outside few stalks and let the center stalks continue to grow. This technique works for leaf lettuce, celery, bok choy, and other leafy greens. Larger leafy greens, like collard greens and Swiss chard, thrive on this method of harvest, and the plants will produce more and more.

Cut-and-come-again. The early 21st century's boom in small-scale market farming has allowed home gardeners to learn and benefit from the techniques these farmers have popularized. Farmers growing baby greens often use a cut-and-come-again method. They plant seeds very close together and harvest handfuls of individual very small (or "baby") leaves, then allow the central growing point of the plant

Succession planting

If garden planning were a college course, Garden Planning 101 would cover how to plan your SFG for one planting per year. Garden Planning 201 is one level up and includes a process known as succession planting. Succession planting involves planting multiple crops per season in the same space, and it takes a little more understanding of plants and their growth habits.

This is where garden planning turns into a jigsaw puzzle. Allowing the squares to guide your succession planning makes this a straightforward process. It can be fun to plan where the pieces fit between and within seasons so you can maximize your harvest.

There are several techniques to succession planting:

Plan for each season. As you just learned, different plants thrive in different seasons. That means when one plant stops producing, it is pulled from the garden and another crop goes in its place. The SFG grid makes this planning easy to visualize.

One method of succession planting is that as soon as one crop is pulled from a square, another one goes in its place.

Succession Planting

Succession planting is using your garden spacing and planting times to maximize and spread out the harvest over time.

Some crops, like this spinach, can be harvested via a cut-and-come-again method. Only the leaves are harvested but the growing points are left intact to sprout new leaves for subsequent harvests.

to regrow, and harvest more baby leaves again and again. As long as you harvest the leaves without damaging the plant's central growing point (known as its crown), you can "cut" and "come again" for another harvest every few weeks. Like harvesting only what you need, this succession planning will keep you in greens for salads and other baby-greens uses. Sample Garden Plan 4: Edible Flowers and Salad Greens, on page 70, features two squares with cut-and-come-again greens: baby arugula and baby mizuna. You'll see the spacing is much tighter for these baby greens than it would be for their full-sized siblings with 36 plants per square.

Succession planting means that when your summer carrots are pulled from the garden, you can replace them with a late-season crop of lettuce or spinach.

Be ready for mid-season changes. Now and then, you'll have a crop that matures quickly or that has held over from the season before but finishes its life cycle mid-season. Once that crop finishes, even if it's the middle of summer, you can replace that crop with another. Garlic is a good example of this, as it has a life cycle that's different from most other garden crops. Garlic is planted in fall and harvested after its leaves start to die back the following mid-summer. With a square now open during a prime growing season, you can pop in a new crop to take its place. In the Sample Succession Garden series on page 73, garlic is replaced with dill, which is a fast-growing herb.

Chart your seasonal succession plan now so you'll be ready to get the most from your SFG come spring, summer, and fall planting time.

Crop rotation

In reading about cool-season crops and warm-season crops, you learned that plants fall within certain families. Plant families carry with them similar characteristics, and they also carry similar nutritional needs, pests, and diseases. This is why crop rotation is important.

You might read this and think, "But Mel's Mix takes care of the nutritional needs of plants and a SFG bed has fewer pests and disease." This is true, but in keeping with good gardening practices, and even in the small space of a SFG, it's best to move plants from one square to the next season after season, particularly if you've faced a disease or pest.

When a pest or plant-health issue does arise in a SFG, you can be quick to quash

One Crop Per Box

While this book focuses on the traditional, diversely planted, 4-foot-by-4-foot SFG box, there are times when you'd want to dedicate a whole box to one crop or one type of crop. If your dream SFG bed includes either of these crops, know they will want their own space:

Blueberries. This beloved fruit requires acidic soil for growth. While most vegetables and fruits need a growing medium with 5.8 to 6.5 pH, blueberries thrive in 4.0 to 5.5 pH. (Read more about pH in Finding pH Balance on page 149.) Blueberries will grow best in their own container or SFG bed with Mel's Mix amended with elemental sulfur or additional peat moss.

Corn. Corn takes up a lot of space. It's not just that their stalks are tall. Corn requires many close companions for ample pollination by wind and good ear production. For this reason, you'll need to plant a whole 4-foot-by-4-foot SFG bed entirely with corn in order to get a harvest. Corn should be planted at 4 plants per square, so your corn-only SFG box should have a total of 64 plants.

You may have your eye on other plants that are extra large or require their own specific-growing-medium conditions. You can grow those crops in their own SFG box or separate container. Mel's Mix can be used in all kinds of raised beds and containers, not just SFG boxes.

Crop rotation is another important component of SFG. However, it's a lot easier to keep track of than in a traditional in-ground garden. Just keep track of what's in each square each year and be sure to rotate to a different plant family next season.

it because your growing space is small and easy to monitor. (Read more about this type of maintenance in chapter 9.) To help prevent crop-specific issues from arising, plant a crop from a different family in that square next season. When the pests awaken from their winter slumber or the fungus hasn't yet been killed off by the sun, it won't find its favorite food in the same place, reducing the likelihood of establishing a problem.

See an example of crop rotation in the northernmost grid row of the Sample Succession Garden on pages 73 to 74. Nightshades and cucurbits follow brassicas from spring to summer, and brassicas and umbels follow nightshades and cucurbits from summer to fall. These families are swapped, rather than planted together back-to-back. The more time you have before returning a crop family to a square, the better.

Perennials, which remain in the garden throughout the years of their productive lives, don't allow for crop rotation in their squares. They'll benefit from regular topping up of nutrients via the addition of compost in their squares, as you'll read about in chapter 9.

Plant Placement

Success in the SFG box depends as much on where you put your plants as it does on which plants you choose. The movement of the sun and the growth habits of the plants dictate the best spot for each crop.

In chapter 3, you sketched how the sun moves across your available garden space to see how the shadows and light changed throughout the seasons. One element that doesn't change is the direction from which the sun enters your garden. In the northern hemisphere, the sun shines predominantly from the south, and tall plants on the south side of your SFG box will shade the short plants north of them. In the southern hemisphere, the opposite is true. This is less of an issue in the summer, when the sun is high in the sky, but you'll notice the difference throughout the other seasons. If there's only one thing you can remember about planning your SFG plant placement, it's that tall plants go on the side of the garden farthest from the sun whenever possible.

Trellising

Upward mobility is the secret to growing great vining plants in a SFG. Growing vertically from the bed, a plant has as much space as you want to give it.

All vining plants can be trained to grow on a trellis—pole beans, cucumbers, melons, squash, and tomatoes included. The beans twine around structures to make their climb, and cucurbits send out tendrils

Square Foot Gardener's Tip

Remember, in the northern hemisphere, tall plants and trellises should always be located on the north side of your SFG box. In the southern hemisphere, tall plants belong on the south side.

There are many different types of prefab trellis you can use in your SFG, and plenty of options you can DIY.

Heavy fruit like this melon may need a sling made from fabric, netting, or, in this case, a nylon stocking to attach them to the trellis and provide additional support.

to wrap around and secure themselves to the structure. Tomatoes will need help with the climb, tied loosely with a piece of twine every few feet.

Heavier fruits, such as melons, might need the additional support of a sling secured to the trellis to help keep the fruit attached to the plants.

Chapter 6 covers DIY trellises that you can customize to fit your SFG bed.

Box edges

The edges of the SFG box allow plants to sprawl out into the space beyond. Picture cascading nasturtium beautifying one corner of the bed, buzzing with pollinators. Let a vining crop run over the edge and alongside the box. Use the edges as breathing room for larger crops or untrellised vining plants, though if left to sprawl on the ground, vining plants may be more prone to pests and diseases.

Top hat box

Top hat boxes invite height and depth. These simple structures are placed on top of your SFG grid and filled with Mel's Mix, elevating the height of the growing space and deepening the volume of soil available to crops with long roots.

Most annual plants—and many perennials you'd want to put in a SFG bed—have shallow root systems, and they'll find all the space they need in a typical SFG configuration. However, there are plants you are growing specifically for the roots. Carrots and late-season potatoes are two common root crops that dig down deep. Fast-maturing early-season potatoes like 'Yukon Gold' don't require the use of a top hat. They aren't as common, but parsnips fit into this category as well. The typical 6- to 8-inch depth of a SFG bed limits their growth. Add another few inches on top of that with a top hat box, and these crops have all the room they need.

A top hat box can raise up a plant, as well. This can be a nice touch to add visual interest—a cluster of multi-colored nigella flowers growing on top, for example—or a top hat can give an extra-large plant a bit more space to run down over the side of the box.

Chapter 6 has easy instructions for building your own top hat.

Here, a top hat is being used to grow a potato plant. Potatoes, particularly late-season varieties, require the extra depth a top hat provides.

Big, Big Plant Placement

Take a look at the sample gardens beginning on page 68. You'll notice that each zucchini plant is placed on the outer edge of the bed, given two squares, and sometimes given a trellis or a top hat. Zucchini can grow into a monster-sized plant. Depending on the variety, it's not unheard of to have a zucchini plant with a 9-foot span. But don't worry, there are varieties with more compact growth habits. Not every zucchini plant will reach so wide. These smaller varieties are great choices for a SFG. Let's say the zucchini you grow reaches 3 feet in width. If you placed that in a center square of your SFG grid, you would need to give up nine squares to this plant for it to have enough room to grow. But if you plant your zucchini in a square along the outer edge or in the corner of the SFG box, the plant can do some of its growing on the outside of the box, away from the other plants, taking up fewer boxes in the grid. Another way to save space is by planting the zucchini in a top hat where you're giving it more vertical space to occupy and allowing it to spill down the side of the top hat. Another option is to grow it on a trellis where it can further use vertical space for its growth.

Extra-large plants like zucchini are challenging in a SFG but not impossible, and they let you get creative with your growing space.

Perennial placement

Your annual plants will come and go each season, but the perennials stay put. Think about where you'd like to place these so they're not in your way. Some gardeners like them in the center squares so they can work on either side of these mainstays. Other gardeners prefer them along an edge so they're easy to plan around. There's no right way or wrong way to position perennials in your SFG bed—just consider your preference and remember they can always be dug up and moved to a new site if the need arises.

Plan for Flowers

Nasturtiums are perfect companions for a SFG.

A lot of the vegetables, fruits, and herbs you're planning for your garden bed will produce flowers on their own. Bumble bees can't get enough of basil flowers, and if you've never seen an okra bloom, you're in for a treat.

With just 16 square feet, can you afford to dedicate a square or two to a plant whose main purpose is to offer showy blooms? The answer is: You can't afford not to. Flowers offer benefits to us humans as well as to the larger ecosystem, including:

- **Attracting pollinators.** Some edible plants, such as squashes, cucumbers, and strawberries, need pollination to produce their fruit. The more flower options your SFG bed offers, the more bees, wasps, and other pollinating insects will visit.

- **Bringing in beneficial insects.** Many of the pest insects that damage your garden plants have predator insects that prey on them, and you can help support those predators by having a diverse array of flowering plants around. Flowers can balance the

Flowers for the Square Foot Garden

FLOWER	BOTANICAL NAME	FAMILY	BLOOM COLOR
Bachelor buttons (cornflower)	*Centaurea cyanus*	Asteraceae	Blue, pink, white
Black-eyed Susan	*Rudbeckia hirta*	Asteraceae	Yellow with black center
Borage	*Borago officinalis*	Boraginaceae	Pink and blue
Calendula (pot marigold)	*Calendula officinalis*	Asteraceae	Yellow and orange
Echinacea (coneflower)	*Echinacea purpurea*	Asteraceae	Purple
Marigold—gem or signet variety	*Tagetes tenuifolia*	Asteraceae	Most often yellow and orange
Nasturtium	*Tropaeolum minus*	Tropaeolaceae	Red, orange, and yellow
Nigella (love in a mist)	*Nigella damascena*	Ranunculaceae	White, purple, blue, and pink
Sunflowers	*Helianthus annuus*	Asteraceae	Typically yellow, but also brown, white, and red
Sweet alyssum	*Lobularia maritima*	Brassicaceae	White
Winged everlasting	*Ammobium alatum*	Asteraceae	Silvery-white with yellow centers
Violet (pansy, viola)	*Viola* spp.	Violaceae	All colors
Zinnia	*Zinnia* spp.	Asteraceae	A rainbow of colors

population of bad bugs by attracting good bugs.

- **Dissuading insect pests.** Some pest insects have a harder time finding their host plants when the garden is interplanted with a mixture of plant species, rather than with a high concentration of a single crop. Adding flowers to your SFG can play a role in creating this type of mixed planting.
- **Adding diversity.** Mixing up plant-family diversity can help break up pest and disease cycles. Most flowers are in a different plant family than most vegetables.
- **Offering edible beauty.** Some flowers are edible, adding color, nutrition, and interest to salads.
- **Providing color and contrast.** Blooming flowers bring something new to a sea of green plants. Go with some long-stemmed flowers, and you can cut and make a bouquet to bring your garden's beauty indoors. Let flowers add whimsy to your SFG bed.

Whether you opt for marigolds, sunflowers, sweet alyssum, or other flowers, it pays big dividends to include some flowering plants in your SFG.

ANNUAL OR PERENNIAL	DIRECT SEED OR TRANSPLANT	# PER SFG SQUARE	NOTES
Annual	Either	4	Can tolerate partial sun Lovely cut flower
Annual	Transplant	1	Perennial in warm climates without freezing temperatures
Annual	Either	1	Attracts bees and butterflies Edible blooms Frost tolerant
Annual	Either	1	Edible blooms Frost tolerant
Perennial	Transplant	1	Attracts bees and butterflies Will grow in clumps and can be divided
Annual	Transplant	1	Edible petals
Annual	Direct seed	1	Avoid vining varieties Attracts hummingbirds and honey bees Edible blooms
Annual	Direct seed	4	Succession sow to have blooms spring through fall Great cut flower
Annual	Either	1	Branching varieties bloom throughout the season
Annual	Transplant	1	Perennial in warm climates without freezing temperatures
Annual	Transplant	1	Perennial in warm climates without freezing temperatures
Annual	Transplant	1	Tolerates light frost Very low growing Edible flowers
Annual	Transplant	1	Choose dwarf varieties Attracts butterflies and bees

Sample Garden Plans

There's a lot of information in this chapter about crop families, crop preferences, crop spacing, and crop placement. It may be easiest to digest it all by looking at examples. One or more of the following plans could resonate with you, making you want to plan the exact same layout for your SFG. At the least, each can serve as inspiration for your own SFG configuration.

These plans are drawn for gardens in the northern hemisphere, with taller plants on the north side and shorter plants on the south side to keep the taller plants from shading the whole box. You'll see how trellises, top hats, and supports maximize the available growing area.

Know that there is no limit to the combinations of crops you can grow in one SFG box. The illustrations here are just a few examples of the creative ways you can plan for your harvest.

In the following plans, the squares are numbered according to the template on this page.

Plan 1: Shade Garden ⤷

This plan is packed with shade-tolerant vegetables and herbs, which also happen to be cool-weather crops. A shade garden still needs to get some sun: 4 to 6 hours is ideal. Because of the lack of sun shining on this garden, these cool-weather crops will have an extended harvest, growing well into the heat of summer much more readily than they would if they were planted in full sun.

Mix and match here. If you want the nutritional density of kale and don't prefer the spiciness of mustard greens, replace mustard greens with more kale or another shade-tolerant crop.

SHADE GARDEN PLANT LIST

Square #	Type of Crop	Quantity of Plants	Square #	Type of Crop	Quantity of Plants
1	Swiss chard	4	9	Spinach (baby)	9
2	Kale (mature)	1	10	Turnips (large)	9
3	Mustard greens	4	11	Kohlrabi	4
4	Collard greens	1	12	Cauliflower	1
5	Beets	9	13	Carrots	16
6	Broccoli	1	14	Parsley	4
7	Radish	16	15	Cilantro	4
8	Cabbage	1	16	Lettuce	4

⤶ Plan 2: Fruit Garden

Homegrown fruits can be even more of a joy than homegrown vegetables. Fruits tend to take up a lot of space, but if you have a family of fruit lovers, dedicating a SFG bed to a few favorites is worth it. Avoid using spreading fruits, like raspberries, in your SFG as they can become invasive. Strawberries are perennials; all other crops in this garden plan are annuals. The five squares of strawberries are placed around the outside of the box so the fruit can hang down over the sides. In the center squares are ground cherries (a slightly sweet, tropical-flavored, husk-covered fruit that's related to the tomatillo), which grow bushy and need the support of a cage or bamboo tepee. Along the north and east edges are melons growing up a trellis. If you fear the trellis on the east side will block too much sun, skip the trellis and allow the melon vines to ramble across the ground outside of your SFG box. Notice in the illustration that the east-side trellis sits along squares 8, 12, and 16, leaving that side of square 4 open so you can access that corner of the SFG bed to tend and harvest it.

FRUIT GARDEN PLANT LIST

Square #	Type of Crop	Quantity of Plants
1 & 2	Watermelon	1 (on trellis)
3 & 4	Watermelon	1 (on trellis)
6 & 7	Ground cherry	1 (with support cage)
10 & 11	Ground cherry	1 (with support cage)
8, 12 & 16	Cantaloupe	2 (on trellis)
5	Strawberries	4
9	Strawberries	4
13	Strawberries	4
14	Strawberries	4
15	Strawberries	4

Plan 3: Stir-Fry Garden →

Crops in a stir-fry garden can be used for much more than just stir-fry, of course. This plan illustrates mid-season succession planting. The northern half of the box is planted in summer vegetables, and the southern half is in cool-season vegetables. Not all of these vegetables will be ready for harvest at the same time, or even in the same season, depending on where you live, but with this collection of plants, you'll enjoy a variety of stir-fry meals for an extended period of time.

The vining zucchini should be trellised so it takes up less room, while the peppers and eggplant benefit from supports.

STIR-FRY GARDEN PLANT LIST

Square #	Type of Crop	Quantity of Plants
1 & 2	Zucchini	1 (on trellis)
3 & 4	Summer squash	1 (on trellis)
5	Banana pepper	1 (with support cage)
6	Bell pepper	1 (with support cage)
7	Eggplant	1 (with support cage)
8	Bush beans	9
9	Carrots	16 (in a top hat)
10	Leeks	9 (in a top hat)
11	Broccoli	1
12	Bok choy (mini types)	4
13	Celery	4
14	Cabbage	1
15	Kohlrabi	4
16	Radishes	16

← Plan 4: Edible Flowers and Salad Greens

A homegrown leafy-greens salad makes a beautiful dish. In this plan, flowers, herbs, lettuces, and greens combine for a diverse, flavorful harvest. This garden would also do well in partial sun, with many of the crops in it preferring cooler conditions.

The baby arugula and baby mizuna are planted more densely than you'd expect. These are fast-growing greens meant to be harvested as cut-and-come-again crops (see page 59). Spinach and komatsuna are also planted close together so they'll produce the smaller baby leaves desirable in salads.

EDIBLE FLOWERS AND SALAD GREENS GARDEN PLANT LIST

Square #	Type of Crop	Quantity of Plants	Square #	Type of Crop	Quantity of Plants
1	Borage	1	9	Bibb lettuce	4
2	Basil	1	10	Komatsuna (baby)	16
3	Napa cabbage	1	11	Spinach (baby)	9
4	Napa cabbage	1	12	Mizuna (baby; cut-and-come-again)	36
5	Romaine lettuce	4	13	Sorrel	1
6	Marigold	1	14	Buttercrunch lettuce	4
7	Kale (mature)	1	15	Nasturtium	1
8	Arugula (baby; cut-and-come-again)	36	16	Green onions/scallions	16

Plan 5: Grocery Store Garden ➜

The International Fresh Produce Association keeps track of the fruits and vegetables most often purchased in grocery stores in the United States. Many crops on that list—especially the vegetables—are easy to grow in a SFG bed. It's possible to spend less money on vegetables from the grocery store by growing them yourself. In this plan, the strawberries are perennials; all other crops are annuals.

GROCERY STORE GARDEN PLANT LIST

Square #	Type of Crop	Quantity of Plants	Square #	Type of Crop	Quantity of Plants
1	Watermelon (bush type)	1 (on trellis)	9	Strawberries	4
2	Cucumber	1 (on trellis)	10	Celery	4
3	Tomato (indeterminate variety)	1 (on trellis)	11	Bush beans	9
4	Bell pepper	1 (with support cage)	12	Broccoli	1
5	Basil	1	13	Onions	9
6	Carrots	16 (in top hat)	14	Lettuce	4
7	Late-season potato	1 (in top hat)	15	Spinach (mature)	4
8	Cauliflower	1	16	Cabbage	1

← Plan 6: Summer Staples

Sliced tomato sandwiches, juicy watermelon on a hot summer afternoon, crunchy dill pickles—these are a few of the foods made possible with a garden full of summer staples. This SFG plan comprises warm-season plants only and should be planted only after any chance of spring frost has passed. Two types of tomatoes here illustrate that it's possible to grow different varieties of one vegetable to serve multiple purposes—the cherry tomatoes for salads, and the slicing tomato for sandwiches.

SUMMER STAPLES GARDEN PLANT LIST

Square #	Type of Crop	Quantity of Plants
1	Cucumber	1 (on trellis)
2	Cucumber	1 (on trellis)
3	Watermelon (bush type)	1 (on trellis)
4	Watermelon (bush type)	1 (on trellis)
5 & 6	Slicing tomato (determinate/patio variety)	1 (with support cage)
7	Dwarf cherry tomato	1 (with support cage)
8 & 12	Zucchini	1 (in top hat)
9	Jalapeño pepper	1 (with support cage)
10	Eggplant	1 (with support cage)
11	Bell pepper	1 (with support cage)
13	Tomatillo	1 (with supports)
14	Basil	1
15	Dill	1
16	Bush beans	9

Plan 7: Dwarf Crops →

Having 16 square feet to work with, small-space crop varieties are a better choice than sprawling varieties. Just for fun, this garden plan uses miniature crops exclusively. Because a plant is small doesn't necessarily mean its yield will be less. One mini cucumber plant can give you as much, by weight, as one plant that produces slicing cucumbers, for example. Try bok choy no larger than your hand, carrots of golf-ball dimensions, and cucamelons—also called mouse melons—that may be the right size for a mouse's cucumber-like snack. Look for varieties with mini, dwarf, and compact in the traits listed in your favorite seed catalog.

DWARF CROPS GARDEN PLANT LIST

Square #	Type of Crop	Quantity of Plants
1 & 2	Baby pie pumpkin	1 (on trellis)
3	Sugar Baby mini watermelon	1 (on trellis)
4	Mini cucumber	1 (on trellis)
5	Dwarf tomato	1 (with support cage)
6	Dwarf tomato	1 (with support cage)
7	Dwarf peas (bush type)	9 (with support)
8	Baby beets	9
9	Mini snack pepper	1 (with support)
10	Mini eggplant	1 (with support)
11	Mini eggplant	1 (with support)
12	Little Gem lettuce	4
13	Scallions/green onions	16
14	Mini bok choy	9
15	Mini romaine lettuce	4
16	Parisian mini carrots	16

← Plan 8: Basic Herbs

This herb bed is heavy on the perennials, as many herbs grow to develop woody stems and come back after each winter. Depending on your climate, perennial herbs can even thrive most of the year. Here, the center squares of rosemary, lavender, sage, oregano, chives, and thyme are perennials, while the others are annuals. You'll notice two common herbs—mint and lemon balm—are missing. These tend to take over growing spaces. Read about how to grow these herbs in Skip the Spreading Plants on page 48.

BASIC HERB GARDEN PLANT LIST

Square #	Type of Crop	Quantity of Plants	Square #	Type of Crop	Quantity of Plants
1	Sweet basil	1	10	Sage	1
2 & 3	Lemon basil	1	11	Oregano	1
4 & 8	Lemongrass	1	12	Thai basil	1
5	Parsley	4	13	Cilantro	4
6	Rosemary	1	14	Chives	4
7	Lavender	1	15	Thyme	1
9	Dill	1	16	Chamomile	1

Sample Succession Garden

This set of sample gardens follows one SFG bed through the seasons, from spring through winter, using succession planting techniques.

Spring →

This spring bed is meant to be planted about a month before the last expected frost. Plants here are cool-weather crops and can withstand some frosty temperatures. Help them along on especially cold nights with some floating row cover. You'll learn how to use season-extension techniques like this in chapter 9. The garlic in this bed was planted in the fall and will continue to grow until early summer. The thyme and chives are both perennial plants, so they live permanently in these squares.

SPRING SUCCESSION GARDEN PLANT LIST

Square #	Type of Crop	Quantity of Plants	Square #	Type of Crop	Quantity of Plants
1	Kale (mature)	1	9	Spinach (mature)	4
2	Broccoli rabe	9	10	Thyme	1
3	Radish	16	11	Chives	4
4	Cabbage	1	12	Garlic	9
5	Beets	9	13	Swiss chard	4
6	Parsley	4	14	Bachelor button	1
7	Cilantro	4	15	Lettuce	4
8	Carrots	16 (in a top hat)	16	Calendula	1

← Summer

Summer's warm-season crops should be ready to go in the ground shortly after your last frost, as the soil warms quickly in a SFG bed. Summer starts out with the garlic still growing. After you harvest the garlic around the summer solstice, plant a fast-growing crop, like dill, in its place. The parsley, Swiss chard, bachelor buttons, and calendula are squares you planted in the spring. These are still in place to produce through the summer. The thyme and chives, too, as perennials, are in their permanent squares.

SUMMER SUCCESSION GARDEN PLANT LIST

Square #	Type of Crop	Quantity of Plants
1	Slicing tomato (indeterminate type)	1 (on trellis)
2	Winter squash (bush type)	1 (on trellis)
3	Cucumber	1 (on trellis)
4 & 8	Zucchini	1 (in top hat)
5	Dwarf tomato	1 (with support cage)
6	Parsley	4
7	Bush beans	9
9	Jalapeño pepper	1 (with support cage)
10	Thyme	1
11	Chives	4
12	Garlic (replaced by one dill after the summer harvest)	9
13	Swiss chard	4
14	Bachelor buttons	1
15	Dwarf Baby Bubba or Blondy okra	1
16	Calendula	1

Fall ➡

Because daylight is decreasing in the fall—as opposed to increasing in the spring—the same plants will grow slower in the fall than they did in the spring. Seed and transplant your fall crops a month to 8 weeks before your first expected fall frost. You'll plant garlic after your first frost; the Swiss chard from the spring can stay in the garden until then. The thyme and chives are still in their squares. The chives will have slowed their growth and may have died back by now.

FALL SUCCESSION GARDEN PLANT LIST

Square #	Type of Crop	Quantity of Plants	Square #	Type of Crop	Quantity of Plants
1	Carrots	16 (in top hat)	9	Turnips (baby)	16
2	Winter radish	16	10	Thyme	1
3	Turnips (mini)	16	11	Chives	4
4	Collard greens	1	12	Kohlrabi	4
5	Buttercrunch lettuce	4	13	Swiss chard	4
6	Bok Choy (mini)	4	14	Beets (baby)	16
7	Arugula (mature)	9	15	Lettuce	4
8	Kale (mature)	1	16	Napa cabbage	1

⬅ Winter

During deep winter with little daylight, plants will not grow more, but as daylight increases, they'll put on growth week over week. All squares can be mulched as an extra layer of insulation and to prevent wind erosion and sun bleaching during the fallow period.

The plants in the northernmost eight squares (squares 1 through 8) are meant to have winter-weight row cover placed over them, or you can cover the entire bed with a covered plastic mini hoop tunnel (see project on page 131) as protection from the harshest weather. You can harvest from these throughout the season. The perennial thyme and chives may look like they've died, but they'll put on greenery come spring.

WINTER SUCCESSION GARDEN PLANT LIST

Square #	Type of Crop	Quantity of Plants	Square #	Type of Crop	Quantity of Plants
1	Carrots	16 (in top hat)	9	Mulch	
2	Winter radishes	16	10	Thyme	1
3	Turnips (mini)	16	11	Chives	4
4	Collard greens	1	12	Mulch	
5	Buttercrunch lettuce	4	13	Garlic	9
6	Bok choy (mini)	4	14	Mulch	
7	Arugula (mature)	9	15	Mulch	
8	Kale (mature)	1	16	Mulch	

It's Your Turn: Plan Your SFG Bed

By now, you may be wondering how to keep all of these details in your head as you plan your own SFG box. The best way to put this information to the test is to try it out. Use a computer program, table, chart, or spreadsheet if you want, but a pencil with an eraser and the blank garden template on page 76 will do just fine—and you may find it's more satisfying. Refer to the Planning & Planting Chart on page 244 to help with your process.

Step 1. Pencil in your favorites.

Fill in each of the 16 squares with the crops you'd really like to grow and eat. Don't over-think it at this point. You'll come back to plant size, crop family, and seasonality in a minute.

Step 2. Sort out your seasons.

For whatever season you're planning, deter-mine whether these crops will grow in that season in your particular growing zone. Erase any crops that don't fall within that season. Jot down these off-season crops so you remember to put them in next season's plan. Fill in the empty grid spaces with seasonal crops or flowers.

Step 3. Arrange your crops by growth habit.

Place your taller crops and those needing trellising on the north side of your grid. Give your extra-large crops a spot along the edge of the bed. Now's the time to give them two grid spaces if they need it.

Planning your garden carefully is important for success, but don't forget to grow your favorites. This gardener has a definite love for all types of peppers.

Step 4. Group crops by plant family.

Within this size arrangement, try to create blocks or adjacent squares of crops that share the same plant family. If you're look-ing at a summer garden, you'll put tomatoes, eggplants, and peppers (the nightshades) in one area; melons, cucumbers, and luffa (all cucurbits) in another. For the beginning SFG grower, this step is not as important as the first three. Don't stress about the plant families in the first season. You'll quickly understand the difference between the families and placing them together will become second nature.

Step 5. Assign the number of plants per square.

Each crop has its own proper number of plants per square to achieve the right spacing. Please reference the chart and illustration on pages 54 and 55. Note that number in each square now.

Square Foot Garden Template

Use the blank templates on the next two pages to plan your SFG bed. Write in pencil so you can easily make changes and rearrange crops as needed.

With this plan in hand, you have a roadmap to your first SFG season. You'll use this plan to purchase your seeds, start your transplants, and dream up future homegrown meals. Now it's time to start building your box.

5

Building Your Square Foot Garden

The thought of *building* anything can be intimidating if you don't have a workshop full of tools. The task of building your Square Foot Garden box is meant to be anything but intimidating. In this chapter, you'll find step-by-step instructions with photos that are easy to follow, even for the beginner DIYer. Assembling the grid for the SFG bed is just as simple. A slightly more challenging project is to build an elevated SFG box, though with the instructions in this chapter, you'll build one that you can be proud of in an afternoon.

You've read several times in this book already that the basic SFG box recommended for new SFG growers is 4-feet-by-4-feet square. The instructions in this chapter focus on this shape. Adapt any of these to fit your needs and space measurements.

Box Depth

When growing crops in a SFG bed, you don't need a lot of depth. All you need is about 6 to 8 inches of Mel's Mix for most vegetables, herbs, and flowers. Choosing a slightly wider-sized lumber for your bed (as discussed in the building plans for a basic bed on page 86) equates to a few more inches of root space, but it also means you'll need more Mel's Mix to fill this slightly deeper bed. Either option is a good one, depending on your budget and goals. Raised beds much deeper than this are more costly and use more resources to fill and maintain.

One circumstance where deeper growing medium is helpful is when growing certain root vegetables, like carrots and parsnips. In the next chapter, Chapter 6, you'll find plans to build your own top hat box, which is essentially a smaller SFG box placed on top of a larger SFG box for growing depth-hungry plants. Top hats also invite visual interest to the garden and give larger plants more space to grow and cascade off the side.

This physical box is essential to the SFG Method for three reasons:

Your SFG box will contain your Mel's Mix. Measuring a 4-foot-by-4-foot square on the ground and planting into it does not make a SFG bed. The Mel's Mix growing medium is an essential component to the SFG Method. This box is the frame you need to contain it.

A SFG box is proportioned to hold a grid with 12-inch-by-12-inch squares. As you read in chapter 4, proper plant spacing is key to growing an abundance of vegetables, fruits, and flowers in a small area. The grid is your visual guide to planning and planting.

The SFG box simplifies gardening all around. A garden contained in this 16-square-foot space is easier to plant, manage, and harvest from than one that spans long rows and large spaces. Even as you become more seasoned and add more boxes to your garden space, you'll find tending to them to be less effort than traditional gardens of the same size.

Box Materials

A traditional SFG box is constructed of wood, but many materials will work. Build your SFG bed from a material that can act as a container for soil, stands approximately 6 to 8 inches tall, can be assembled in four straight lines with plumb corners, and poses no soil-contamination risk. The right material for you will depend on what's most available in your area, what fits your budget, and what fits your style.

Here are some materials commonly thought of as SFG bed options:

Wood

Standard 1×6 or 2×6 dimension lumber is an easy choice of building material. Many Square Foot Gardeners prefer to use 1×8 or 2×8 lumber for greater root depth. Lumber of both sizes is available at any home-improvement store. You can even have the wood cut to size there—sometimes free of charge. See the sidebar on page 85 for more information about lumber dimensions.

The type of wood you use can make a difference to your project. The choice you

make may depend on what's readily available in your area, your budget, and other characteristics that are important to you. Here are some types of wood you might consider:

Black locust. The heartwood of black locust trees is among the most resistant to rot and insects. The density of the wood requires predrilling holes before installing screws (which is our recommended practice for all types of wood anyway). It's difficult to find black locust lumber commercially.

Cedar. The oils and tannins in cedar trees give the wood a natural resistance to rot. A cedar SFG bed could last ten years or more. Cedar is widely available and is the go-to material for the Square Foot Gardening Foundation's box-building needs.

Cypress. Cypress tends to be more expensive and probably needs to be sourced from a lumber yard rather than a home-improvement store. It may not last as long as cedar, but it is more rot-resistant than pine.

Fir. The heartwood of this species is lightweight and slightly decay resistant. It's a soft wood, making it easy to use in constructing beds. Fir lumber is inexpensive. Note that fir is different than Douglas fir.

Oak. For such a hard wood, you'd think oak would be a rot- and insect-resistant choice, but it's not much sturdier than pine. It's a beautiful choice but an expensive one that will probably only last a few years.

Pine. Pine is readily available and by far the most inexpensive wood option in the United States. It's structurally strong and easy to work with but has little resistance to rot and insects. Pine is a good wood to start with if you're on a tight budget. It will last six to seven years before it needs to be replaced.

Redwood. This beautiful wood is moderately priced and highly available in the Western United States. There's some concern that redwood is being overharvested. It resists decay and insect damage but splits easily.

There are many types of wood you can use to make your SFG, just be sure to avoid chemically treated lumber options if possible.

Treated Lumber

Of course you want your SFG box to last for seasons to come. Being an organic material, wood is subject to rotting and to wood-digesting insects. This is especially an issue in warm and wet environments. Wood can be treated to withstand these elements, but commercial treatments carry risks.

Treatments for wood intended for home use may consist of copper, boric acid, fungicides, and other chemicals meant to limit damage from pests, mold, and decay. The National Pesticide Information Center states it's difficult to predict what amount of compounds could be leached from the wood into the growing medium and be absorbed by plants. Leaching and absorption could depend on the type of plant, the type of treatment chemical used, and the organic-matter content of the growing medium. The SFG Foundation cautions against using pressure-treated lumber for any SFG box that will be used to grow edible crops.

Railroad ties, utility poles, and pilings are usually treated with creosote and other chemicals not intended for residential use. You should **never** use materials treated with creosote in a SFG bed.

If you have big gardening dreams and hope to certify your garden as USDA Certified Organic, or with another organic certifier, check their guidelines for using treated wood before choosing your wood source.

Plastics are a possible material option for your SFG bed.

Composite lumber

The synthetic composite lumbers that we've come to know as decking and fencing materials are actually recycled plastics bonded to wood byproducts, such as sawdust. The wood ingredients can decay and are typically treated with zinc borate, which may leach into the soil. Composite lumber's use in raised beds hasn't been studied at the time of the writing of this book.

Plastic lumber

High-density polyethylene (HDPE) lumber is a plastic lumber usually made from recycled plastics, like milk jugs and plastic bags, that carry the recycling symbol #2. This thermoplastic polymer resists degradation and could last a millennium, giving it the ultimate durability rating. This is an expensive building material.

Concrete and cinder blocks

Concrete blocks and cinder blocks are two different materials, but their names are often used interchangeably. Concrete blocks are made of water, cement, and aggregate, such as fine sand and stones. They are very heavy. Cinder blocks are made of those same materials plus fly ash—cinders—which is a byproduct of burning coal that includes heavy metals and other hazardous waste. This ingredient is added as a cost-effective, lightweight aggregate that makes cinder blocks less heavy than concrete blocks but still durable. Without talking to the manufacturer, it's difficult to know whether the building block you're looking at is a concrete block or a cinder block, and there's little research on the safety of cinder blocks' fly-ash content in garden beds.

These blocks are long-lasting, easy to source, and very inexpensive. Building a bed using cinder or concrete blocks would require few tools.

Retaining wall blocks

Concrete retaining wall blocks are meant to be attractive additions to a landscape, and they're meant to stand the test of time. These are also cumbersome—often weighing 50 pounds or more—and expensive but can be found secondhand for sale from landscapers or posted on online message boards.

Bricks

Another nearly ubiquitous building material, bricks make a beautiful raised bed. This bed-building material takes more effort. One brick layer is not tall enough to contain all of the Mel's Mix you need for a SFG bed. Additional brick layers make the structure less stable, so you should adhere the layers using mortar. This requires a level construction area and becomes a semi-permanent structure.

Concrete blocks are better than cinder blocks for building a SFG, but it can be tough to know which is which.

Galvanized beds offer a modern design, though you may have to search for one with a suitable exterior dimension for Square Foot Gardening.

Metal

Metal raised beds are a trendy garden asset, bringing the modern industrial interior design style outdoors. Prefabricated options are available, though they may not measure the required 4 feet x 4 feet exterior dimension or have the proper depth. Metal garden edging may be an alternative material for framing a bed if you can source it at the proper depth. It is pliable and will require staking along the length to keep straight linear walls. Other than garden edging, you may be able to find metal sheets that are 2 feet or more in width, but they will require extensive cutting that results in sharp edges. Do not use rusty metal as SFG box material.

Reclaimed materials

It always feels good to be able to reuse something you already have on hand. If that material isn't listed here, ask yourself: Is it durable? Nontoxic? Is it 6 or 8 inches tall, and can it be assembled to create a 4-foot square?

You're encouraged to be creative with your SFG bed-building materials as long as they can offer a safe place to grow in a square-foot grid system.

BOX MATERIAL OPTIONS

With a lot of options available to build a SFG bed, this chart outlines their features. The wood lumber is assumed to be untreated.

Material	Durability	Affordability	Availability	Nontoxic	Ease of Use
Black locust lumber	X			X	X
Cedar lumber	X	X	X	X	X
Cypress lumber	X			X	X
Fir lumber		X	X	X	X
Pine lumber		X	X	X	X
Redwood lumber	X		X	X	
Oak lumber			X	X	X
Composite lumber			X		
Plastic lumber	X		X	X	X
Concrete/cinder blocks	X	X	X		X
Retaining wall blocks	X		X	X	
Bricks	X	X	X	X	
Metal edging	X		X	X	

The Bottom of the Box

So much attention is paid to the dimensions and construction of the SFG box itself. It's worth understanding what's happening beneath the box, too.

If your SFG bed is on the lawn, you don't need to worry much about the bottom of the box, except to lay landscape fabric underneath. Landscape fabric is a woven polypropylene sheet—usually black or gray—that you can find at any home-improvement store or farm-supply store. Sometimes you can even find small rolls of landscape fabric at the grocery store during gardening season. This material is water permeable and breathable.

Lots of gardeners like to use cardboard or newspapers for weed suppression. Cardboard and thick layers of newspaper are also options for the bottom of the box, though they will eventually break down. Both the landscape fabric and cardboard or newspaper will help to keep insects, weeds, and grass from coming up into the bed from ground level.

There are a few instances where you need a more significant box bottom than what landscape fabric offers:

An elevated SFG bed. If you're building an elevated SFG bed, you'll need a well-supported plywood or metal bottom with ample drainage holes in addition to the landscape fabric to contain the Mel's Mix. The building plans on page 89 include those instructions.

Garden pests. If moles, voles, and gophers frequent your yard, the landscape fabric will be no match for them. These ground-dwelling pests have foiled many a gardener's harvest. Exclude them from your SFG box with a piece of hardware cloth or $1/4$-inch wire mesh secured to the bottom of the bed frame beneath the landscape fabric. The pests can't dig through this material.

A more stable base. If you just can't get the ground level enough to provide a stable base for your SFG box, a plywood bottom can help shore up the structure. Using $1^1/_2$-inch galvanized deck screws, attach a 48-inch-by-48-inch piece of $^3/_4$-inch-thick plywood to the underside of the box. Drill $1/4$-inch drainage holes every 12 inches across the board.

DIY Square Foot Garden Building Projects

The projects on the next few pages are your blueprint to assembling various SFG beds. Talk about a feeling of accomplishment when this is done! Not only will you be growing your own food, but you'll have built the bed it's growing in. Whether you're a seasoned construction pro or this is your first time using a power drill, this is something to be proud of.

About Lumber Sizes

Dimension lumber—the kind of wood you source commercially—is easy to work with because it's dry and uniform in size, no matter which store you purchase it from. It also has one misleading quality—dimension lumber's actual size is smaller than its stated size. A piece of lumber sold as a 2×6 is not exactly 2 inches wide by 6 inches tall; it's 1½ inches wide by 5½ inches tall. A 1×6 is actually ¾-inch wide by 5½ inches tall. Keep this in mind as you make your measurements for the projects in this book.

Build a Basic Square Foot Garden Box

This classic Square Foot Garden box is a simple 4-foot-by-4-foot cedar box, though you could opt to use a different type of wood. This building plan uses a butt joint to secure the ends. (The end of one board is "butted" against and attached to the side of another.)

The materials list lets you choose 1×8 boards or 2×8 boards. If you want a less expensive option, use 1x6 or 2x6 boards. The 1-inch thickness option will cost much less, but it will also be less durable. Choose the size screws for this project based on the size of lumber you're working with. The screws need to be long enough to reach through one board and bite into the next.

Build your box on a level surface, like a flat yard, driveway, or the floor of a garage, to ensure a level and square finished product.

Materials and Tools →

- ○ 4 - 4' 1×8 or 2×8 untreated cedar boards (alternatively, 1×6 or 2×6 can be used, see note above)
- ○ 1½" or 3" deck screws
- ○ 4'×4' landscape fabric
- ○ Staples
- ○ Rafter (or speed) square
- ○ Pencil
- ○ Drill
- ○ ⅛" drill bit
- ○ Staple gun
- ○ Eye and ear protection
- ○ Work gloves

Building a basic 4-foot-by-4-foot SFG bed only takes a few hours to complete.

Assembly

Step 1: Prepare the corners.

1a. Stack the four boards as shown here, to give yourself space to drill pilot holes.

1b. Using the rafter square, outline the butt joint. To do this measure and mark the width of the lumber on one end of each board. This is your reference for drilling the pilot holes.

1c. Drill three pilot holes in the end of each board. Stack the next board on top of the pile and repeat.

Step 2: Assemble the corners.

2a. Position the boards in a square so the pilot holes are aligned with the end grain of the adjoining board. One end of each board should overlap another board. See illustration in Perfectly Square on page 88.

2b. Secure each corner with three deck screws, using the pilot holes.

Step 3: Arrange your box.

3a. Move the box to its final location.

3b. Lay landscape fabric on top of the box, and staple it to the box.

3c. Flip over the box so the landscape fabric is on the bottom.

Step 4: Finish your box.

Your box is ready for its finishing touches. In chapter 7, you'll get the Mel's Mix recipe, and later in this chapter, you'll find instructions for building a SFG grid.

Perfectly Square

You'll notice that these instructions call for holes to be drilled in one end of each board. This joinery method gives you a perfectly square box.

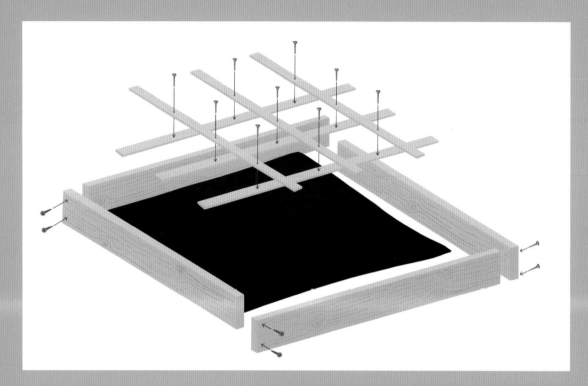

It's important to join the corners of your box properly in order to form a perfect square.

If you were to drill holes in both ends of two boards, you'd end up with two slightly longer and two slightly shorter sides—almost square, but not quite.

Another joinery method that results in a perfectly square box is one using corner braces. A wide brace or two narrow braces on the inside of each corner can replace the screws at the butt joints in this project. Be sure to use the same method of arranging each board so it overlaps with another just once to keep your box square. All metal will eventually corrode when in constant contact with wet growing medium. Stainless steel and galvanized steel may be the most corrosion resistant.

Metal corner joiner brackets are an inexpensive way to secure the corners of your SFG bed.

Build an Elevated Square Foot Garden Box

Follow this project to build a 16-square-foot SFG box elevated to 36 inches.

An elevated SFG box serves a number of purposes. Gardeners with physical limitations or aging bodies and those using wheelchairs have easier access to an elevated bed. An elevated garden keeps out pests like rabbits, armadillos, and dogs—even your own dogs.

MATERIALS AND TOOLS →

- 4 - 4-foot 2×10 cedar boards
- 4 - 3-foot 2×2 cedar balusters
- 4 - 3-foot 2×6 cedar boards
- 4 - 3-foot 2×4 cedar boards
- 2 - 51-inch 1×4 cedar boards
- 2 - 45-inch 1x4 cedar boards
- 2½" galvanized deck screws
- 1⅝" galvanized deck screws
- 1 - 46½" x 46½" x ¾" exterior-grade plywood sheet
- 56" x 48" landscape fabric
- Staples
- Exterior-grade wood glue
- 4 - 4" × 4" cedar post caps (optional)
- Pencil
- Tape measure
- Drill
- ³⁄₁₆" drill bit
- ¼" drill bit
- Rafter square
- Scissors
- Staple gun
- Eye and ear protection
- Work gloves

Building this elevated SFG bed is a bit more complicated than a basic ground-level bed, but it makes a beautiful and productive gardening structure.

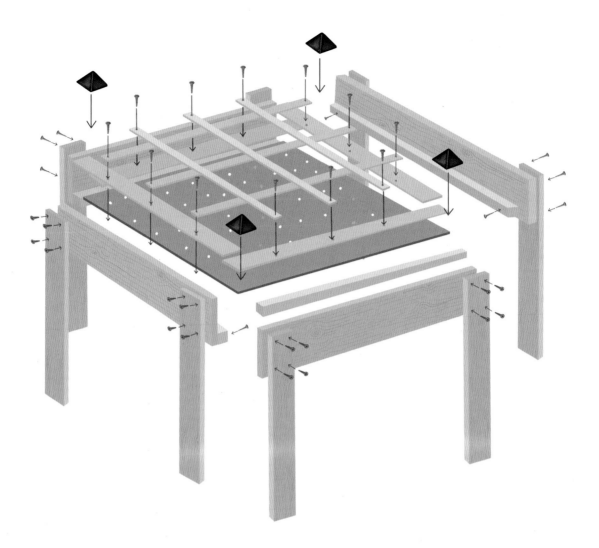

ASSEMBLY

Step 1: Prepare the corners.

1a. Outline the butt joint. Measure and mark the width of the lumber on one end of each 2×10 board. This is your reference for drilling the pilot holes.

1b. Drill three ³⁄₁₆″ pilot holes in the end of each board.

Step 2: Prepare the bottom frame.

2a. Center one baluster along the bottom edge of each 2×10.

2b. Drill five ³⁄₁₆″ pilot holes spaced evenly along each baluster.

2c. Secure each baluster with 2½-inch deck screws, using the pilot holes.

Step 3: Assemble the corners.

3a. Position the 2×10 boards in a square so the pilot holes are aligned with the end grain of the adjoining board. One end of each board should overlap another board. Be careful to keep the balusters along the bottom edge. Use the rafter square as a guide to ensure a 90-degree-square box.

3b. Secure each corner with three 2½" screws, using the pilot holes.

Step 4: Assemble the legs.

4a. Position a 2×6 board over a 2×4 board at a 90-degree angle with the edges aligned. Be sure the 2×6 board overlaps the 2×4 board, not the other way around. The width of one side of each leg will be 5½ inches, and the width of the other side of each leg will be 5 inches.

4b. Drill five ³⁄₁₆" pilot holes from the side of the 2×6 into the edge of the adjoining 2x4.

4c. Secure the boards with 2½" deck screws, using the pilot holes.

4d. Complete all four legs.

Step 5: Attach the legs.

5a. Flip the assembled box upside down so the balusters are now on the top side.

5b. Position the assembled legs around each box corner. Be sure the top of the leg is flush with the top of the box. (The "top" is currently resting on the ground.)

5c. Drill three ³⁄₁₆" pilot holes on the outer edge of both sides of the leg, into the box.

5d. Secure the leg to the box with 2½" deck screws, using the pilot holes.

5e. Complete all four legs.

Step 6: Assemble the bottom of the box.

6a. Flip over the box so it's standing on its legs.

6b. Insert the plywood sheet so it rests on the balusters.

6c. Screw three 1⅝" deck screws through the plywood into each baluster.

6d. Draw a grid on the plywood with lines intersecting every 6 inches. Drill a ¼" hole at each intersection for drainage.

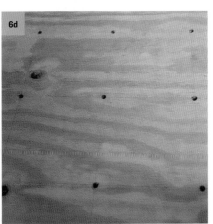

6e. Lay landscape fabric in the bottom of the box. The edges will come up two of the sides. Secure with the staple gun.

Step 7: Assemble the top plates.

7a. Set a 51" 1x4 on top of the box, one long edge flush with the inside of the box and both short edges flush with the outside of two legs.

7b. Drill five ³⁄₁₆" pilot holes along the top plate, into the edge of the box below.

7c. Secure the top plate with 2½" deck screws, using the pilot holes.

7d. Repeat with the 51" 1x4 on the opposite side of the box. Attach the 45" 1x4s on the remaining two sides.

Step 8: Attach the post caps.
Use wood glue to attach the post caps to the corners of the box, flush with the edges of the top plates.

Step 9: Finish your box.

Move the box to its final location. You can now fill it with Mel's Mix and top it with a grid. You'll get the Mel's Mix recipe in chapter 7, and later in this chapter, you'll find instructions for building a grid.

Elevated SFG Box Adaptations

The plan offered here can be altered to match your specific SFG box use. Here are two examples:

Adjust the height. The instructions build a SFG box that's 36 inches tall. Raise or lower this by sizing the leg boards to the height that works for you. In the materials list, the 2×6 and 2×4 boards form the legs.

Modify the box for balcony use. In cases where you don't want water running out of the bed, such as on a balcony where it can drip on people below, modify the box height and the bottom of the box.

While a level SFG box is generally preferred, a small slope will allow the water to drain toward the low side of the box. Construct the legs so one side sits an inch or 2 shorter than the other. An alternative to altering the box construction is to build the box legs as instructed, then set the legs of one side of the box on a 2×6 board to raise them slightly.

In the plywood sheet that makes the bottom of the box, don't drill holes throughout. Instead, drill holes only on the low end of the box, and place buckets or other vessels underneath to catch the draining liquid.

Build a SFG Box with Oldcastle Blocks

As far as construction projects go, this one is as easy as it gets, requiring no power tools or small parts. If you rent your space or are setting up a SFG bed in a temporary spot, building an easy-to-disassemble bed is a smart idea.

Oldcastle blocks are inexpensive, non-composite concrete blocks available at most home-improvement stores. At about 20 pounds each, these blocks are heavy but possible for one person to manage. Oldcastle blocks have a groove in each of the four sides, making the block look like, well, an old castle. The grooves are sized for 2×6 dimension lumber.

Unlike the freestanding-bed projects in this chapter, you'll assemble this bed in its final location. If you plan to do any wood finishing, such as painting or staining the exterior of the box, do so before assembling it. It's especially important to pay attention to leveling the area for an Oldcastle-block SFG bed so the boards sit flush with the ground and the blocks.

MATERIALS AND TOOLS →

- 4 - 7¾" x 5½" x 7¾" Oldcastle concrete blocks
- 4 - 46" 2x6 cedar boards
- Landscape fabric
- Level
- Work gloves

Oldcastle blocks make building a SFG bed extra quick and simple.

ASSEMBLY

Step 1: Place the Oldcastle blocks.

1a. Place an Oldcastle block to form the first corner of the box. Be sure this is set level and square to the rest of the box.

1b. Place each block in the box configuration.

Step 2: Assemble the sides.

Slide each board into the block grooves, making four box walls.

Step 3: Lay the landscape fabric.

Lay a cut-to-fit piece of landscape fabric in the box, and tuck it under the corners and sides.

Step 4: Finish the box.

Your completed box is ready to be filled with Mel's Mix and topped with a grid. In chapter 7, you'll get the Mel's Mix recipe, and later in this chapter, you'll find instructions for building a grid.

Square Foot Gardener's Tip

Make your SFG bed your own with finishing touches, like paint or stain. Just be sure to paint or stain the exterior, not the interior. You don't want those substances in contact with the growing medium.

Build a SFG Box with Prefab Corners

This sturdy bed is easy to assemble, requiring just a few screws to hold boards in brackets. This is a great temporary bed option, as it's easy to disassemble, as well as pick up and move when empty.

There are several kinds of prefab corners available from various manufacturers. The rust-proof aluminum prefab-corner brackets shown here have a clean, contemporary look. They are built to fit dimension lumber, each board snugging into its slot for tight and tidy corners. You can find these prefab corners from specialty garden retailers online. They are a more expensive option than Oldcastle blocks.

In case you use prefab corner brackets that are different than those shown here, you may need lumber of a different length. These prefab brackets don't lose any length in assembly, making the box exactly 4-feet square. If your brackets cause the boards to overlap, adjust the length of the boards.

MATERIALS AND TOOLS →

- 4 prefab corners
- 4 - 4' 2×6 cedar boards
- 1¼" galvanized deck screws
- 4'×4' landscape fabric
- Staples
- Drill
- ⅛" drill bit
- Staple gun
- Eye and ear protection
- Work gloves

Prefab corners, made especially for DIYing raised garden beds, are a great way to set up your SFG bed.

ASSEMBLY

Step 1. Assemble the sides.

1a. Insert the end of a board into the metal corner bracket.

1b. Using the predrilled holes in the brackets, drill pilot holes.

1c. Secure the board to the metal corner bracket with the deck screws.

1d. Repeat so the boards and brackets make a square.

Step 2: Arrange your box.

2a. Move the box to its final location.

2b. Flip the box so it's upside down. Lay landscape fabric over it and staple the fabric to the box.

2c. Flip over the box so the landscape fabric is on the bottom.

Step 3: Finish your box.

Your box is ready for Mel's Mix, a grid, and planting.

Using Raised Bed Kits

Because gardening in raised beds has become quite popular, ready-made kits for building raised beds are easy to find in all price ranges.

While all SFG beds are raised beds, not all raised beds are SFG beds. If you choose to purchase a kit to make your SFG box, be sure it meets your needs: durable, nontoxic, about 6 to 8 inches tall, and able to create a box with square-foot increments.

The white beds in this SFG were made from a kit. They offer an attractive option for non-DIYers.

The grid is a critical piece to SFG spacing.

The Square Foot Garden Grid

Your SFG box isn't finished until it has a grid on top. The grid makes the garden, transforming your box into a SFG bed. Having a box without a grid is like having a parking lot without parking-space lines. Chaos ensues.

Set in 1-square-foot sections, the grid visually divides the growing space so you can focus on the planting and harvesting needs for each crop without overthinking plant placement. Along with the plan that you created in the second step of the SFG Method, this grid tells you where to plant which crop and how many seeds or transplants belong in each square. The grid guides you in amending your Mel's Mix each season, because you know that every time you take out one plant and put in another, you should mix a few cups of compost into that square. Having this clear visual guide also helps you to rotate crops from season to season.

Grid materials

You can make a grid from a variety of materials. The instructions on page 98 use specially cut cedar boards. The SFG Method says there must be a grid, but there's nothing that says the grid must be made of wood or must be made of cedar slats.

Wood

If you want to stick with wood for your grid but can't spring for specially cut cedar boards, a few precut options are common in home-improvement stores. Look at the wood lath and furring strip options.

A wood lath is a narrow strip of softwood originally intended for use in lath-and-plaster construction. You might also recognize these thin boards from snow or beach-erosion fencing. They're usually untreated but durable enough to last as a

Rebar

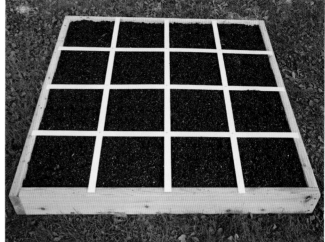

Vinyl lattice

PVC

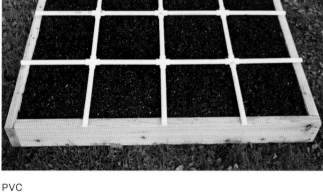

Bamboo

garden grid for several years. Laths are 1¹/₂ inches wide.

Furring strips are also made of softwood and are thicker than laths in both width and depth. They may last longer because of their thickness. They'll also be bulkier to store in the off season. Furring strips can be treated or untreated, so be sure to ask before you buy. You want the untreated furring strips.

Precut options like these may come in 4-foot or 8-foot lengths. Here you have a decision. A grid that's 4 feet long will fit inside your 4-foot-by-4-foot SFG box and rest on the soil. It's not long enough to attach to the sides of the box. This is not a bad option, but it does differ from the grid-building instructions you'll find in this chapter.

If you're making your own wood strips for a grid, cut them to 50 inches so you can screw them to the top of the SFG box—or cut them to 48 inches if that's what is most effective for your budget and available materials.

Wood alternatives

Go ahead and be creative about the material you select to construct your grid. This structure should fit your budget and complete the look of your SFG bed.

Square Foot Gardener's Tip

String, yarn, twine, and rope are not long-lasing grid materials. You can make straight lines with these materials and secure the ends with nails or round-headed screws in the box edges, but they're not long-lasting enough to make a permanent SFG grid. These materials may even break down before the growing season is over.

Whatever material you use to create your grid, it should be:

- Durable
- Nontoxic
- Narrow
- Straight

The examples of alternative grid materials pictured here are bamboo, PVC, rebar, and vinyl lattice. These materials are easily sourced from home-improvement stores. It's possible you already have them in your own garden shed. The pieces are joined at the intersections to make a solid structure to top the SFG bed.

As above, if you want your grid to nestle into the box, make the length 48 inches. If you intend to attach it to the top of the box, size the pieces to 50 inches each.

Attaching the grid

It's not essential to attach your grid to your SFG box, but there are a few reasons you would want to. If your grid is constructed with lightweight material, you certainly don't want it to blow away. And while you're working in your SFG bed, you don't want to bump the grid and have it knock into plants or to skew your planting pattern.

If your SFG box is constructed of wood, attaching most grid materials to it will be easy enough with screws. If you chose bricks, blocks, or metal to make your bed, some creative thinking could be required. A construction adhesive is a strong but permanent choice. Driving wood stakes into the inside of the bed gives you a wood attachment point.

If your grid fits into your SFG bed, sitting on top of the soil, landscape staples can help to secure it in place.

You don't have to attach the grid to your SFG box if you don't want to. You can rest it on top of the soil like this gardener has done.

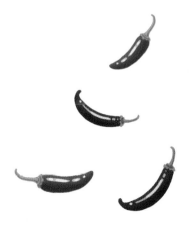

How to Build a Traditional Square Foot Garden Grid

Six pieces of untreated cedar slats can be assembled in an hour with these instructions. These slats are not standard-issue home-improvement store materials. You can have these cut for you—or you can cut them yourself, if you have a table saw—from 50-inch cedar boards.

This grid will fit a 4-foot-by-4-foot SFG box.

You can assemble this grid on the bed, on the ground, or on a work surface. It's light enough that you'll be able to move it when it's complete.

The grid will be a part of your garden throughout the whole growing season. If you only grow two or three seasons out of the year, you can remove this grid and store it indoors. It's even collapsible.

MATERIALS AND TOOLS

- 6 - ¼" × ½" × 50" custom cut cedar slats
- 9 - ¼" × 1" bolts with washers and nuts
- 12 - 1" exterior screws
- Drill
- Tape measure
- ¼" drill bit
- ⅛" drill bit
- Eye and ear protection
- Work gloves

This simple grid is easy to make and attach to your SFG bed's frame.

ASSEMBLY

Step 1. Arrange the first three slats.

1a. Position three slats perpendicular to one another.

1b. Space the slats 12" apart from center to center.

Step 2. Arrange the second three slats.

2a. Position the remaining three slats on top of the first layer to form a grid. Place the center of the outermost slats 13" from the ends of the slats in the first layer.

2b. Place the middle slat halfway between the outer slats.

Step 3. Secure the grid.

3a. Drill a ¼" hole at each intersection of lattice pieces.

3b. Slide a bolt through each hole, secure it with a washer and nut.

Step 4. Attach the grid.

4a. Before attaching the grid to your SFG bed, fill the box with Mel's Mix. (You'll do this in chapter 7.)

4b. Position the grid on top of the box so 1" of the grid overlaps the box on all sides.

4c. Drill ⅛" pilot holes through the end of each cedar slat into the edge of the box.

4d. Secure the cedar slats to the box with screws.

Step 5. Get planting.

Grid assembly is the last step in getting your new SFG box ready for the Mel's Mix. You're almost ready to put some seeds and plants in the bed!

Your SFG project is taking shape now. A SFG box with the grid is a key element to growing a lot of crops in a little space. The next step is to construct any add-ons that your SFG bed needs to support and protect your plants.

Extend the Life of Your SFG Grid

The wood-slat grid you're building here is collapsible, making it easy to bring indoors when it's not in use.

Push the outside slats together to fold it into a structure that's about 6 feet tall and a few inches around. You can store this in the rafters of your garden shed, mounted on the wall behind a door in the garage, or even under your bed—anywhere that gets it out of the elements and out of your way during your garden's off season.

Regardless of whether the grid is in direct contact with the soil or raised above it, rainwater will soak into and run off the grid, into the Mel's Mix in your SFG box. For this reason, painting or staining the grid is a bad idea.

The grid is easy to fold closed for winter storage. Simply grab the grid as shown and squeeze it in on itself.

6

Building Your Square Foot Garden Add-Ons

The box is just the beginning of the framework for your Square Foot Garden growing space. With a little more time, you can construct accessories to boost your growing power. On the horizontal plane, your 4-foot-by-4-foot SFG box offers 16 square feet to work with. Going vertical, you have much more space. Easy trellises allow you to grow vining plants that would otherwise dominate your SFG bed. SFG boxes give most plants sufficient space for their roots, but some deep-rooted crops, like carrots, need a little extra room to grow down, which is where SFG accessories known as "top hats" are useful. A few accessories are meant to protect your plants, too—from the elements, from insect pests, and from critters. Because your SFG box is compact, so are these protective structures. In this chapter, you'll learn about vertical growing and pest protection and get step-by-step instructions to build your own SFG bed add-ons.

Grow Up (and Down)

When you think about plants growing in nature, vertical growing has always been a feature. A forest comprises different layers of plants, from ground covers all the way up to canopy trees. In between, there are various leafy plants, shrubs, and smaller trees. And don't forget about the vines. Grape vines, poison ivy vines, Virginia creeper, and more are rooted in the earth and climb the plants around them to go vertical. Adding a vertical dimension to your SFG bed isn't a new idea, rather it's one that mimics some plants' natural inclination.

There are a number of reasons for growing your garden vertically:

It makes for an easier harvest. Plucking waist-height cucumbers from a vine is less work than bending over and hunting under leaves for the fruit.

Plants are healthier. Growing on a trellis, plants are exposed to more airflow and sunlight. This boosts their photosynthesis and strengthens their production. Getting them off the ground reduces the pathogens that might splash onto them from the soil when it rains. The airflow limits pathogens' opportunity to settle on the plants. You'll see fewer fungal and bacterial issues than you would if vining plants grew over the garden bed and ground. It also keeps crawling pests at bay, such as slugs and earwigs.

It saves garden space. One reason gardeners growing in rows need so much space to garden is because their vining plants are taking up a lot of space on the ground. Giving these plants a way to grow up frees the ground level area for more plants.

Produce is cleaner. Tomatoes and cucumbers that are growing in the air will naturally have less growing medium clinging to them than those that grow along the ground.

Trellises and structures are visually interesting. This is another opportunity for you to exercise creativity in your SFG bed. Vegetables, fruits, and flowers growing vertically add beautiful touches to your garden space, and you can build trellises and supports using interesting materials.

Your garden is more productive overall. If you left the vines to sprawl over your garden bed, they'd smother other plants growing around them. Letting the climbing plants climb benefits them as well as your other crops.

➙

Nothing could be simpler than using wooden 1" x 1" stakes with nylon garden netting stretched between them to grow vining crops vertically.

Plants That Vine

Think about the plants that have a long and sprawling growth habit: tomatoes, melons, squash, pole beans, cucumbers, sweet potatoes, peas, etc. While they all vine, they have different means of vining. There are four ways a plant climbs:

- **With tendrils.** Cucumber, melon, squash, and pea vines send out tendrils. These thin, surprisingly strong plant extensions essentially allow the plant to reach out and grab onto objects around it. With proper planning, that object will be your trellis, and the tendrils will help the plants climb it. Plants with tendrils sometimes need help finding their support, but once they get started in a vertical direction, they will keep going on their own.

- **By twining.** Twining plants climb as their vines encircle upright supports. Pole beans are a good example of a twining plant.

- **In a sprawl.** These plants don't so much climb or wind, but they do grow long and viny. Tomatoes and sweet potatoes are sprawling plants. They need to be tied to their trellises. You can also weave their branches or vines through the trellis, but be careful—you don't want to accidentally break them.

- **With aerial roots.** Some plants have tiny adhesive "feet"—which are actually aerial roots—that they use to cling to surfaces. These are not edible plants that you'd grow in a SFG, though, and some are even considered invasive in certain regions, including English ivy and trumpet vine.

Beans climb structures by twining. They'll easily wrap themselves around trellises and fencing, but it never hurts to give wayward stems a helping hand.

The top hat

Vertical growth goes the opposite direction, too. In the forest, what we don't see is all the growth happening below ground. Plants' roots tunnel deep into the earth to find water and nutrients. Even in an ecosystem as crowded as a forest, there's plenty of vertical below-ground space for everyone.

In your SFG bed, plant roots don't need quite the area that forest plants require. Your average garden plant will do fine in a 6- to 8-inch-deep SFG bed because its roots will grow outwards into the Mel's Mix. Those whose below-ground growth we want to encourage can find extra vertical growing space with the help of a top hat box set on top of the SFG bed. The sky isn't exactly the limit when growing in this direction, but this additional depth goes a long way for potatoes, sweet potatoes, carrots, leeks, ginger (if you plan to hill it), and others.

By providing a top hat on just one, or several, squares of your SFG bed, you're being efficient with your use of resources. Instead of building up the whole SFG box to 12 inches, filling that space with Mel's Mix, and watering that volume of growing medium, you're only filling and watering the area that needs it.

Trellis types

In this chapter, you'll find instructions for building a flat wooden trellis and an A-frame trellis—two trellis options sized to fit your 4-foot-by-4-foot SFG bed. These are not the only trellis options available to you, of course.

Setting up your vertical-growing space is another way you can make your SFG bed your own.

Choose a trellis that:
- Is durable
- Can be securely anchored
- Is nontoxic
- Has a structure that allows plants to wind and climb
- Is strong enough to support the weight of the plant and the fruit

This top hat is being used to grow leeks. Giving them extra depth means whiter, more tender stalks.

You can build your own trellis using bamboo, metal conduit pipe, rebar, wood, string netting, or PVC. If you would rather sit out this building project, there is no shortage of commercially made trellises sold at garden and home-improvement stores. These come in all sizes and colors.

You might even find creative upcycled trellis ideas around your house, at a yard sale, or somewhere surprising. Here are a few ideas that could work:

Wooden ladders make logical trellises—trellises are essentially ladders for your plants—though plants may need your help to reach from one rung to the next.

Tree branches are beautiful garden trellises. Use them on their own for a wild look or weave them into a frame.

Wood pallets will serve as trellises, too. Check the stamp on the pallets first. This indicates how the wood was treated. Pallets marked HT, KD, or DB have been heat treated, kiln dried, or debarked—respectively—and are safe to use in a garden. Pallets stamped with MB have been treated with methyl bromide and should never be used. Pallets without a stamp haven't been treated.

Prefab bamboo A-frame trellises work to not only provide a climbing structure for pole beans and other vining crops, but they also provide summer shade to any lettuce and other heat-sensitive greens growing beneath.

Stakes are useful for tying up a plant that needs help standing upright. Sometimes top-heavy plants like sunflowers need a stake, as well as peppers or eggplants that are falling over. Look for wooden stakes at least 1 inch thick to be able to hold up growing plants. Bamboo poles are good staking materials, too.

Woven supports are easy to make with a stake in each corner of the square—or in each corner of a set of squares—and sturdy garden twine wrapped around them to create a system for propping up the plants. Better yet, place the supports on the outside of the SFG box. Pound rebar into the ground on opposite sides of the box. Slide PVC or metal conduit over the rebar— or use the rebar itself—as support stakes for weaving twine. Peppers, eggplants, tomatillos, bush beans, and the like can be propped up this way.

Chicken wire is another easy DIY support system. Place one stake in each corner of the square (or squares) or install rebar on the outsides of the SFG box, and secure chicken wire to the stakes to create your own cage. It'll be harder to harvest from the plants in a chicken-wire cage— you can't reach your hand through those holes—so be sure you can reach down through the top come harvest time.

A tepee structure can be an attractive addition to a SFG bed, and an easy one to build—or to buy—using bamboo or wood. If the plant you're supporting with the tepee needs additional help, wrap hefty garden twine around the tepee legs to create an obelisk-like structure.

An arched trellis is a beautiful addition to a set of SFG beds. By bending a piece of cattle panel into an arch, or by properly positioning a few pieces of arched rebar with welded-wire fencing stretched between it, you can create a walkway between two SFG beds with plants growing over top. Before you get wrapped up in the whimsy of this project, consider your plants' access to sunlight. This trellis will cast a lot of shade. Arches are great for pole beans, climbing peas, winter squash, cucumbers, gourds, and other vining crops. Orient your arch in an east-west direction so that each side gets either morning or afternoon sun.

Other supports

While top hats are the best option for growing deep-rooted crops, trellises are not the only way to support tall plants. Sometimes the issue is less that the plant is tall and more that the plant is bushy or that the plant is unstable.

In these cases, you can reach for other types of supports:

Round or square tomato cages found at home-improvement and garden-supply stores are not good supports for indeterminate tomato plants—these tomato plants are just too big for these—but they do a good job of propping up smaller bushy plants, including determinate tomatoes, peppers, and eggplants.

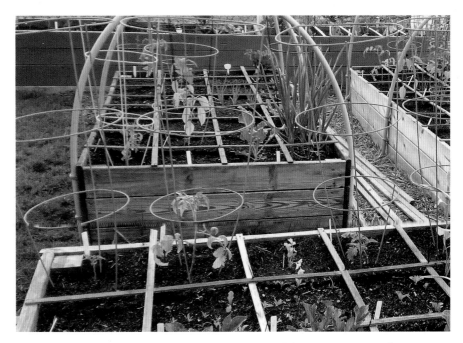

These round wire cages will soon be filled with pepper and determinate tomato plants.

Cattle panel arches positioned between two beds and over walkways extend your growing space and look beautiful. They also make harvesting a snap.

This clever Square Foot Gardener has DIYed a unique arch with PVC pipes and galvanized wire fencing. The sky is the limit when it comes to creating possibilities.

Holding It Down

Whatever vertical-growth tool you're using, a strong anchor is vital. Plants loaded with fruit get heavy, and one gusty thunderstorm can take out a flimsy support structure.

Pound metal or wooden trellis support legs 18 to 24 inches into the ground on the outside of the SFG box, or secure the trellis to the exterior of the SFG box using screws or pipe straps.

Cage- and stake-support systems should reach the depth of the SFG box, but try to not breach the landscape fabric underneath the box. Let's say you use a round metal tomato cage to help support a pepper plant. The cage will be most stable with its bottom ring resting on the surface of the Mel's Mix. You may need to trim the cage legs so they don't pierce the landscape fabric at the base. You can put in a couple of landscape staples to anchor the bottom ring of the cage in the Mel's Mix. If you're using multiple cages in a row, tie the tops together so they're less likely to topple over.

Tepee structures are easy to make and help support plants. They can be constructed from branches, bamboo poles, or metal or wood garden stakes.

Build a Flat Wooden Trellis

This all-purpose trellis is a common-sense addition to any SFG bed. It's durable, and at 5 feet tall, it will accommodate extra-large vining plants, including indeterminate tomatoes, melons, squash, cucumbers, and more. This plan will fit a 4-foot-by-4-foot SFG box. Tailor it as needed for other box sizes.

As you select the fencing for this project, keep in mind that any galvanized-metal fencing will withstand years of outdoor use. Welded-wire fencing is more sturdy than woven-wire fencing, but either will do. This type of fencing comes in rolls, and you will have to cut your own 5-foot pieces with wire cutters. Look for wire fencing with 4" by 4" squares, which allow plants with tendrils to grasp the structure while also providing enough space for sprawling and twining plants to weave throughout.

Attach this trellis structure to the SFG box after your box is in its final place. It will be much more difficult to move your SFG box once this trellis is attached. In fact, you should detach the trellis from the box if you need to move it, so you don't accidentally damage the trellis—or your back.

This trellis is the perfect place to grow pole beans, cucumbers, and other vining crops. Building it is quick and easy.

MATERIALS AND TOOLS

- 2 piece of 66" 2×4 lumber
- 1 piece of 41" 2×4 lumber
- 4 - 2" × 4" galvanized mending plates
- 1½" galvanized deck screws
- 4' × 5' galvanized wire fencing
- Fencing staples
- 2½" galvanized deck screws
- Rafter square
- Drill
- Hammer
- ³⁄₁₆" drill bit
- Eye and ear protection
- Work gloves

ASSEMBLY

Step 1. Assemble the frame.

1a. Lay the 2×4s so the 66" pieces are parallel to one another and the 41" piece is perpendicular between them.

1b. Align the 41" piece so its short edges are in between the long edges of the 66" pieces. Use the rafter square to be sure these joints are 90 degrees.

1c. Join the 41" crossmember board to the 66" upright boards using mending plates with 4 1½" deck screws each.

1d. Turn over the structure. Attach mending plates to this side of the joints, as well.

Step 2. Attach the trellis fence.

2a. Align the fencing with the top and side edges of the frame.

2b. Attach the fencing piece to the trellis frame with fencing staples driven in every 8" apart.

Deterring Birds

Birds are a beneficial part of a gardener's ecosystem and, at the same time, a nuisance.

Birds are important to have around because they eat insect pests and weed seeds from around the yard.

In a vegetable, fruit, and herb garden, birds have some negative effects, as well. Birds do eat insect pests, but they also eat beneficial insects. Birds eat fruits right off the vine and love berries. Larger birds can snatch whole plants out of the ground.

Perhaps the largest downside to having birds around your SFG bed is their droppings. Bird waste carries pathogens that are harmful to humans. This is especially dangerous on produce that will be eaten raw.

Unfortunately, trellises and other garden structures make great landing pads for avian friends, inviting their droppings into the vicinity of your plants. Bird netting, such as the kind used for the Perimeter Crop Cage on page 128, will exclude birds from the garden space, but this doesn't stop them from landing on your structures. Plus, birds and other small critters can get trapped in it. It's up to you to convince birds that your garden structures aren't a safe place to hang out.

Movement deters birds. They especially don't like reflective objects in motion, including pinwheels, CDs or aluminum pie plates on strings, and mylar streamers. All of these will move in the breeze. Eventually, the birds become used to these objects and start to ignore them. It's best to keep them guessing. Put up pinwheels this week, spinning CDs next week, and so on.

Some birds are protected species, meaning you can't kill, injure, or harass them. Lethal means, chemicals, and auditory effects are not good bird deterrents in your garden.

Step 3. Attach the trellis to the box.

3a. Drill four ³⁄₁₆″ pilot holes in the lower 6″ of each leg of the trellis.

3b. Raise the trellis structure so it is flush against the SFG box.

3c. Be sure the edges are square and secure the trellis to the box with 2½″ deck screws, using the pilot holes.

Build an A-Frame Trellis

An A-frame trellis is a versatile vertical-growing option for SFG beds. When you have a plant that needs even more support, when you're intentionally creating a shady microclimate, and when you have more vining plants than a single trellis will support, an A-frame trellis could be the solution. Essentially two ladders built on a hinge, this trellis can be installed in a variety of ways.

This trellis is an exception to the rule that says a trellis belongs only on the north side of the SFG bed. An A-frame trellis straddles two or more rows of squares in the SFG bed. You can also use it between two beds. Depending on what you're growing, you may need to set up the A-frame trellis in a north-south—instead of an east-west—orientation to allow one side of the trellis to get morning sun and the other side of the trellis to get afternoon sun. See "How to Use the A-Frame Trellis" on page 119 for examples.

Use the instructions here to build an A-frame trellis that fits inside your 4-foot-by-4-foot SFG box. Adjust the measurements to fit SFG boxes of other sizes. You can also adapt this trellis by replacing the wood slats in this project. Instead, use galvanized-wire fencing leftover from the Flat Wooden Trellis project on page 114 or install a premade wood trellis from a home-improvement store, or use one material on one side and another material on the other.

A-frame trellises are a fun way to add more vertical growing space to your SFG.

MATERIALS AND TOOLS

- 4 - 6' 1×4 cedar boards
- 4 - 46½" 1×4 cedar boards
- 1¼" galvanized deck screws
- 10 - 46½" 1×2 cedar boards
- 2 galvanized hinges with hardware
- Rafter square
- Drill
- ¼" drill bit
- Tape measure
- Pencil
- Eye and ear protection
- Work gloves

Square Foot Gardener's Tip

You can create an A-frame trellis in just about any size by using shorter and/or smaller pieces of lumber and following the same building method. Just be sure to drill pilot holes for all the screws, use a rafter square to maintain all angles, and attach the hinges at the top in a manner that allows the legs to be spread as far apart as needed.

ASSEMBLY

Step 1. Assemble the frames.

1a. Lay two 6'-long leg pieces on your work surface. Space them parallel to one another, with outside edges 46½" apart.

1b. Lay one 46½" 1×4 cross rail perpendicular across the top of the first pair of legs. Be sure the top and sides of the cross rail are flush with the top and sides of the legs. Use the rafter square to confirm a 90-degree angle.

1c. Drill two ¼" pilot holes from the top cross rail into each leg.

1d. Secure the top cross rail to the legs with 1¼" deck screws using the pilot holes.

1e. Lay another 46½" 1×4 cross rail perpendicular across the legs, 12" from the bottom of the legs. Secure the bottom cross rail as you did the top.

1f. Repeat this process with the second set of 6' leg pieces and 46½" 1×4 cross rails.

Step 2. Assemble the bodies.

2a. Measure and mark each leg 10" from the bottom of the top cross rail.

2b. Align the top of one 46½" 1×2 cross rail with that mark.

2c. Drill one pilot hole through the cross rail into each leg.

2d. Secure the cross rail to the leg with 1¼" deck screws using the pilot holes.

2e. Measure and mark each leg 10″ from the bottom of this cross rail, and attach the next cross rail.

2f. Repeat for the remaining cross rails on both frames. Each frame will have five 1×2 cross rails evenly spaced between the 1×4 top and bottom pieces.

Step 3. Assemble the A-frame trellis.

3a. Position the frame pieces so their tops butt up, even on both sides, with the cross rails facing up.

3b. Place the hinges on the top cross rails, just inside the legs, and attach using the provided hardware.

Step 4. Place the trellis.

Your trellis is ready to use in your SFG bed. Plan ahead to place this in the bed while plants are small or, better yet, before you plant them. You don't want to accidentally knock over or damage a plant while moving the trellis.

How to Use the A-Frame Trellis

The A-Frame trellis is a creative support for many SFG crop plans. Here are just a few ways you can put it to work:

- Place the legs in two adjacent rows of box grids and grow vining plants up both sides. Set up the trellis in a north-south orientation along the east side of the box so all sides get some sun.

- Let very long vining crops take over both sides of the trellis. Place the trellis in an east-to-west orientation with legs in the first and second rows on the north side of the box. Plant the crops—indeterminate cherry tomatoes, cucumbers, or pole beans, for example—in the second row, and let them grow up and over the top.

- Grow large indeterminate tomato plants, which will need space and support, under the trellis. Set up the trellis running east to west on the north side of the SFG box. Place the trellis legs in the first and third row, and plant the tomatoes in the second row.

- Create a shady microclimate to grow lettuce, cilantro, arugula, and other cool-season or shade-garden crops in the warmer months. Place the trellis legs in the first and third row on the north side of the box, oriented east to west. Plant the cool-season crops under the trellis, in the second row. Plant warm-season vining crops over the trellis, in the first and third rows. You don't want to block all light from the crops growing underneath the trellis, so choose moderately sized crops here. Good warm-season vining candidates are vining zucchini or summer squash, cucumbers, melons, and Malabar spinach. The plants on the north side of the trellis will get less direct sun than the plants on the south side, and they may grow slower and produce less.

Build a Top Hat Structure

Think of the top hat as a frame that adds extra growing space and visual interest to a SFG bed. A top hat structure can be built to raise up one SFG growing square or multiple growing squares. Position it where it makes the most sense for your crop plan: in the middle, along one edge, in the front, or in the back.

The top hat is a useful SFG add-on, and you'll likely want to build a few of varying sizes. The plans here are for building a top hat that fits into one SFG square. The top hat created by following these instructions is sized to fit perfectly with the building plans for the basic SFG bed and the lattice grid shown on pages 86 and 100.

Adapt these plans to build top hats that span two squares (21¼" × 10¼") or four squares (21¼" × 21¼") to create your ideal SFG bed. If your top hat covers more than one square, you'll need to install a grid pattern on the top hat as if it were a SFG box—because it is a SFG box, just a smaller, elevated one.

MATERIALS AND TOOLS →

- 4 pieces of 10¼" 1×8 lumber (you can also use 4", 6", or even 10" lumber widths depending on how deep you want your top hat to be)

- 1½" galvanized deck screws

- Rafter square

- Pencil

- Drill

- ⅛" drill bit

- Work gloves

- Eye and ear protection

This top hat-building project is a quick and simple way to extend the root space for deep-rooted crops.

ASSEMBLY

Step 1. Prepare the corners.

1a. Using the rafter square, outline the butt joint. Do this by measuring and marking the width of the lumber on one end of each board. This is your reference for drilling the pilot holes.

1b. Stack the four wood pieces as shown in the photo, to give yourself space to drill pilot holes.

1c. Drill three pilot holes in the end of each wood piece. Stack the next piece on top of the pile and repeat.

Step 2: Assemble the corners.

2a. Position two wood pieces so the pilot holes in one piece are aligned with the end grain of the adjoining piece.

2b. Secure the corner with three deck screws, using the pilot holes.

2c. Repeat with all pieces to make a box. One end of each wood piece should overlap another wood piece.

Square Foot Gardener's Tip

1×6 lumber is also an option for creating a top hat, though the resulting box won't be as deep. But if you have 1×6 lumber scraps sitting around, feel free to use them.

Step 3: Place the top hat.

The top hat should fit nicely inside a grid square, though if you used a different grid material than shown in the grid building project on page 100, it may fit a little differently. If you want your top hat to fit perfectly snug within a square, you'll need to alter the dimensions of the lumber used to build it accordingly, depending on the thickness of the grid material you're using. Rest assured that even if it doesn't fit perfectly, a top hat will still be fully functional. Put the top hat in its place and fill the top hat with Mel's Mix. (You'll learn about Mel's Mix in chapter 7.)

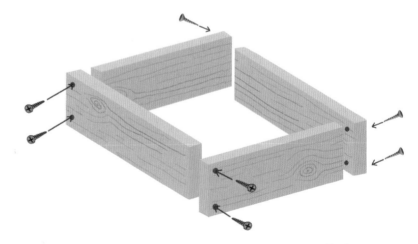

Top hats are perfect for giving long root crops, potatoes, and sweet potatoes more room to grow. Building them is easy.

Top Uses for a Top Hat

A top hat addition can be used on your SFG bed in a number of ways. Some crops are especially well-suited for a top hat.

Deep-Growing Plants

The primary use for top hats is to provide much-needed extra room for root crops to grow. Some root crops are natural candidates for deeper growing medium provided by a top hat. These include:

- Carrots
- Daikon radishes
- Ginger (if you plan to hill it)
- Leeks
- Parsnips
- Potatoes (especially late varieties)
- Sweet potatoes
- Turmeric (if you plan to hill it)

Visual Interest

One secondary use for top hats is to add visual interest to your garden. Even if a plant doesn't "need" the extra root room, using top hats on a few squares adds depth and dimension to your SFG. Try growing cascading flowers, like sweet alyssum or nasturtiums, in a top hat and let them tumble down over the top edge. Herbs are another good choice for top hats if you're hoping to increase visual interest. A curly or flat-leaved parsley plant looks great in a top hat, as do chives or tarragon.

If you can't build a perimeter fence around your entire garden like this gardener did, protect a single SFG bed with one of the projects on the following pages.

Pests, Pests, Go Away

It won't take long after you plant crops for creatures in your neighborhood to take notice. This goes for wild animals, neighborhood cats, neighbor's dogs, and insects of all kinds. There are few things more disappointing to a gardener than to watch a squirrel run across a telephone wire with one of your tomatoes in its mouth, to realize the neighborhood cat has been using the warm Mel's Mix in your SFG bed as its own bed, or to notice cabbage looper caterpillars are munching your broccoli leaves.

The next three building projects focus on excluding pests from your garden. The Critter Exclusion Cage and Perimeter Crop Cage will keep out the birds and animals. The Basic Plastic Mini Greenhouse Tunnel can be adapted to keep out insects, as well as birds and animals.

Build a Critter Exclusion Cage

A simple cage of chicken wire and a wood frame goes a long way in protecting your garden from animal pests. This cage is light enough for you to lift on and off the SFG bed so you can work with and harvest from your plants regularly.

These building plans are flexible, in that you get to choose the height of the Critter Exclusion Cage. Chicken wire is found at home-improvement and farm-supply stores in 2- to 6-foot tall rolls in varying lengths. Choose the fence height that meets your needs. The cage needs to clear the tallest of your plants. You don't want plants growing up through the cage, because once they become entangled, it will become impossible to take off the cage. The trade-off is that the taller the cage, the more cumbersome it will be to work with each day. If you're mostly growing greens and other low-growing vegetables or herbs, a 3-foot-tall cage might do. If you're growing peppers and any plants that require supports, you'll want a 5- or 6-foot-tall cage. You might want to have cages of several sizes that you can swap out as your crop plan changes and your plants grow to new heights.

The chicken wire also comes in varying mesh sizes. It's common to find 1-inch or 2-inch mesh openings; sometimes you'll even find ¾-inch mesh. The smaller the mesh, the sturdier the wire.

If you've ever worked with chicken wire before, you know it's pliable and easy to cut. You also know the ends are sharp once you cut them. Be sure to wear work gloves.

Keep neighborhood pets and wild animals such as deer, chipmunks, and groundhogs away from your garden with this easy-to-build protection cage.

MATERIALS AND TOOLS

- 4 pieces of 4' 1×2 lumber
- 2" galvanized deck screws
- 20'+ chicken wire of your preferred height
- Heavy-duty staples
- Zip ties
- Tape measure
- Pencil
- Drill
- 3/16" drill bit
- Wire cutters
- Staple gun
- Eye and ear protection
- Work gloves

ASSEMBLY

Step 1. Assemble the frame.

1a. Measure and mark ¾" on one end of each board. Drill two pilot holes within this space.

1b. Using the pilot holes, secure the side of one board to the end of the next with 2" screws to make a square. (See Perfectly Square on page 86 for more about joining corners.)

Step 2. Assemble the sides of the cage.

2a. Roll out and cut 16 feet of chicken wire.

2b. Stand the frame upright on one edge.

2c. Stretch and staple the chicken wire to the frame. Bend the wire sharply to form corners for the cage.

2d. Set the cage upright on the ground. Secure the loose ends of the chicken wire together with zip ties to close the side of the cage. Bend the cut edges to the inside so there are fewer sharp edges sticking out.

Step 3. Assemble the top of the cage.

3a. The height of your chicken wire will dictate the number of pieces of chicken wire you need to create a cage top. Do your own math, then cut one piece or multiple pieces of chicken wire from the roll to cover the 4'-by-4' cage.

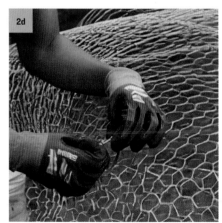

3b. Secure the top of the cage to the sides of the cage with zip ties. If using multiple pieces of chicken wire to form the top, secure those to one another using zip ties, as well. Bend the cut edges to the inside so there are fewer sharp edges sticking out.

Step 4. Place the cage.

Your Critter Exclusion Cage is ready to be put to work. Place it on top of your SFG bed, using care to not knock over or damage any plants as you set it on the box edges.

This versatile cage can be used on top of any 4-foot-by-4-foot SFG bed, even elevated ones.

Square Foot Gardener's Tip

Use this cage as a temporary protective cover for your plants. Attach shade cloth, row cover, or plastic sheeting to the cage to protect your garden from cold snaps or to shield delicate seedlings from harsh sun. Clip on the material with clothespins, large binder clips, or spring clamps, and secure the frame to the SFG bed with a couple of screws on each side so it doesn't blow away. You can even add a handle or two to the frame to make it easier to lift.

How to Build a Perimeter Crop Cage

When a simple Critter Exclusion Cage doesn't provide all the protection your garden needs from the animals visiting your SFG bed, this Perimeter Crop Cage is another option. Bird netting attached to 2×2 wood frames goes the extra step of excluding birds and small rodents from the garden. For added protection, use thicker deer netting or even plastic snow fencing. For even more protection, replace the bird netting with chicken wire or another type of metal fencing..

The sides of the Perimeter Crop Cage are intended to be temporarily screwed together simply so you can quickly remove them for garden access. At the end of the season, the frame can be disassembled and panels can be stored flat in your garage or shed, taking up much less space than a full cage would.

The instructions here are for a 4-foot-tall cage on a 4-foot-by-4-foot SFG box. This is tall enough to keep browsing deer away from your crops. Adjust the dimensions as needed for your project.

A cage top, SFG-box attachment points, and reinforced side panels are optional. See "Extra Security" on page 130 for these considerations.

Keep browsing deer away from your garden with this perimeter crop cage. Add more netting to the top, and you'll exclude birds as well.

MATERIALS AND TOOLS

- 16 pieces of 4' 2×2 lumber
- 2½" galvanized deck screws
- 16 L-brackets and hardware
- 4 sheets of 4' × 4' nylon mesh bird netting, deer netting, or snow fencing
- Heavy-duty staples
- Drill
- ³⁄₁₆" drill bit
- Staple gun
- Eye and ear protection
- Work gloves

ASSEMBLY

Step 1. Assemble the panels.

1a. Using the rafter square, outline the butt joint by measuring and marking the width of the lumber on one end of each board. Drill one ³⁄₁₆" pilot hole in this space.

1b. Using the pilot holes, secure the square with 2½" screws. (See "Perfectly Square" on page 86 for more about joining corners.)

1c. Reinforce these joints with L-brackets screwed to each corner of the frame, using the screws included with the brackets.

1d. Repeat with each set of 2×2 boards to build four side panels.

Extra Security

The Perimeter Crop Cage acts like a fortress around your SFG bed. Beyond the plan shown here, you can further reinforce the structure. Here are some extra security precautions:

Add a Lid

A cage this tall will keep out most of the ground critters that would bother your SFG bed. A lid will secure the bed's contents from birds and persistent climbing pests, as well. Build a lid frame using 2×2s and bird netting in the dimensions of your SFG box. Secure the lid with four large spring clamps, one in the middle of each side. You could screw the lid onto the cage, but at this angle, using a drill will be cumbersome. The clamps are easy to attach and remove as needed.

Reinforce the Sides

If chewing pests are extra motivated to get to your vegetables, nylon bird netting will slow them down but not stop them. Take the extra step of covering the side panels with chicken wire in addition to the bird netting. Rodents won't be able to chew through the wire.

Anchor the Cage

The Perimeter Crop Cage has more structure to it than other crop-protection methods. A frame this tall may catch the wind. It's possible to anchor the cage to your SFG box. Just run two screws from each side panel straight down into the top edge of your SFG box. Remove these as you do the side-panel screws when it's time to access the bed.

Step 2. Cover the panels.

Lay one sheet of nylon mesh bird netting over each panel frame. Stretch the netting and secure it with staples.

Step 3. Assemble the cage.

3a. Stand up two side panels along the edge of the SFG box so the end of one panel butts up against the side of another panel.

3b. Drill four ³⁄₁₆" pilot holes along the side of one 2×2 into the other. Secure the side with four 2½" screws, using the pilot holes.

3c. Repeat for the remaining sides.

Build a Mini Hoop Tunnel

A mini hoop tunnel serves several purposes for your SFG, and this project could not be simpler. Create a mini greenhouse for starting and protecting plants in the springtime by covering the tunnel with clear plastic. The same can be done in the autumn to extend the growing season and protect plants from early frosts. You can also use polypropylene floating row cover over the supports to keep out insects and animals throughout the growing season, provide a windbreak, and extend the growing season by adding a few degrees of insulation. In the heat of summer, cover the tunnel with shade cloth to grow heat-sensitive plants, like salad greens and cilantro. The options are many. Read more about growing-season extension and insect-pest protection in chapter 9.

MATERIALS AND TOOLS →

- 2–10' piece of ½" PVC pipes
- 1–4' piece of ½" PVC pipe
- Staples
- Zip ties
- Hoop tunnel cover (plastic sheeting, row cover, shade cloth, etc.)
- 2 weights to hold the ends closed (bricks, sandbags, wood posts, etc.)
- Tape measure
- Drill
- Twist bits
- Staple gun
- Eye and ear protection
- Work gloves

A mini hoop tunnel is perfect for extending the season and protecting plants from animals and insects.

ASSEMBLY

Step 1. Drill center hole in hoop supports.

1a. Use the tape measure to mark the center point of each 10'-long PVC pipe.

1b. Drill a hole through each pipe at these marked points.

Step 2. Drill a hole at each end of the central support pipe.

2a. Use the tape measure to mark ½" from each end of the 4'-long pipe.

2b. Drill a hole through these marked points.

Step 3. Bend the hoop support pipes into place.

3a. Insert one end of one 10'-long PVC pipe into the SFG box against one corner, pushing it down until it meets the landscape fabric beneath the Mel's Mix.

3b. Bend the PVC pipe toward the opposite corner on the same side slowly, making sure it does not buckle or kink. Insert that end of the pipe into the box against that corner, again pushing it down through the Mel's Mix until it meets the landscape fabric. This should create an arch.

3c. Repeat with the second 10' PVC pipe in the two remaining corners on the opposite side of the box. The tension of the pipes against the box will hold them in place.

Step 4. Secure the cross brace.

4a. Place the 4'-long piece of PVC pipe across the top of the tunnel created by the two arches so it rests on top of them.

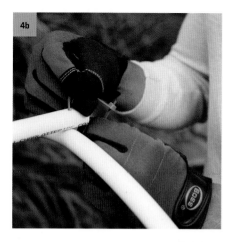

4b. Thread a zip tie through the hole in the end of the cross brace and then through the hole in the center of the hoop support, securing it tightly.

4c. Repeat with the other side.

Step 5. Cover the dome.

Drape your cover material of choice over the tunnel. Wrap it so there are no gaps where warm air can escape—for cold-air protection—or insects can enter—for pest protection.

Step 6. Secure the cover.

6a. A large piece of fabric or plastic can act as a sail in the slightest breeze. Use a staple gun to fasten the covering material to the bed's frame along the two sides that are parallel to the central cross brace. Pull the material as taut as possible.

6b. On the two open hoop ends, fold over the material neatly to close the end and weigh it down with heavy but easily moveable objects, like bricks, sandbags, or pieces of lumber. When you need to work in your garden bed, remove the weight and fold open the covering material. Just be sure to close it back up again when you're finished.

Accessories like the ones you learned to build in this chapter will allow you to extend your growing season, grow vining plants, and keep your crops away from pests. Now that your SFG bed is equipped to handle weather and pests of all kinds, it's time to fill the bed with Mel's Mix—the final step between preparing and planting.

Square Foot Gardener's Tip

If you're covering your dome with plastic sheeting, vent it on warm days to prevent the plants inside from getting too hot. To vent, simply remove the weights and fold open one side of the dome. Close it again when nighttime or cold temperatures arrive.

7

Filling Your Square Foot Garden Bed

Mel's Mix is a key element of a Square Foot Garden. This growing medium is a result of years of formulation and experimentation to find the right combination of plant nutrition and soil friability. Adding Mel's Mix to your SFG bed means you don't have to use soil from your garden space to grow your plants. By filling your SFG box with this mix just once to start, and amending it with compost as you rotate through the seasons, you know your plants will have the conditions they need to thrive.

Mel's Mix is simple, and it's convenient to use. This growing medium consists of one part compost, one part peat moss, and one part coarse vermiculite.

Mel's Mix works for a number of reasons:

Mel's Mix simplifies soil science. There are whole university classes dedicated to what makes soil ideal for growing crops. You shouldn't need a PhD to have a great garden. Mel's Mix has the proper pH and nutrients for nearly all plants you'd want to grow in your SFG bed. There's no need for additional fertilizers or soil amendments, and you don't need to perform soil tests, making gardening simpler.

Mel's Mix doesn't require digging. Sourcing your Mel's Mix ingredients from home-improvement and garden-supply stores, you don't need to engage in the

Mel's Mix is light and friable and the ideal growing medium for growing vegetables especially when your native soil is less than perfect.

labor-intensive digging and amending of soil that traditional in-ground gardening requires. Even in places with rocky soil—or pavement instead of soil—Mel's Mix in a SFG box means you don't have to touch the ground underneath.

Mel's Mix is safe to use when existing soil isn't. Some areas have soil that contains heavy metals that pose a danger to human health. Crops grown in soils with high lead, arsenic, and other heavy metals can take up these compounds, making those crops unsafe to eat. You know what's in your Mel's Mix, and heavy metals aren't on the ingredients list.

Mel's Mix balances moisture. With this combination of ingredients, Mel's Mix is able to retain moisture while draining away excess water, ensuring plants have consistent access to water without drowning their roots.

Mel's Mix is friable. This growing medium is always ready for planting, even during times when you wouldn't want to work in your in-ground garden soil, such as after a rain. You're not dealing with heavy clay clumps or a sticky, sandy mess. Mel's Mix is loose and easy to work with.

Mel's Mix will last for years. While you may have to top up your Mel's Mix every few years, the contents of the box as a whole will last 7 to 10 years (see Caring for Your Mel's Mix on page 151). Every time you harvest a square, you'll replenish the nutrients in that square with the addition of some compost.

Compost

Compost makes up one-third of the Mel's Mix formula, and it's the one ingredient that you'll replenish each time you harvest a grid square.

Looking at a handful of this Mel's Mix ingredient, you might think it's nothing special. It looks like a handful of dirt. Despite its lackluster appearance, "dirt" is not actually any part of compost. Compost is what's left behind when organic matter—like plant materials, kitchen scraps, cardboard, and farm animal manures—break down. It is both a marvel of nature and a common-sense process. Good compost is rich in nutrients as well as microbes—the beneficial bacteria and fungi that support the function of plant roots. It makes sense that something that was once living will decompose back into the elements that living things need to grow.

Compost is one of the three main components of Mel's Mix. It's good stuff!

Properly made compost is friable and nutrient rich. The pH of compost changes as the organic materials in the pile decompose. Finished compost usually has a pH of 6 to 8.

The best compost you can use in your Mel's Mix is the compost you make yourself with a diversity of ingredients. If you don't have enough of your own compost available, you can also purchase a few different bagged composts made from various sources and blend them together for a diverse, ready-made compost.

How compost works

Composting itself is a simple act, though to get to a finished product, organic materials undergo complex processes. Two natural reactions can take place as these materials break down: anaerobic decomposition and aerobic decomposition.

Anaerobic composting takes place when there's a lack of oxygen. This is otherwise known as rotting, and it's messy and smelly. An example of anaerobic composting is when you've forgotten about a head of lettuce in a sealed plastic produce bag in the back of your refrigerator crisper drawer. When you find it a month later, its leaves are slimy and partially broken down, and when you open the bag, it smells like rotten lettuce. A successful compost pile avoids the anaerobic process—with one exception, bokashi composting, which you'll read about in this chapter.

In contrast, aerobic composting involves microbes digesting plant material in an oxygen-rich environment. The process creates heat, which helps to further support the microbes in their decomposition work. Aerobic composting is odorless and efficient. An example of aerobic composting in nature is leaves that have fallen from trees breaking down into nutrients in the ground below. It doesn't smell bad, it doesn't look bad, and you don't even realize this process is happening under your feet.

Aerobic composting can take place in all kinds of compost bins and locations as long as it has a few basic elements:

Nitrogen. Nitrogen (N) in the compost bin comes in the form of "green" materials. These include fresh plant materials, plant scraps from the kitchen, and manure.

Carbon. The carbon (C) compost ingredients are referred to as "brown" ingredients. Brown materials are things like cardboard, dead leaves, and straw.

Air. The microbes that create aerobic compost require adequate air.

Water. The microbes also need water, just like any other living organism.

Ways to compost

There are several different ways compost is made. You may choose to use one or more of these methods at home, depending on your space and resources. The information in this book focuses on the hot composting method, but multiple processes can work in tandem.

Hot composting. Hot composting, or rapid composting, is the backyard composter's goal. This method makes compost efficiently and quickly. It will take some attention to do it properly. In addition to being on top of the carbon-to-nitrogen ratio, the pile requires the right amount of water and regular turning—every couple of days. It's possible that you'll start to see decomposition in fourteen to thirty days, depending on the particle size of the ingredients added to the pile.

Cold composting. Cold composting, or static-pile composting, happens when you dump a bunch of organic matter into a pile and pay no further attention to it. Regardless of the carbon-to-nitrogen ratio, the moisture content, or how frequently the pile is turned, this pile of organic matter will break down into compost eventually—perhaps in 3 months or more. This type of compost will contain nutrients and beneficial microorganisms but may also contain weed seeds and pathogens that could have been eliminated in a hot compost pile.

Vermicomposting. Worms are valuable partners in the garden and in the compost bin. Vermicomposting entails worms consuming decaying food waste and leaving behind a partially digested, dark, and nutrient-rich compost. Vermicompost

Why Compost at Home

Having your own homemade compost on hand is nice because you'll continue to reach for this Mel's Mix ingredient throughout the year.

Making your own is a good idea from a food-waste standpoint. In the United States, about 95 percent of discarded food ends up in landfills. As this waste decomposes in the anaerobic atmosphere of a landfill, it releases methane. When broken down with aerobic processes in a compost bin, it does not produce this byproduct. Composting turns organic trash into organic treasure.

Some municipalities have ordinances outlining the kinds of organic materials that can and cannot enter the waste stream. If you live in a place that prohibits lawn and garden waste or foods from being put in the trash, you have extra incentive to compost your own.

As one-third of your Mel's Mix recipe, and the only amendment you'll add to your SFG bed each season, making your own compost results in significant cost savings over purchasing it. By making your own, you also know exactly what goes into the compost.

Kitchen scraps are a nitrogen-rich ingredient for composting.

is also called worm castings. Red wiggler worms (*Eisenia fetida*) are the stars of vermicomposting. They need a worm bin to live in, shredded paper for bedding, and kitchen scraps to digest.

A worm bin needs a tight-fitting lid so your charges can't escape, ventilation, drainage, and humidity. You don't want it to get too hot or too cold—worms live and work in here. You can build your own vermicompost bin using a sturdy plastic bin with a lid, or you can purchase one designed for this purpose.

You'll need several vermicompost bins, or you'll need to supplement your worm castings with other compost sources, as 1 pound of red wigglers can only eat up to 2 pounds of food scraps each week.

Vermicompost is a good option for SFG users who don't have room outdoors to set up large compost bins. You can put a worm bin indoors, in the garage (as long as it doesn't freeze), and even under the kitchen sink.

Bokashi composting. This composting method uses an inoculated bran to ferment organic materials in an anaerobic environment—one without oxygen. Unlike the microbes in an outdoor aerobic pile, the beneficial microbes doing this work thrive in anaerobic and acidic environments. The organic materials ferment in the bucket for about 2 weeks. This results in not traditional compost but a fermented "pre-compost" that can be added to a compost bin for finishing. The benefit of this extra step is that bokashi composting can digest the dairy, meat, and cooked foods that regular aerobic compost cannot.

You can make your own bokashi composter using a 5-gallon bucket with a locking lid, or you can purchase one. You also need to purchase the inoculated bran to get started.

Countertop composting. Gadget lovers may be interested in this form of composting. In the 2020s, a small kitchen composting appliance came on the market, scaled down from huge commercial versions. Countertop composters accept your food scraps—including meat and some bones but excluding fruit pits and oil—and grind and dehydrate them using high heat and moisture extraction. The resulting organic matter pellets are ready in just a few hours for the compost bin, where they can be dispatched by the compost microbes.

This appliance is costly, and again adds another step to a compost routine, but it could make sense for SFG users with limited outdoor space for a full-size compost bin.

Hot compost made easy

There are whole books written about composting—even Master Composter certifications offered by universities and municipalities. At its most basic, there are just four things you need to know about compost—the 4 Ms.

Mix. The ideal C:N ratio in a compost bin is 30 parts carbon (brown ingredients) to 1 part nitrogen (green ingredients). Unfortunately, it's not quite as simple as needing to add 25 pounds of straw for every one pound of vegetable scraps, because all organic matter contains some carbon and some nitrogen in varying amounts. For example, coffee grounds have a 20:1 C:N ratio, while tomato scraps have an 11:1 C:N ratio. These are both common green compost ingredients, but one has more brown content than the other.

If you spend too much time worrying about how to achieve the perfect C:N ratio in your compost bin, you'll never actually get around to composting. The important thing is to have a diversity of ingredients to maintain an active and balanced compost pile. A 30-to-1 ratio of green ingredients to brown ingredients, using the Compost Ingredients chart on page 141 as a guide, will get you close to the ideal.

Take your greens and browns from varying sources. Don't use all grass clippings as your nitrogen source or only dried leaves as your carbon source. Mix it up. The greater the diversity of ingredients you incorporate, the greater the diversity of microbes and nutrients your compost will contribute to your Mel's Mix.

Mash. Mash—that is, break down—the green and brown materials into smaller pieces before incorporating them into your compost pile. The organisms breaking down your compost pile are essentially chewing and digesting each piece. This is the difference between taking a giant bite of a sandwich versus a reasonable bite. You'll have an easier time chewing and digesting the smaller bite, and so will your compost organisms. You'll have finished compost in faster time with smaller pieces.

Moisten. Proper moisture is essential for composting, to keep the microbes alive. Your compost should be neither overly wet nor excessively dry. Technically, you're looking for 50 percent to 60 percent moisture by weight, which is to say, aim for the dampness level of a wrung-out sponge.

Wet your pile with a hose if the moisture content gets too low.

Excessive sun or rain can disrupt the moisture balance in a compost pile. Monitor the pile, and add water when necessary. In addition to the water you may add from a hose or rain barrel, some compost ingredients are high in moisture and will boost the dampness of the pile. Consider putting a roof over the top of the pile, if too much rainfall is consistently an issue, so you have more control of your pile's moisture content.

Move. Regardless of whether you make compost in a compost tumbler or in an open-air bin, regularly turning your compost accelerates the decomposition process. This action brings outer materials to the pile's interior, where the heat is concentrated and organic matter breaks down more quickly. Turning the pile ensures the microbes get the oxygen they need to thrive and distributes the moisture throughout the pile.

Frequently turn your compost to keep it "cooking." Use a pitchfork, shovel, or a compost-aerator tool for the job.

A shovel or pitchfork is a simple compost-turning tool that you probably already have in your garden shed. You can also use a compost-aerator tool—which looks like a giant corkscrew on the end of a long handle—to turn and mix your pile. If you have multiple compost bins, you can fork the contents of one into the next as a means of turning. If you're working with one bin, you'll work on your ingredient-mixing and -turning skills.

As the microorganisms do their decomposition work, they generate heat. You might even see steam coming from the pile as you turn it. The ideal temperature for a hot compost pile is 140°F, the temperature at which weed seeds and pathogens can break down. Temperatures above 160°F slow down the composting process and may kill off the beneficial microbial life and result in charring or burning. A compost thermometer will help you keep an eye on your pile's progress.

Compost Ingredients

Technically, all organic materials—meaning everything made of organic matter—will eventually compost.

Just because it can be composted doesn't mean it should be composted. This chart shows which organic materials are considered brown/carbon, which are considered green/nitrogen, and which should be skipped altogether.

Brown Ingredients	Green Ingredients	Do Not Compost This
Wood chips	Uncooked fruit and vegetable scraps	Cooking oil or grease
Straw	Grass clippings	Baked goods
Paper	Coffee grounds	Diseased plant material
Cardboard	Tea bags	Plant material sprayed with herbicides or pesticides
Leaves	Healthy garden vegetation	Insect-infested plant material
Sawdust (avoid sawdust from plywood which may contain glues)	Manure from herbivores	Seeds or seed heads
Corn stalks		Manure from carnivores or omnivores
Eggshells		Dairy
		Meat
		Bones

You'll see manure is in two different lists in this chart. Manure from herbivores—chickens, horses, alpacas, rabbits, etc.—is considered a green compost ingredient, and it should be used with caution. Manure from carnivores and omnivores—dogs, cats, humans, pigs, etc.—should never be composted because it can contain parasites that are harmful to humans and difficult to kill in home composting setups. Herbivores' manure also contains pathogens, as well as weed seeds, but at the right temperature, these can break down in the compost pile.

If you choose to use manure from herbivores as a compost ingredient, look at the USDA National Organic Program guidance and instructions for animal manure in compost. It says a compost pile must reach a temperature of 131°F to 170°F for 15 days and must be turned at least five times during that period. This is for human health and safety.

In selecting all ingredients for your compost pile, understand their source. Manure from animals that ate forage treated with herbicides or pesticides, as well as vegetative materials contaminated with these chemicals, can hold onto their residues, even after composting. These chemicals can wreak havoc on your SFG bed by preventing germination and causing stunted plant growth.

Finished compost looks good, smells good, and feels good. None of the original ingredients are recognizable.

If large chunks of materials remain in your compost, screen it prior to use.

Square Foot Gardener's Tip

Let your compost bin tell you what it needs. If the contents are slimy and smelly, increase the brown ingredients in the bin, turn the pile, and water it less. If the compost is stagnant and slow to break down, add green ingredients to the bin, water it, and turn it to wake up the microbes and restart decomposition.

Finished compost

After all the watering and turning, you're no doubt anxious to put this compost to use. You'll know your compost is finished when it has a dark brown, crumbly texture and a rich, earthy scent. The pile will have shrunk by one-half or more of its original size, and you'll no longer recognize what you once put in there. Also, the compost pile will stop generating heat.

If your compost fits this description but some chunks remain—maybe larger woody pieces that aren't totally decomposed—remove them by hand or sift them out using a piece of $\frac{1}{4}$-inch-mesh hardware cloth from a home-improvement store (see the tip on page 143). Left to pass, these larger wood pieces will complicate the environ-

ment of your SFG bed. They'll continue to decompose in your Mel's Mix, which sounds like a good thing because that will add more nutrients, but in the process, the microbes digesting them will tie up nitrogen that your plants need. When you screen out the larger pieces, toss them back into your compost pile to continue their decomposition.

Once your compost is ready, you should use it as soon as possible. If you won't be able to incorporate the compost into your Mel's Mix right away, store it out of the direct sun and rain so the nutrients don't leach out. The compost won't "expire," but it could lose some of its nutritive value. The microbial activity of compost will decrease over time, as well, but when you wet it again, life will return to the compost.

Your compost bin

To make enough compost to first create your Mel's Mix and then replenish the compost in your SFG box each season requires some outdoor space. Don't attempt to build a compost bin in an enclosed space, like a garage or a garden shed, because an active pile can generate a lot of heat and, if it is not properly attended to, it can pose a fire danger indoors.

The minimum size for an active aerobic compost pile is 3 feet wide by 3 feet long by 3 feet tall. This volume of decomposing organic matter can hold enough moisture and create enough heat to keep the compost microbes active.

Compost will happen, whether you have a compost bin or not, but efficient composting happens in a bin, which keeps the materials together, allowing heat buildup and moisture retention. What this bin looks like is up to you, and there's no shortage of ways to construct one.

Compost bins that are open on the bottom and sit on the ground invite in earthworms and other soil-dwelling organisms, which are great allies in breaking down organic materials. Those that are enclosed are useful when you're concerned about wildlife—or pets—getting into the compost pile. Plastic bins will heat up in the sun, which is great for getting the compost up to temperature, but the compost can get too hot in the summer and require venting.

Look for these features in a compost bin:
- Ventilated
- Ease of adding new ingredients
- Ease of turning the pile
- Lidded, in areas with heavy rain or heavy wildlife activity
- Constructed of material that won't leach contaminants into the compost
- Meets any requirements of your homeowner's association
- Fits your budget

There is no shortage of compost-bin choices available, with building plans online, bins for sale at home-improvement and garden-supply stores, and even municipalities and non-profits hosting bin-building workshops. In the end, the best compost bin for you is the one that fits your living and gardening situation.

Consider a few of your compost-bin options:

DIY fence compost bin. Create a convenient compost bin using snow fencing, chicken wire, or welded-wire fencing—left over from your Flat Wooden Trellis project on page 114 or the Critter Exclusion Cage on page 125.

This type of bin is not the most attractive, but it is simple to construct and allows for great airflow throughout the pile. Determine the desired diameter for your compost bin and multiply it by 3.2 to calculate the length of fencing needed to create the cylinder. Fasten the ends together to enclose the cylinder. Stand it on end, and attach this structure to two T-posts pounded into the ground opposite one another.

You have two options to turn this pile. One is to use a compost aerator, working from the top. The other is to create a modular two-bin system. Install another two T-posts next to this bin. Detach the cylinder from the original set of posts, pull it off of the compost heap, and reattach the cylinder to the new set of posts. Now use a shovel or pitchfork to move the compost into this new bin.

Square Foot Gardener's Tip

Build a simple compost sifter by stapling hardware cloth to a 1' × 2' wooden frame. Place the sifter over the 5-gallon bucket you're using to measure Mel's Mix ingredients, and sift right into the bucket.

Wire fence–enclosed bins are a quick and simple way to get a compost pile started.

Wood pallet bin. Construct compost bins using wood pallets as the sides. If you live in an area with heavy rainfall, you can even make a lid frame out of a pallet to prevent your compost pile from getting too wet. Build a 3-sided bin, or attach the front so it's easy to remove for access to turn the contents with a shovel or pitchfork.

Read Trellis Types on page 110 for important considerations about using wood pallets for garden projects.

Tumbler bin. These clever, self-contained compost drum bins are convenient. They look like large, plastic drums suspended horizontally on a spit. To add ingredients, you slide open or unlatch a door, and to mix the ingredients, you turn a crank. It can be challenging to turn the crank when the bin is full and heavy. You'll find these for sale and can build your own using a food-safe 50-gallon drum. Tumbler bins are ideal for patios and other small-space environments.

Compost tumblers are aerated by turning a crank and spinning the ingredients around.

Trash bin. A trash can is an inconspicuous and inexpensive compost bin, and with some ventilation holes drilled throughout, it does the trick. The trash can needs to be weighted or otherwise secured so it doesn't blow around in the wind. You can even partially bury a trash can, allowing soil-dwelling organisms to visit your compost through the ventilation holes. Use two trash cans side-by-side to dump the bin contents back and forth as a means of pile turning.

Multi-bin system. If you really have the space to dedicate to composting, it's hard to beat a multi-bin system. Using three or more bins, you can regularly turn composting materials by shoveling or forking from one bin into the next. Use the third bin to store material to be added when you need it.

A multi-bin system will have you making oodles of compost. Just be sure to turn the bins regularly.

When You Can't Make Your Own Compost

For all of the benefits of making your own compost, time, resources, and living arrangements can get in the way of the process.

Even if you are making your own, it's possible you aren't able to make all that you need for your SFG beds. Lucky for anyone gardening today, various forms of compost are readily available in many parts of the world.

The Ingredients Label

You're looking for compost with the most diversity of nutrients and microbes possible. Before you put the bag of compost into your cart, figure out what's inside.

You might find compost that comes from one specific source, such as cattle manure, mushroom production, or vermicompost. These single-ingredient composts don't offer the full range of nutrients and microbes that will make the most successful garden. If a blended compost isn't available, choose a mix of single-ingredient composts—ideally four to six different types—to blend your own for your Mel's Mix.

Also on the ingredients list, check for peat moss. Peat moss is one of the three ingredients in Mel's Mix. You don't want to throw off the ratio by adding compost that also includes peat moss. Skip any compost with peat moss as an ingredient.

Buying Bulk Compost

Purchasing your compost means you're trusting others to supply your SFG bed's nutrients. You can be as selective as your compost options will allow. Before ordering a pickup-bed full of bulk compost from a garden center,

If you can't make your own compost and have to purchase this Mel's Mix ingredient, blend 4 to 6 different types together for an ideal and well-balanced blend. This image shows worm castings, leaf compost, lobster compost, mushroom compost, and seaweed compost.

Commercially bagged composts are available for purchase if you can't make your own.

Municipalities and Private Composters

Some cities and counties offer compost—sometimes for free—and you should scrutinize that source as you would any bulk compost. There are also private composters, especially in cities in the United States, that collect food scraps from residents and food businesses and return finished compost for a fee. These operations range from college entrepreneurs with compost bins in city lots to full-scale commercial composting facilities. This is a great way to recycle your garden, vegetable, and yard scraps without having your own compost setup. Here, too, learn about their compost ingredients and process before signing on.

The OMRI Label

OMRI is the Organic Materials Review Institute, the keeper of the list of inputs approved for USDA Certified Organic agriculture. When you're questioning the safety of various compost ingredients, look for the OMRI label. This means it's OK for use by certified organic farmers and gardeners and does not contain synthetic or biohazardous ingredients—or, if it does contain synthetic ingredients, they've passed the National Organic Program's muster.

a local farm, or your municipality, inspect the product. You want a compost that:

- Is free from debris, such as plastic, metal, or glass
- Has few pieces that have not fully decomposed, such as stems or bark chunks
- Smells good
- Is not infested with flies or maggots —but earthworms are great

Ask about the ingredients and the composting process. Some composts might include biosolids, which are organic materials from municipal wastewater-treatment plants. This ingredient is not approved for use in U.S. Department of Agriculture Certified Organic production. It's up to you whether you want to use it in your garden.

If buying compost from a farm, ask about the source of the livestock's feed. Avoid compost that could pose the risk of herbicide contamination.

Be particular about the difference between compost and aged manure. Composted manure was made in a pile with a temperature that was monitored and recorded so weed seeds and pathogens have most likely been killed off. Aged manure is manure that has sat in a pile—cold composted, essentially— and may or may not have reached the necessary temperature. Aged manure is not an appropriate or food-safe alternative to compost of any kind, so it should not be used in your Mel's Mix. You can fully compost manure yourself with other ingredients in your own compost pile, if you aren't sure of its source or safety.

Peat Moss

Mel's Mix ingredient No. 2 is peat moss. This organic material is the result of tons of vegetative matter decomposing over millions of years. It comes from wetlands where living mosses got buried, slowly dried out, and became preserved over thousands of years.

Peat moss has long been used by gardeners. While it doesn't have nutritive properties, it lightens the Mel's Mix, improves friability, and boosts water-holding and -draining ability.

Peat moss is hydrophobic, meaning it has trouble absorbing water when it's dry. Think about the first big rain after a period of hot, dry summer weather when the water runs right over the ground without being absorbed. This is the same phenomenon. With the right attention paid to your SFG bed, the only time you would need to think about peat moss's hydrophobic nature is when you're getting started with a new box or after you've let your box go fallow for a season. When filling a new SFG with Mel's Mix, all ingredients need to be thoroughly mixed and wetted prior to filling the bed. Pre-moistening Mel's Mix is an important step.

If you've paid no attention to the garden for a few months, it may have dried out and needs to be rehydrated again. Because all of the Mel's Mix ingredients work together, the compost and vermiculite in the mix will hold onto the water, allowing the peat moss to absorb it from them a little at a time until the peat moss is fully hydrated again. You'll need to water a little at a time to allow the water to fully soak in.

Peat moss's pH varies by source. You may find peat moss with a pH of 3.5, which is acidic, or you could find it with a pH of 6.4, which is more neutral. Because compost tends toward a higher pH, this is generally okay, as they even out one another.

You may be familiar with peat moss as a questionably renewable resource. Peat wetlands provide habitat for numerous plants and animals, purify water, and absorb carbon dioxide. In Canada, where 80 percent of the peat for sale in the United States is harvested from, the industry is required to rejuvenate the bogs it is harvesting from by following strict restoration regulations. Using a moss-layer transfer technique to restore post-harvest peat bogs to functioning ecosystems takes less than 10 years for the reclaimed wetlands to return to their previous function.

In the United Kingdom, where peat bogs have been severely damaged by overharvesting for cooking, heating, and manufacturing fuel, The Royal Horticultural Society plans to be peat-free by the end of 2025.

Peat moss is sold at home-improvement stores and garden centers in most of North America. You'll find it in compressed bales of 1 to 3 cubic feet in volume. Peat moss is less readily available in other parts of the world.

When reaching for a bag of peat moss, be sure you're not purchasing dried sphagnum moss. Most peat moss is, technically, a decomposed sphagnum moss, but the product sold as dried sphagnum moss is not the same. Dried sphagnum moss are the long strings of brown moss used to decorate potted plants and flower arrangements.

Page 150 discusses a few alternatives to peat moss if you decide against using it in your Mel's Mix.

Fallow

To let a garden go fallow is to not plant anything for a season. The fallow time is most often during the season when the weather is not ideal for growing crops.

Peat moss is an essential ingredient to Mel's Mix.

Coarse Vermiculite

The third essential component in Mel's Mix is coarse vermiculite. This product is produced by heating a mined mica-like silicate ore to an extraordinarily hot 1,600°F. The mineral expands, and lightweight, accordion-like particles with high water-holding capacity are formed. Mixed into a growing medium, these particles boost aeration and excess-water drainage. As a mineral, vermiculite also contributes potassium, magnesium, and calcium to Mel's Mix.

Vermiculite's high pH of 7 to 9 makes it even more alkaline than compost. This is balanced with the lower-pH peat moss.

You'll find vermiculite comes in grades from fine to super coarse. Coarse or super coarse vermiculite is ideal for Mel's Mix. The particle sizes of other grades are too small, which may be appropriate for indoor plant pots or propagating plant cuttings but not for SFG beds. The finer grades of vermiculite don't provide the aeration benefit that the coarse grades allow. Over time, vermiculite particles will compress and lose their aeration and water-holding capacity.

Before the 1990s, there was concern about asbestos contamination in vermiculite. This is no longer an issue. Today's vermiculite is tested, ensuring its safety, and the mine where contaminated vermiculite was sourced is no longer active. Regardless, vermiculite is a dry, dusty mineral product. When you're opening bags and making your Mel's Mix, you should wear protective gear—including gloves and a particle mask—to avoid inhaling or becoming irritated by its fine particles.

Coarse vermiculite is the third ingredient in Mel's Mix.

The accordion-like structure of vermiculite boosts drainage and water-holding capacity at the same time.

The Importance of pH

While you don't have to study the science behind Mel's Mix (we've already done that part for you), the acid-alkaline balance is one thing to be aware of. Measured by pH, the range is 0, which is extremely acidic—think battery acid—to 14, which is extremely alkaline or basic—like liquid drain cleaner. A neutral pH is 7, and most garden plants do best in growing media with a neutral or slightly acidic soil pH. Blueberries and azaleas are two examples of plants that like really acidic soil with a pH of 5.0 to 5.5.

Soil pH affects the availability of nutrients in the growing medium. Your compost could be as rich and fertile as possible, but if your pH is off, it will be of little use to plant roots. A pH that's too high or too low can stunt plant growth, cause spots on the leaves, and even cause plants to wither. Part of the beauty of having the three ingredients in your Mel's Mix is that they work together to create a balanced system.

Mel's Mix Substitutes

Mel's Mix was carefully formulated with SFG trials to arrive at the one-third compost, peat moss, and vermiculite recipe you're reading about. Supply chains are different everywhere, and sometimes specialty garden items can be hard to find in the quantity needed. If you run into challenges sourcing a Mel's Mix ingredient, all is not lost. No alternative is as good as the original ingredient, but some will do.

Compost substitutes

Looking at the first ingredient, compost, there is no actual substitute. Compost is a natural way to provide the nutrients your plants need to thrive. But you aren't locked into using any one kind of compost. In fact, it's the mix of four to six compost types—unless you're using compost you've made yourself with a diversity of ingredients—that is the key. It's not possible to replace the value that blended compost offers to Mel's Mix.

Peat moss substitutes

Think about peat moss's main attributes—aeration and water retention. Peat moss is the ideal material for this purpose in Mel's Mix. If peat moss isn't available in your area or you have another reason for seeking out an alternative, there are two options that can do similar work. These are coconut coir and more compost.

Coconut coir. Made from coconut shells, coconut coir is the fiber of coconut hulls—a byproduct of the food industry. The coconut fibers are milled and screened to less than ³/₄ inch, then dried and compressed into blocks for easy shipping and handling. Early coconut coir sometimes had a high salt content, but processing improvements may have remedied this. Similar to peat moss, coconut coir holds water, breaks down slowly, and doesn't compress easily. Its 5.8 to 6.9 pH is ideal for most garden crops. Coir is considered a renewable agricultural product, though the environmen-

Lightness and fine particles make coconut coir a substitute for peat moss.

tal impact of shipping the product long distances should be taken into consideration. Coir breaks down slightly faster than peat and will need to be replenished in 3 to 5 years.

More compost. Compost and peat moss serve different purposes in Mel's Mix—crop nutrients versus moisture management—but if you must fill in for peat moss and have no other option, compost will do. At two-thirds compost, you may notice the SFG bed is wetter after a heavy rain event than if you were using true Mel's Mix.

Coarse vermiculite substitutes

Vermiculite is a fairly typical garden amendment. Finding the right grade of vermiculite is another story. Coarse and super coarse vermiculite aren't as readily available as medium and fine grades. In this case, you're looking for an amendment that promotes aeration and water drainage, plus provides a mineral source. Rice hulls and compost don't offer the minerals that vermiculite does, but they cover the other needs.

Rice hulls. A product of the rice-milling industry, rice hulls are the seed coverings removed from the rice you may cook for dinner. The hulls are parboiled during processing to kill any grains of rice—which are actually seeds—so they can't sprout and

Rice hulls add aeration and drainage, much like coarse vermiculite does, making them a reasonable substitute for vermiculite in Mel's Mix.

become weeds. Rice hulls create space for aeration and water drainage. They have pH that's near neutral to slightly alkaline, but they're not likely to influence the pH of the surrounding growing medium.

More compost. Compost is a viable alternative for vermiculite, as well. It's possible, in fact, to use compost alone in your SFG bed, though you will miss out on the important water drainage, water retention, and aeration benefits of using a combination of Mel's Mix ingredients.

This wheelbarrow is filled with an alternate blend of rice hulls, coconut coir, and compost. It's ready to go into a SFG bed.

Caring for Your Mel's Mix

Mel's Mix is designed to last for years—as many as ten years, in fact. There are a few things you can do to help prolong the life of this growing medium.

Add compost. Each time you harvest one of your SFG grid squares, top off the square with more compost. This ensures that no matter how "hungry" the previous crop was for nutrients, you're replenishing them for the next crop.

Conserve Mel's Mix. Each time you pull roots from the SFG bed, knock off as much of the Mel's Mix as possible. You want to keep that in the bed.

Protect it in the off-season. If you let your SFG bed go fallow for a season, cover the bed with mulch of some kind. This blanket covers the bed to protect it from sun bleaching, erosion, and the intrusion of weed seeds. Mulch will also help to stabilize the temperature of the Mel's Mix and retain moisture so your SFG bed will be ready to plant into next season. You'll read about mulching in chapter 9.

Top it up. A growing medium naturally settles over time. As the Mel's Mix ingredients dry out and rehydrate, are exposed to the sun, are blown by the wind, and naturally decompose or compress, you'll notice an inch or so difference over the years. Every few years, add back as much Mel's Mix as you need to get your SFG bed back to its original depth. Incorporate the new Mel's Mix into the existing Mel's Mix so there's fresh growing medium throughout.

Store it properly. When you whip up a batch of Mel's Mix, you will invariably have some left over. Keep it in a lidded container in a cool location, preferably in a garage or other covered space. If your only storage option is in a pile outdoors, mulch the pile and water it now and then. This will keep the microbes alive, and you'll have Mel's Mix ready for the next time you need to fill a top hat or top up your SFG bed. If your Mel's Mix has dried out, mix in some more compost and water it well to rejuvenate it before putting it to work.

Mel's Mix is straightforward to blend and easy to work with, but it should be amended with new compost each time a new crop is planted.

Sourcing Mel's Mix Ingredients

The experience you have sourcing your compost, peat moss, and coarse vermiculite will vary based on where you live. This might be the only example of when living in a big city doesn't mean you have the easiest access to the must-have items of the moment. You're more likely to find these materials at a farm store than you are in a major city.

If you make your own blended compost, checking that ingredient off your list is a matter of walking into your backyard. If you're purchasing some or all of your compost, as well as the other Mel's Mix ingredients, here are a few places to start:

- Independent garden centers
- Home-improvement stores
- Landscape supply yards
- Feed stores
- Co-op buying clubs and stores
- An internet search

If you come up empty-handed locally, talk with the folks at your local stores. They may be able to special-order products for you.

If you find Mel's Mix ingredients online but shipping costs are prohibitive, see if you can combine shipping with others to bring down the cost. Look to your friends with SFGs, garden clubs, community organizations that have gardens, and other similar groups. Sometimes it just takes a larger order split with a few people to make the math work.

As you start researching Mel's Mix ingredient sources, you may find the ingredients are more expensive than regular bagged garden soil. Your initial investment pays off quickly. Regular bagged soil requires soil tests and amendments each year. Using Mel's Mix, it'll be a few years before you need to add more growing medium to your SFG box—besides the small amount of compost you'll replenish after you harvest—and you don't need to test or amend the soil.

This community SFG gets a truckload of bulk compost delivered at the start of every growing season. They use it to top up their SFG beds and get the growing season off to a great start.

With Mel's Mix there's no need to add supplemental fertilizers. All the nutrition your plants need is already present in the mix.

Don't Add That Fertilizer

Mel's Mix is formulated to provide all the nutrition and support that garden plants need to thrive. When you're browsing the garden amendments and fertilizers in your favorite seed catalog or garden store, restrain yourself. There are several reasons why you don't need to—and shouldn't—add more fertilizer or other amendments to your Mel's Mix.

Don't change the pH balance. As you read in Finding pH Balance on page 149, you don't want to mess with the pH of your Mel's Mix. Fertilizers and amendments can throw off the pH balance.

Don't disrupt the nutrient balance. The balance of nutrients in Mel's Mix is already perfect for growing vegetables. Adding unnecessary fertilizers could result in nutrient excesses or deficiencies that can have detrimental effects, including too much foliage and not enough fruit, stunted growth, discolored leaves, nutrient run-off, etc.

Don't waste your money. Quality blended compost, aeration, water-retention, water drainage, and mineral content are already included in Mel's Mix. You can spend a lot of money on additional resources that your plants don't actually need.

Don't waste your time. Part of the appeal of the SFG Method is that it simplifies gardening. You can browse soil amendments for hours and then have to go through the effort of figuring out when and how to apply them. It's not necessary.

Formulating Your Mel's Mix

The recipe for Mel's Mix could not be easier. You don't need a scale or fancy equipment. The ratio is one part blended composts to one part uncompressed peat moss to one part coarse vermiculite by volume. A 5-gallon bucket is the perfect measuring tool.

Sourcing the right amount of each product can be confusing because none of them are sold in the same unit of measurement. You may find these come in pounds, cubic feet or yards, or quarts. Maybe they'll even be compressed into bales and then loosen up to expand into a much larger amount. You need to know the volume of each bale, bag, or pickup truck bed full, and from there, the math is easy.

Calculating the volume of Mel's Mix you'll need for your SFG box requires some math, but nothing you can't do with a smart-phone calculator. All of the formulas you need to do your own calculations follow, along with a chart that breaks down common SFG box sizes into cubic feet and 5-gallon-bucket measurements.

How much Mel's Mix you'll need to fill your SFG bed depends on its height, width, and depth. Use the formulas and charts in this section to determine how much Mel's Mix you'll need.

Calculate the volume of the box

The volume of your SFG box is found by multiplying the length by the width by the depth. Before you make this calculation, convert all of the measurements to the same unit. The end goal is to find the cubic feet of the SFG box, so your starting measurements need to be in feet. Here's the formula:

SFG box length in feet x box width in feet x box depth in feet = box volume in cubic feet

Using the dimensions of a 6-inch traditional SFG box—4 feet by 4 feet by 6 inches—this formula looks like:

4 x 4 x 0.5 = 8 cubic feet

It's okay that the actual height of a 6-inch dimension lumber is $5\frac{1}{2}$ inches. The 6-inch measurement, which is half of a foot, will get you close enough.

If you opted to use 8-inch lumber, you'll need to adjust your calculations accordingly to get:

4 x 4 x 0.66 = 10.56 cubic feet (again, the actual height of 8-inch lumber is $7\frac{1}{2}$ inches, but this will get you close enough)

Calculate the volume of materials needed

Each Mel's Mix ingredient is needed in equal measure. Determine the cubic feet needed of each ingredient by dividing the box's volume by 3.

Box volume in cubic feet / 3 = cubic feet of each ingredient

For the traditional 6-inch SFG box, this is your calculation:

8 / 3 = 2.66 cubic feet per ingredient

If you used 8-inch lumber, the calculation would be 10.56 / 3 = 3.52 cubic feet per ingredient.

Calculate the number of buckets needed

A 5-gallon bucket is a convenient measuring cup for Mel's Mix ingredients. Each 5-gallon bucket holds 0.668 cubic feet of material. Now you can use this formula to arrive at the number of buckets you'll need for each ingredient:

Cubic feet needed / cubic feet of measuring scoop = number of 5-gallon buckets needed

Put this to work for your traditional 6-inch SFG box:

2.66 / 0.668 = 3.98 5-gallon buckets of each ingredient

The precise answer to this equation is 3.98 buckets, which we can call 4. The recipe for Mel's Mix is not the same as a recipe for baking bread. You want to get your measurements close, but a bit of rounding up or down will serve the purpose without overcomplicating things.

If your bed has an 8-inch depth:

3.52 / 0.668 = 5.25 5-gallon buckets of each ingredient

Square Foot Gardener's Tip

Some of your Mel's Mix ingredients will come to you in a compressed form. Release them from their bags and bales and aerate them before measuring. Compressed peat moss can expand by another 50 percent when released and aerated, turning a 2-cubic-foot bag into 3 cubic feet of usable material.

Mix a large enough batch of Mel's Mix to fill your bed. How much of each component you need depends on the size of the box.

Mel's Mix Measurements

Use the formulas on page 154 to calculate the amount of each ingredient needed to fill your SFG box, or find the numbers you need for common SFG box sizes in this chart. The first chart is for beds built with a depth of 6 inches. The second chart is for beds built with a depth of 8 inches.

Box dimensions using 6" lumber	Box volume in cubic feet	5-gallon buckets of each ingredient (rounded)
4' × 4'	8	4
4' × 8'	16	8
4' × 12'	24	12
4' × 16'	32	16
2' × 4'	4	2
2' × 8'	8	4
2' × 12'	12	6
2' × 16'	16	8
1' × 4'	2	1
1' × 8'	4	2
1' × 12'	6	3
1' × 16'	8	4

Box dimensions using 8" lumber	Box volume in cubic feet	5-gallon buckets of each ingredient (rounded)
4' × 4'	10.56	5½
4' × 8'	21.12	10½
4' × 12'	31.68	16
4' × 16'	42.24	21
2' × 4'	5.28	3
2' × 8'	10.56	5½
2' × 12'	15.84	8
2' × 16'	21.12	10½
1' × 4'	2.64	1½
1' × 8'	5.28	3
1' × 12'	7.92	4
1' × 16'	10.56	5½

Create Your Mel's Mix

Now you know all about the three ingredients that go into your Mel's Mix, you learned how to calculate the amount you need of each, and you are ready to make this recipe.

Using this manual-mixing method, it's best to work in one-SFG-box increments. Your arms will really get a workout if you're trying to combine the Mel's Mix ingredients for multiple boxes at the same time.

The best place to make Mel's Mix is close to your SFG box. Be sure you're happy with the SFG box's location. You won't want to move the box once it's filled. It's best to work outdoors on a calm day, as the Mel's Mix ingredients can be dusty when dry.

MATERIALS AND TOOLS

- Screened compost
- Coarse or super coarse vermiculite
- Uncompressed peat moss
- Watering can or hose with sprayer nozzle
- Tarp
- 5-gallon bucket
- Rake
- Shovel
- Particle mask
- Work gloves

This tarp-mixing method allows you to mix large quantities of Mel's Mix without making a huge mess.

PROCESS

Step 1. Spread the tarp over the ground as close to your SFG bed as possible.

Step 2. Alternately add ingredients.

2a. Empty the measured amount of compost onto the tarp. If you're using your own blended compost, no mixing is required. If you're using single-source compost, pile on all four to six different kinds.

2b. Add the measured amount of peat moss to the compost on the tarp. Wet it thoroughly.

2c. Add the measured amount of vermiculite to the mixture on the tarp. Wet it thoroughly.

2d. Use a shovel to preliminarily mix the ingredients together.

2e. Add another measure of each of the three ingredients. And mix with a shovel again.

Step 3. Wet the mixed materials.

3a. Mist the pile to keep down dust.

3b. Use a rake or shovel for further mixing.

3c. Mist again, if needed.

Step 4. Mix the mix.

Drag or lift the ends of the tarp back and forth to mix the materials thoroughly. A second person can make the mixing easier.

Step 5. Transfer Mel's Mix to your SFG box.

5a. Pick up opposite sides of the tarp to cradle the Mel's Mix, and dump a 1- to 2-inch layer into the SFG box, using the tarp like a funnel. You can also use the 5-gallon bucket or a wheelbarrow to make the transfer.

5b. Repeat layers until the SFG box is full and the Mel's Mix is thoroughly wet, with no dry spots, and evenly distributed, with no clumps.

Step 6. Complete your SFG box.

Now you're ready to add the grid and plant your first season of crops.

Now you've not only filled your SFG box with Mel's Mix, but you understand the mechanics behind the Mel's Mix ingredients and why these are essential to your SFG success. Next, you get to put your plan into action and start planting.

Mix It Up

Using a tarp as a mixing tool is an efficient way to combine a quantity of Mel's Mix ingredients, but it's not the only way. If you're doing this project solo or you don't want to deal with a heavy load all at once, mix smaller quantities of your ingredients in a wheelbarrow or a cement mixing bin. Keep the same equal ratio in each batch so the ingredients are evenly spread throughout the SFG box.

Wheelbarrows make great mixing bins for smaller quantities of Mel's Mix.

8

Planting Your Square Foot Garden

You now have a plan, a Square Foot Garden bed and add-ons, and Mel's Mix for producing plants. This chapter digs in to the joy of starting and planting your garden. You'll be sowing seeds, selecting transplants, and transforming your SFG bed in no time.

A Planting Primer

If you've gardened using other growing styles before, you'll need to resist the temptation of planting too closely or too far apart. The SFG Method typically yields a larger harvest in a smaller space than other styles of gardening. Stick with the plan you created in chapter 4. Putting this plan into action starts with gathering your seeds and transplants.

Sourcing seeds

There are more reputable sources of seeds now than ever before. In addition to large, international seed sellers, you'll find smaller, regional seed catalogs with varieties suited to specific growing regions; those dedicated to certain heritage-crop varieties; and some that only deal in certified-organic seeds. Purchasing your seeds from a reputable seed seller should yield good results.

For gardeners with a very tight budget, some communities have seed libraries—often at the actual library or the regional Cooperative Extension office—where you can "borrow" seeds. Many communities host seed swaps, where gardeners can share seeds they've saved themselves and extras from seed packets they've purchased. At seed swaps and seed libraries, you can often find local heirloom seeds and cultural or heritage seeds with interesting stories.

What's Inside a Seed?

Learning about the science of seeds demystifies seed starting. It's easy to answer the question, "What are seeds?" Seeds are plants' source material. But it's what's inside a seed that matters.

You might think of a seed as one whole plant, but actually a seed is a whole packet of organic matter.

On the outside, the seed coat is the protective layer, keeping the delicate insides safe from insects, disease, and moisture. Inside the seed coat is the genetic material of a new plant, plus the carbs, proteins, and fats the new plant needs to develop roots and leaves. Once the first leaves (the cotyledons) are formed, plants exhaust the nutrients from the seed and turn to sourcing nutrients using photosynthesis and their root systems.

The seed will germinate when its interior workings receive the environmental signals that say it's go time. Each type of seed has its own germination requirements: proper temperature, light, and moisture. Given the signal, the seed undergoes a series of changes, cells elongate and divide, and the first tiny plant root (the radicle) breaks through the seed coat. While it may take weeks to get to this point, depending on the type of seed, the process unfolds quickly from here.

Cotyledon
The cotyledon is also called the "seed leaf." It's the first leaf or pair of leaves that emerge from the seed after germination. The cotyledon may look nothing like the plant's true leaves.

Planting from seed is a very economical way to grow a SFG, plus you'll have access to more varieties.

True Leaf

A plant's true leaves form after the cotyledon. These leaves may be very different than the cotyledon, and will match the appearance of the leaves to come.

Source transplants from quality sources such as a local nursery or farm.

Sourcing transplants

Selecting a source of young plants (called transplants) is similar to looking for seeds. You want to find a source you trust. Local nurseries and farmers have most likely grown varieties that do well in your climate. At farmers markets, you'll often find farmers selling the extras of the seedlings they didn't have room to plant in their own gardens. Here, you can ask about the varieties available and what to expect from them.

Transplants are also available at many home-improvement stores, grocery stores, and big-box stores. It's possible these varieties were chosen because they'll thrive in your region and are easy to grow. But it's also possible they were chosen because this is what the store is offering nationwide. See if someone at the store is knowledgeable enough to answer your questions about these plants before you decide to purchase them.

Wherever you source your transplants, examine them carefully before taking them home. Pests and disease can be transported to your SFG bed by an innocent, 3-inch-tall seedling.

Direct seeding vs. transplanting

Whether you plant your seeds directly into your SFG bed or you plug transplants into your SFG bed depends on a few factors.

The time of year. Your location and weather dictates some of your seeding decisions.

In colder climates with shorter growing seasons, starting a garden with transplants can give you a jump start on growing warm-weather crops by 6 weeks or more. This can mean the difference between cherry tomatoes in June or not until August.

The same is true for cool-weather crops you'd like to plant in the fall. In some climates, it can be too hot outdoors at the end of summer for lettuce seeds to germinate without taking measures to protect them in some way. For fall gardens, you're often better off plugging transplants into the garden when it's time.

Your garden plan. Swapping plants out in between seasons takes a bit of coordination. Your written garden plan tells you which plants to put in each square each season. Sometimes a square won't be ready to harvest before it's time to start growing the plant for the next season's square. Look at the Sample Succession Gardens on pages 73 to 74. The squares that house a zucchini

plant in the summer will have collard greens and kale in the fall. Your zucchini plant may still be producing come late summer when it's time to direct seed the collards and kale. You can start your collard and kale plants indoors instead, and they will be nice-sized seedlings when the zucchini plant is ready to be pulled in early fall.

The plant's preferences. Some plants do better than others during transplanting. Tap-root vegetables, including carrots and daikon radishes, prefer to be direct seeded. Cucurbits, like winter squash and watermelons, have sensitive root systems that don't like to be disturbed and require very gentle transplanting. Shallow-rooted crops, like beans and peas, don't transplant well. These plants may be more susceptible to transplant shock. Look at the Planning & Planting Chart on page 244 to see crops' preferences.

The crop's use. When planting cut-and-come-again crops (see page 59)—usually greens and herbs—you're putting 36 plants in each 12-inch grid square. It makes the most sense to direct seed these.

Some crops, like lettuce for example, can be planted either by direct seeding or from transplants. Other crops prefer one method or the other.

Starting your own seeds vs. buying seedlings

For the transplants you need to start your SFG bed, you can choose whether to start them yourself from seeds or to purchase them. Starting your own seeds is an economical means of gardening and can provide a lot of variety. You can purchase a whole packet of seeds for the cost of one seedling from a nursery, and that packet may last for several years, if stored properly (see page 185).

If you're just starting out, you might do a little of each to ease into the process. There are some other reasons behind the decision to start your own or to purchase seedlings:

Crop and variety availability. Some crop transplants are easier to source than others. Callaloo, or amaranth, for example, will not be an easy seedling to find in many parts of the United States. Tomatoes, on the other hand, are ubiquitous, but you may be looking for a specific variety. Whether you are starting seeds yourself or purchasing plant starts from others could depend as much on the variety you're looking for as it does on any other factor. For the most success, seek out varieties that are suited to your region.

Your time. Tending to seedlings isn't difficult, but it is an item for your daily to-do list. You don't want to plan any trips away while you have seeds germinating and seedlings in your care.

Your indoor space. Seedlings are small but require specific conditions to thrive. You need a seed-starting space that's warm, gets direct sunlight or can accommodate a grow light, and is out of your way. Not everyone has an abundance of space that matches this description, and sometimes this is the dividing line between starting seeds yourself and letting someone else start them for you. You'll read more about how to set up your indoor seed-starting space later in this chapter.

Spotty germination. Some plants are notoriously difficult to start from seed. They might have low germination rates, specific environmental requirements, or take a long time. You may be better off sourcing seedlings from someone who has starting those plants figured out.

Seasonal timing. Sometimes the growing season can sneak up on you. Even with the best of intentions, you might want to start your tomato seeds inside but realize it's already time to put tomato plants out into the SFG bed. In these cases, it's a good thing that others start seedlings to sell and share.

Transplant Shock
Stresses affecting newly transplanted seedlings are known as transplant shock. These can slow the growth of the plant and make it more susceptible to pests and disease. Read about how to reduce transplant shock on page 181.

Whether you plant from seed or transplants, a successful SFG is close at hand.

Planting root stock or other plant parts

Not every plant you grow will start with a seed. In these cases, you're planting root stock or another plant part, rather than seeds or transplants. Ginger, turmeric, potatoes, sweet potatoes, and asparagus are some crops grown this way. In this case, you'll plant all or a piece of these roots, rhizomes, crowns, or slips into your SFG square, just as you would a seed or transplant. Refer to the Planning & Planting Chart on page 244 for details about how to work with these crops.

You can source root stock for these crops from grocery-store foods, but you know very little about their history. You don't know if they're disease free, whether they've been treated with a growth retardant that will delay sprouting, and whether they'd even produce in your region. As you do for seeds and transplants, look for reputable sources of root stock.

Planting bulbs and sets

Ornamental gardeners will think of perennial tulips, daffodils, and hyacinths when the idea of planting bulbs comes up, but crops in the allium family—including onions, garlic, and shallots—also grow from bulbs or sets. Alliums can be started from seed, but they take a long time to mature this way. Starting with bulbs or sets is a simpler and quicker process.

Garlic gets started with the cloves of a head saved from the season before. You only want to plant garlic that's free of pests and disease. Once something like onion maggot sets up in your SFG bed, you'll have a heck of a time getting rid of it. Growing onions and shallots this way involves ordering sets—which are dormant bulbs—or plant starts from a catalog or picking them up at a gardening center.

Onions are most often planted from sets. These have sprouted and will continue to grow throughout the season. Notice the 9-plants-per-square spacing? If this gardener were growing green onions, the spacing would be 16.

Seed-Germination Basics

Whether being direct seeded into the garden or started indoors, different seeds have specific conditions required to germinate. Seed packets are helpful in guiding this process, as well as the Planning & Planting Chart on page 244.

Seed-starting medium

The right seed-starting medium puts seeds in contact with the moisture needed for germination. Nutrients aren't important in the germination stage, but once the cotyledon emerges, the seedling's roots want to be in a nutrient-rich environment. Though there are many options for seed starting, using vermiculite or Mel's Mix to start seeds is a great choice. You'll learn more about both on page 170.

Soil temperature

You'll find some seeds are picky about the soil temperature they need to emerge, while others will germinate in a range of temperatures.

Starting seeds indoors, most seeds will germinate in their growing medium at room temperature. Some warm-weather crops—like peppers and tomatoes—benefit from an electric seedling heat mat under the seeding trays to speed germination, especially if your house is cold. The cooler-weather crops—especially lettuce and peas—might be better off germinating without a heat mat beneath.

When direct seeding outdoors, the Mel's Mix in a SFG box will heat up faster in the springtime than regular garden soil. You can use a soil thermometer if you'd like to be precise. In your SFG box, check the temperature of the Mel's Mix at the same time each morning for a week and take the average. You are interested in the temperature in the top couple of inches of soil, because this is where the seeds germinate.

When starting from seed indoors, Mel's Mix made with fine- or medium-grade vermiculite makes a great growing medium for your new plant babies.

Light requirements

Some seeds will germinate in darkness, and others need light. The general rule for sowing seeds is to plant them 2 to 4 times as deep as the seed's diameter. Sometimes a seed packet will instruct you otherwise—to sow on the soil surface or to cover lightly with growing medium. A thin layer of Mel's Mix or vermiculite over the seeds will give them the darkness necessary for germination as well as prevent the seed from drying out.

After the seedlings emerge, they need light. We'll cover details on how to do this in an upcoming section on page 175.

Moisture

Consistent moisture is necessary for germination and early seedling growth. There's a balance here though. Too much water will cause the seeds to rot, and too little won't penetrate the seed coat. Humidity is a friend to seeds that haven't yet germinated. You can increase humidity with a simple clear plastic lid over the seed-starting tray, creating a tiny greenhouse. When the seeds germinate, remove the lid. At this point, too much humidity can cause fungal issues.

Days to germination

While some seeds seemingly instantly germinate when placed in a growing medium—radishes are a good example—others can take weeks and require special treatment to get there—parsley, for example. The waiting can feel interminable.

Know your seeds' days to germination so you can calculate the date to start your seeds and know when to start looking for emergence.

If it's taking much longer than the estimated germination time, try again to seed this crop. The issue could be operator error or the seeds could be from a less-vigorous batch. If you're planting outdoors, the problem could be that wildlife or birds found the seeds in your SFG bed and thought you put the seeds there for them to enjoy. Some kind of critter protection could be in order. If the issue persists, a germination test as described on page 186 can help you determine whether the seed is still viable.

Germination rates

Seed packets will sometimes state the germination rate as a percentage. For a seed with 77 percent germination, such as leeks, 77 out of 100 seeds are likely to sprout under proper conditions. Pad your chances at getting the number of plants you want by seeding more low-germinating seeds than you intend to grow.

Seed treatments

Some seeds need to be fooled into thinking they've gone through certain environmental processes before they'll germinate. You might read on a seed packet that a seed needs stratification or scarification. Special treatment before sowing might involve freezing the seeds (stratification), soaking them in water for a day, or scratching the surface with sandpaper (scarification). Now the seed believes it's gone through a winter outdoors or passed through an animal's digestive tract, and it's ready to break dormancy. Seeds that germinate best with pretreatment include echinacea, nasturtium, and beets.

Some seeds germinate very quickly, while others take a long time. These radishes are among the fastest germinating seeds for the vegetable garden.

Deciding which varieties to grow starts with a careful review of the seed selections available to you in catalogs and at garden centers. Purchase quality seeds and the result will be quality plants like this bok choy.

Selecting Varieties

Just how do you choose between the twenty-plus varieties of green beans in a seed catalog? There's a lot that goes into this decision, and the choice comes down to personal preference, variety performance, and what grows best in your region.

Organic seeds

If organic integrity is important to you, organic seeds should be where you start. USDA Certified Organic seeds are produced according to the National Organic Program standards, which limits the use of synthetic chemicals found in many fertilizers and pesticides and prohibits the use of genetically modified seeds and soil amendments.

Genetically modified seeds

Genetically modified (GM) seeds are those that come from plants that have been genetically altered in a lab environment to impart a new trait on the plant that originated in an entirely different organism. One example of a GM seed is *Bt* corn, which is a dry corn that has been altered with genetic material from the *Bacillus thuringiensis* (*Bt*) bacterium. *Bt* kills corn borer caterpillars as they feed on the corn plant, limiting damage to the crop.

Most crops a home gardener would be interested in planting are not commercially available as GM varieties. As of this writing, only fourteen crops are approved for production using GM seeds. Of that list, eggplant, potato, zucchini, and summer squash are the ones home gardeners would be likely to grow. Until recently, in the United States, GM crop seeds were only commercially available from seed dealers in large quantities, and you would have to sign a contract to purchase them.

However, in 2024, the first genetically modified tomato became available to the general public. Named Purple Tomato, it has cherry-sized fruit and scientists have incorporated genes from a snapdragon into the variety so it produces bright purple tomatoes filled with antioxidant anthocyanin pigments. Future GM crops may be available to home gardeners, however as of this writing, it's virtually impossible to purchase GM seeds and not know it.

Many seed companies label their seeds as GM-free, and some seeds carry the Non-GMO Project label—GMO meaning genetically modified organism—but don't assume the seeds that don't carry these labels are genetically modified.

Hybrid seeds

There tends to be a confusion between hybrid seeds and GM seeds. While GM seeds are the result of laboratory-driven genetic alterations, hybrid seeds come from controlled, intentional plant breeding. Plant parents are crossed to strengthen or to downplay a particular trait. Plant breeders might choose to create hybrids for better disease resistance, higher yields, drought tolerance, or larger fruit. Hybrids are developed over years until the plant breeder gets the result they want. Only then do they release their hybrid variety to farmers and gardeners.

Seeds collected from hybrid plants won't "breed true"—meaning they won't produce the same plant that they came from. If you save and plant the seeds of a sweet, large, hybrid orange tomato, you could end up growing a small, bitter orange tomato from those saved seeds. There's no way of knowing how the hybrid will breed back the next year. If you grow a hybrid variety and like it enough to grow it again the next year, you have to start with new seed from a commercial seed company each season.

Heirloom seeds

Heirloom seeds are from varieties that have been developed by gardeners over time. Some horticulturists consider a variety to be an heirloom if it was developed before 1951, which is when hybrids first came into production. Others call a variety "heirloom" if it's been cultivated in localized conditions and passed down over the years through family or community lineages. Many gardeners choose to plant heirlooms to carry on the story of the seeds and the people who've grown them.

Heirlooms are open pollinated. (See more about that below.) Home gardeners saving seeds and sharing them are typically how they're passed around, though more heirloom varieties are available for sale all the time. Heirloom varieties often have a distinct appearance or flavor, but they rarely have the disease resistance of newer varieties.

Open pollinated

An open-pollinated label means the variety will breed true year after year, and you can save your own seeds from this crop—with care. (See page 187 for seed-saving advice.) While all heirloom plants are open pollinated, not all open-pollinated plants are heirloom.

Treated seeds

Some seeds come with a coating or a treatment to help correct some common issues with the seed. Some treated seeds are considered okay for organic growing, and some are not. Treated seeds will always be labeled.

A few examples of when a seed could be treated or coated are:
- Very small seeds, like lettuce or carrots, may be pelleted, or coated, so the seed size is larger and easier to handle.
- Seeds that are prone to fungal issues may have a fungicidal treatment or coating. You'll find this for a range of vegetables, from peppers to pumpkins.

- Legumes, like beans and peas, may come coated in an inoculant that will help them draw nitrogen from the air and fix it into the soil with their roots.

If you choose to plant treated or pelleted seeds, wear a mask and gloves when handling them to protect yourself from the coating. Pelleted seeds are only meant to be viable for one year.

Hybrids, like this dwarf tomato, have been purposefully bred to have particular traits. In this case, the desired trait is a compact growth habit.

There are many considerations that go into what seeds to grow for your garden. The good news is that it's okay to experiment and have fun with it.

The most important considerations

Regardless of the label on the seed packet—the fun name, the certifications, the pretty picture—the most important consideration when selecting seed varieties is whether they will work in your SFG bed.

Size. Compact and dwarf varieties do well in SFG beds because they're bred for small spaces. Determinate tomatoes are shorter and bushier, and indeterminate tomatoes are viny and tall, so they need vertical area to grow with trellises or supports.

Your climate. Think about your growing conditions to select the best varieties for your garden.

If you typically have 90 frost-free days in the growing season, select varieties that mature in less than 90 days. Cilantro and greens that are slow to bolt are smart choices in hot climates. Basil and cucurbits that are resistant to fungal issues work well in humid places. You will find other characteristics appropriate for your area.

The season. You can choose the variety based on when you are planting it. For example, reach for short-day onions if you're planting in the fall to overwinter for a spring harvest—because the days are shorter then—but long-day onions if you're planting in spring to harvest in summer.

Maturity cycle. Sometimes, you need a crop to be ready for harvest sooner, and

sometimes you need it to be ready later. In chapter 4, you read about succession planting techniques. One of those is to plant different varieties of the same crop that mature at different times. Choose varieties based on when you hope to harvest them.

Your personal taste. Let's say you love red tomatoes only, and no other color of tomato will do. By all means, don't choose a

yellow tomato. If you must have a seedless watermelon, don't reach for the seeded variety. If you've always wanted to grow a maroon sunflower, you can do that with the right seed choice. None of the other considerations on this list actually matter if you don't enjoy what you're growing.

Starting Seeds Indoors

Starting your own seeds is an additional step in the gardening process, and it's a rewarding one. By starting your own seeds, you have full control over how your food is grown—from selecting the seed to harvesting the resulting crop. It's hard to find a greater feeling of empowerment.

There are a few different ways you can start seeds indoors to grow your own seedlings for transplanting. The premise is the same for each. Two methods are shown here: starting seeds in seed trays using vermiculite and starting seeds in soil blocks using Mel's Mix.

Dwarf and compact varieties do very well in a SFG. Check out the super-compact dwarf tomatoes in the third row from the left in this backyard garden. Perfect!

Square Foot Gardener's Tip

Always label your seed trays and seedlings so you know the crop, variety, and date planted. Wooden craft popsicle sticks or plastic plant label are ideal for this because they poke easily into seed-starting medium.

Start Your Seeds in Vermiculite

By using vermiculite as your seed-starting medium, you're surrounding your seeds with an airy, moisture-filled medium to aid in their germination. For small seeds, you'll want to use a finer grade vermiculite. For large seeds, use a fine or medium grade. This is a good method for starting seeds, because the vermiculite is so lightweight, the newly germinated seedling has little resistance in its emergence. From here, you'll pot them up into Mel's Mix to continue their growth.

Pictured here is a standard seed-cell tray that you can find at home-improvement stores and garden centers. These are handy for starting seeds because each seed has its own cell, and each cell has a drainage hole so excess water can drain away. Just starting out, you may not use every cell in a tray like this. These trays are reusable and will last for many years. As you expand your garden with more SFG beds, you may eventually fill the tray with seeds to start all your plants.

If you'd prefer to use vermiculite to start your seeds but don't want to invest in a seed tray, you can also use a shallow plastic bowl, tray, or clam shell container with holes poked in the bottom—like a hummus or deli-meat container. The instructions below will work in any well-draining container.

MATERIALS AND TOOLS

- Fine- or medium-grade vermiculite
- Seed-starting tray
- Water
- Clear plastic tray cover

Vermiculite used to start seeds can then be added to a new batch of Mel's Mix.

Method

Step 1: Fill the seed tray or container with vermiculite.

Leave ⅛ inch or so of space at the top of the tray. You'll want this space in case you add too much water so your seeds don't float away.

Step 2: Hydrate the tray.

Gently pour water over the vermiculite so it's fully damp. The vermiculite will change to a darker color as it hydrates.

Step 3: Place your seeds.

Pour a few seeds from the packet into the palm of your hand. Poke a shallow hole in the center of the cell, and place one or two seeds inside.

Square Foot Gardener's Tip

When you're finished starting seeds for the season, add the vermiculite from your tray to your next batch of Mel's Mix. Even though you are using fine- or medium-grade vermiculite instead of coarse grade for your seed-starting efforts, it can be added to Mel's Mix. This small amount of vermiculite will constitute such a minor percentage of the overall vermiculite in the blend of Mel's Mix that its finer grade does not cause a significant change in the overall texture.

Step 4: Cover your seeds.

Read the instructions for this seed type. Either leave the seed exposed so it can germinate in the light or cover the seed with vermiculite.

Step 5: Cover the tray.

Place the clear plastic greenhouse cover on top of the tray.

Step 6: Keep the seed tray watered.

Mist the seed tray with water every day, or set the bottom of the seed tray in a tray of water for an hour a day so it can soak up the moisture it needs.

Step 7: Transfer seedlings into Mel's Mix after sprouting.

Depending on the seed you planted, the first part to emerge may be a spindly, pale string of a stem or it could be a more robust, bright-green stalk. Check on the seedling every day, and when the first true leaves appear, transfer the seedling into a seed tray or other container with Mel's Mix.

Seed-Starting Alternatives

From this chapter, you should gather that you have many options in seed starting.

In addition to the seed-starting techniques outlined here, you can use seed trays filled with Mel's Mix. Because Mel's Mix is coarser than fine grade vermiculite, these work best for medium and large seeds. When the seedling is a few inches tall, you can pot it up into a new container. (See Potting Up on page 175 for more about this.)

You also can reuse yogurt cups—punch holes in the bottom first—to start seeds.

Over time, you'll develop your own preferred method. This is a place to experiment and find out what works best for you.

Start Your Seeds with Soil Blocks

Soil blocking involves making a batch of Mel's Mix and using a soil blocker—a hand-held contraption that looks like a big cookie cutter—to stamp out blocks of soil. These soil blocks have an indentation in the center for the seed to sit in.

Soil blocking is more work on the front end of seed starting because you have to combine the Mel's Mix and stamp the soil block. This is less work come germination time, because—unlike seed starting in vermiculite—you don't have to transfer newborn seedlings out of this growing medium. They're already planted in the Mel's Mix with the nutrients they need for their early seedling stage. This method also reduces plastic waste by not relying on nursery pots or other containers.

Because they're not surrounded by solid sides, plants growing in soil blocks get a lot of oxygen to their roots and are less likely to become rootbound, which happens when the roots run out of space in the container and start growing in circles. When being transplanted directly from a soil block into the garden, plants have less transplant shock because their roots aren't being disturbed during removal from a container.

Soil blocks may dry out faster than vermiculite or Mel's Mix in plastic seed trays. The upside to this is that it's hard to overwater soil blocks because they drain well.

MATERIALS AND TOOLS

○ Mel's Mix (Find this recipe on page 135.)

○ Compost or soil sifter (See the SFG Tip on page 143.)

○ Water

○ Tray with drainage holes

○ Tub to hold Mel's Mix

○ Soil blocker

Starting seeds in soil blocks reduces plastic waste and keeps the roots of your seedlings well aerated.

Process

Step 1: Sift the Mel's Mix.

To remove larger particles that may impede germination, sift the Mel's Mix through a soil or compost sifter, discarding any larger chunks of materials.

Step 2: Moisten the Mel's Mix.

The sifted Mel's Mix needs to be the right consistency to hold the soil block shape. Add enough water so that it holds together when you ball up a fistful and excess water freely runs out. Add more Mel's Mix or water as you work to maintain the right consistency.

Square Foot Gardener's Tip

Soil blockers come in various sizes. The 4-square blocker is a good all-purpose size. Find soil blockers at garden-supply stores or in seed catalogs. You might convince gardening friends to go in on a purchase of a soil blocker together, because this is a tool you'll each need just a few times a year. Some libraries even have soil blockers that can be checked out from their "library of things."

Step 3: Make the soil blocks.

3a. Push the soil blocker into the tub of Mel's Mix. Keep your hands on the blocker itself, and not on the plunger.

3b. Wiggle the soil blocker back and forth to pack the Mel's Mix in there.

Step 4: Place the soil blocks.

4a. Scrape excess Mel's Mix from underneath the blocker so the bottoms of the soil blocks are level.

4b. Transfer the soil blocker to the tray. Press down the plunger while pulling up on the soil blocker to deposit the blocks in their place. It's okay if it takes a few tries for you to get the hang of this. If this doesn't work as you'd hoped, return the Mel's Mix to the tub and try again.

4c. Place the next row of soil blocks right up against the row before it, both to fit as many blocks as you can in the tray and so they keep one another from drying out. Make only as many soil blocks as you need.

Step 5: Place your seeds

Pour a few seeds into your hand. Place one seed in each block's indent.

Step 6: Cover your seeds.

Read the instructions for this seed type, and either leave the seed exposed so it can germinate in the light or cover the seed with the right amount of sifted Mel's Mix. You could also cover the seed with fine grade vermiculite instead of Mel's Mix. Place a clear plastic greenhouse cover or a piece of plastic wrap on top of the tray.

Step 7: Keep the soil blocks watered.

Mist the tray with water every day, or set the bottom of the soil block tray in a tray of water for an hour a day so the soil blocks can soak up the moisture they need. Letting them soak up water from the bottom will prevent the growing medium from splashing onto the seedlings and reduce fungal issues. Do not pour water over the top of the blocks or they may fall apart.

Square Foot Gardener's Tip

When soil blocking, always start with more Mel's Mix than you think you'll need. An impressive amount packs into the blocking gadget, and you want to have enough growing medium to fully fill out all blocks.

Bring the light

Most home windowsills don't provide all the light that seedlings need to thrive. You could try to place your seedlings in east- and south-facing sunny spots. You'll know if your seedlings aren't getting enough light. They will become "leggy"—long and spindly, with weak-looking stems and pale leaves. They're putting their energy into reaching for the light rather than growing strong.

Grow lights are an easy way to solve this. The energy-efficient bulbs put out a wide spectrum of light, mimicking sunlight. Follow the manufacturer's recommendation regarding how close to the plant tops to position the lights, and raise the lights as the plants grow. The plants will do best with 16 hours of light per day from a grow light. A simple timer can turn the lights on and off so you don't have to.

You'll find a range of grow lights, from whole shelving units to a bulb for a simple shop-light fixture that you may already have. Shop around at home-improvement and garden-supply stores and catalogs to see what setup works for your available space and the number of seedlings you hope to grow.

Potting up

As seedlings grow, they may need to be put into larger containers. This is called potting up or up potting. There are generally two times you would up pot seedlings:

Seedlings started in vermiculite need to be moved into a container with Mel's Mix. The seeds that germinated in vermiculite will need nutrients and structural support for their roots soon after they develop leaves.

As your seedlings grow, they may need to be moved into progressively larger containers until they are ready to go out into the garden. This tomato was grown via soil blocking and then up potted into a larger pot for several weeks before being moved into the garden.

Insert a plastic knife or a wooden craft stick into the vermiculite alongside the seedling. Scoop out the seedling and transfer it into a seed tray or other well-draining container of Mel's Mix. Be careful not to handle the stem too much because it's very fragile at this point. Firm up the Mel's Mix around the seedling, and water it well.

Seedlings started in small seed trays or soil blocks need to be potted up as their roots grow. This is especially true for tomatoes and the larger cool-season crops—like broccoli and cauliflower—that you'll start indoors some time before planting into your SFG bed.

This process is straightforward. Fill a larger container that has good drainage with Mel's Mix, and make a hole in the Mel's Mix about the size of the seedling plug. When potting up a soil block, separate the block from its companions. When potting up a seedling from a seed cell, squeeze the sides of the cell, or if the hole underneath is large enough, poke your finger up through the hole to pop out the plug. Settle the seedling into the larger container, and pat down the soil around it. Water it well.

Timing it all

You could think of starting your garden as conducting an orchestra. If you were on stage, you'd want the flutes to start the piece, the drums to come in at just the right time, and the trumpets to arrive with a flourish. This is the same, except your flutes are the seeds you started indoors, the drums are the seedlings you've up potted, and the trumpets are the seedlings you purchase from the nursery.

Square Foot Gardener's Tip

Purchase flowerpots for up potting, or make your own potting containers. Plastic cups, yogurt containers, and other pint and quart containers with holes poked in the bottom for drainage all work great.

No book can tell you exactly when you need to start seeds or source seedlings, because the timing of all of this will depend on your climate and your crops. Seeds started too early will be ready for transplanting before the garden space is available or the weather is appropriate. These could require several rounds of potting up to hold off transplanting them outdoors. Seeds started too late will delay the start of your gardening season. You are aiming for the sweet spot in between.

Rootbound
Rootbound plants have roots that have outgrown their container's volume. The roots begin to overlap and circle around the container. When planted in the SFG box, root-bound plants may be slow to establish themselves.

Orchestrate your seed-starting timing by planning backward from the time you wish to start planting into your SFG bed. Depending on the season and the crop you're growing, you'll want to start your seeds indoors 4 to 8 weeks before you need to transplant them into the garden.

Time your warm-season crops to be ready to transplant outdoors after the last average frost date and when the soil and weather are warm. Your cool-season crops should be ready for transplanting in time to produce their first crop before the heat of summer arrives for spring plantings or before the arrival of regular hard freezes for fall plantings.

For example, let's say you're in the United States, in southern Kentucky which is USDA Zone 6b. Your average last frost is around May 7, and you're starting seeds indoors for your summer garden, including sweet basil, slicing tomatoes, and peppers. Looking at the Planning & Planting Chart on page 244, you can see how long it should take for seeds to germinate and how long the seedlings need to grow before transplanting them into your SFG bed:

- Basil takes 8 to 14 days to germinate and should be started 4 to 6 weeks before transplanting.
- Tomatoes need 7 to 10 days to germinate and need at least 6 to 8 weeks before transplanting.
- Peppers have a 7- to 21-day germination window, depending on whether a heat mat was used, plus need 6 to 8 weeks before transplanting.

By counting backwards from the target May 7th outdoor planting date, this tells you to start your basil seeds indoors at the end of March or the first week of April, your tomatoes indoors at the beginning of March, and your peppers indoors in early to mid-February.

Timing your planting dates is a careful dance. Don't worry. You'll get the hang of it when you have a season or two under your belt.

Dividing Your Squares

You'll most commonly plant your squares with 1, 4, 9, or 16 plants each. The 12-inch-by-12-inch grid space makes it easy to mark your spacing.

Plant Spacing in Practice

Here are easy-to-follow guidelines to keep your spacing on track:

16 very small plants. To have 16 plants in one grid square, first draw a plus sign in the Mel's Mix to divide the square into quarters. Then draw lines to divide each quarter into quarters.

9 small plants. For a square with nine plants, draw a hashtag in the Mel's Mix. One plant goes in each section.

4 medium plants. A four-plant square is simple to divide. Draw a plus sign in the Mel's Mix with your finger to divide the square into quarters. Place one plant in the center of each quarter.

1 large plant. You'll typically plant a single-plant square with one plant in the center. If you're planting a large plant in a square along the outer edge of the bed, place the plant toward the outside of center to give it a few inches of extra room.

The Outliers

1 extra-large plant. An extra-large plant will take up two or more squares on its own. You'll put the plant or the seed in one grid square but plan for it to grow so large that it'll cover two or more squares. These plants do best in the outer squares of the SFG box so they can grow over the side.

36 cut-and-come-again plants. The only time you'll put 36 plants in a square is when you're planting leafy greens as cut-and-come-again crops, most often direct seeded (see page 178). This spacing is intentionally tight because you're harvesting them when they're very small. The spacing doesn't have to be perfect for cut-and-come-again-style plantings but aim for 36 evenly spaced holes while planting your seeds.

Direct Seeding

Some crops respond well to direct seeding into the SFG bed, while others need to be transplanted, and some pay little mind either way. The Planning & Planting Chart on page 244 includes a guide.

When the soil is the right temperature for germination and you're ready to start tending this season's SFG bed, head outside with your garden plan and seed packets in hand. Direct seeding is a simple task. Here are the steps.

Step 1: Divide your squares.

Use the Dividing Your Squares guide on page 177 to draw an outline for your seeds in the Mel's Mix. Make a small indentation in the center of each division.

Step 2: Seed your squares.

Drop one to three seeds in each indentation. (As they grow you may have to thin out the planting. See Thinning Seedlings at right for instructions.)

Step 3: Cover your seeds.

Follow the seed-packet instructions to either cover the seeds with Mel's Mix or to leave the seeds exposed so they can germinate in the light.

Step 4: Water in your seeds.

Gently water the area around the seed so that the seed is soaked but not in standing water. The mist setting on a multi-setting hose nozzle gently moistens the Mel's Mix without displacing the seeds. Water the seeds every day for the next several weeks—don't let the Mel's Mix dry out while seedlings are getting established.

Step 5: Await germination.

Mark your calendar for the day you expect germination. The hardest part of direct seeding is having to wait patiently for the seedlings to emerge.

The SFG Method is easy enough for kids. Let them help place and plant your seeds. It's a good lesson in math, too.

Thinning Seedlings

From other parts of this book, you know that following spacing instructions is important for plant health and productivity. These may seem like competing ideas. This is where thinning comes in. From these instructions, you know to drop up to three seeds per hole.

You will have better odds of germinating all the plants you want by starting with multiple seeds. When more than one seed germinates in that spot, let them grow until they develop their first set of true leaves. Then use scissors to snip the weakest-looking seedlings, and save the best-looking seedling to grow in your SFG bed.

Trimming with scissors is preferred to pulling the tiny plants, because you don't want to disturb the roots of the remaining seedling.

Thinning is especially important for many beets and chard. They are unique as they produce a cluster of seeds grouped together. Sowing what you think is a single seed might result in a group of seedlings.

These seedlings need to be thinned down to only 9 plants. Use a pair of garden snips or scissors to cut off the weakest-looking seedlings.

Transplant Time

After starting seeds indoors or choosing your transplants from the farmers market or nursery, it's time to give them a home in your SFG bed. As is the case with seeding, timing is everything. The first week your plants spend getting established in the SFG bed will set them up for a season of strong growth and production. Wait until the time is right—the soil is warm enough and, in the case of warm-season plants, your expected last-frost date has passed.

Easing transplant transition

It's a jarring experience for seedlings to go from a controlled environment—probably indoors, surrounded by a protective plastic pot—into the wilds of your SFG bed. In fact, some seedlings experience transplant shock, which is a plant's physiological response to the transition. Transplant shock is a bit like going into survival mode. This might look like extreme wilting within hours of transplanting and reduced or no growth for a period of time while the plant diverts its resources to protecting itself for a couple of weeks. While in transplant shock mode, seedlings can overheat and are more prone to sunscald. The plant will likely recover, though its growth is now behind.

Ease your plants into their new environment with thoughtful planning.

Hardening off. Hardening off is a gardener's version of "tough love." Hardening off your plants is the process of transitioning them from an indoor life to an outdoor life, a little at a time.

Assuming temperatures are above freezing—or above 50°F, for warm-season plants—move your seedlings outside a week or 2 before you plan to transplant them into your SFG. Put them in a shady spot so they're not shocked by immediate direct sunlight. If it's raining, keep them under cover, like a roof awning. If it's very windy, don't put them outside, because you don't want tender stems to break. Water them less than usual, but don't allow them to wilt. The seedlings will become accustomed to breezes and

Some crops perform better when directly seeded into the garden. Others do better when grown from transplants.

Whether your transplants were started in your living room or at a local nursery, good timing is everything when it comes to planting them out in the garden.

changes in temperature throughout the day. Each passing day, give them more time in direct sunlight, but bring them back inside each night. Over the course of a week or two, they will slowly become accustomed to outdoor growing conditions and can even be left outdoors overnight. They are now ready to transplant into your SFG.

Plant at the right size. This tip is a hard one to plan for. Larger seedlings are more prone to transplant shock than smaller seedlings. If you live in a place with a shorter growing season, some plants, like tomatoes, will have to be on the larger side when you plant them, because you're increasing the length of their growing season by starting them earlier indoors. A transplant with a smaller root mass will transition better than one that already has a complex vascular system. This is especially true for plants that don't like to be transplanted in the first place, such as watermelons or cucumbers. Timely transplanting also reduces the chance that the seedling would become rootbound.

Tend to them well. After hardening off, transplant when the forecast looks safe—more on this below—for the coming days. Water them well in your SFG bed so they don't have to struggle to find the moisture they need. Extra care now will aid their transition.

When to transplant

Choose a cloudy day, and transplant late in the afternoon when the sun is less intense, or do it when your SFG bed is in shade. Try to time your transplanting for a period that's not too cold at night, not too windy, and not too much rain in the immediate forecast. This is a list of conditions that are out of your control, and sometimes you just have to plant at a less-than-ideal time. If you choose one just-right condition, let it be the temperature. Transplants can bounce back from most everything else.

Choose a cloudy day to settle your transplants into your SFG bed. Then promptly water them in well.

Square Foot Gardener's Tip

To use a trellis that sits in the SFG bed, such as the A-Frame Trellis on page 117, place the trellis before you plant your seedlings whenever possible. There's less likelihood of knocking into and damaging a plant if the trellis goes in first.

How to Transplant

Transplanting is a straightforward-enough process—remove plant from pot, insert plant into SFG bed, cover the root mass with Mel's Mix, and water. While that's the summary version, there is a bit of finesse that goes along with the process.

Transplanting is not a challenging process, but it does involve care and caution.

Step 1: Divide your squares.

Following your SFG plan, use the Dividing Your Squares guide on page 177 to draw an outline for spacing and placing your plants in the Mel's Mix.

Step 2: Dig your hole.

Make a hole for your transplant using your hand or a trowel, moving soil aside so you can slide in the transplant. A trowel is useful to make bigger holes for transplants with larger root systems. Mel's Mix is friable and easy to work with, so there's no hard digging required. Make the hole as deep as the container your seedling is in now. (For planting tomatoes, see Trench-Plant a Tomato on page 184.)

Step 3: Place your plant.

Plants' stems and root systems are fragile. Handle the transplant by the mass of Mel's Mix rather than by the stem as much as possible.

3a. Remove the seedling from its pot. If you're using small seed cells, squeeze the sides of the cell, or use a pencil or your finger to push up through the hole in the bottom of the cell to pop out the plant. If you're using a stand-alone pot, hold the pot upside down with your hand covering the top with your fingers on either side of the plant stem. Squeeze the sides and tap on the bottom so the Mel's Mix and root mass falls gently into your hand. If you're transplanting a seedling in a soil block, just separate one block from the others. You may have to tear some roots apart—do so gently, and they'll be fine.

3b. Place the plant into the hole in the grid square. The top of the root mass should be just under the surface of the Mel's Mix in the SFG bed. The exception to this is tomatoes, which can be planted deeper (see page 184).

Step 4: Settle in the plant.

4a. Firm the Mel's Mix around the transplant.

4b. Water it well.

Step 5: Water regularly.

New transplants should be watered daily or as often as needed to keep the transplant's roots consistently moist. Never let the Mel's Mix dry out completely.

Trench-Plant a Tomato

Tomato plants want to be deeply rooted. In How to Transplant, on page 183, you learned how to settle a transplant into the SFG bed so the top of its root mass is just below the surface of the Mel's Mix. Tomatoes are an exception to this planting method.

Look at the stem of a tomato plant. All of those hairs and nodules become roots when in contact with growing medium. One way to make your tomato plant more stable and allow for a larger root system that can pull in more nutrients—resulting in a healthier plant and more tomatoes—is to use the trench-planting method. This is an especially useful way of planting tomatoes if your seedling grew tall before planting.

MATERIALS AND TOOLS

○ Tomato plant

○ Water

○ SFG bed, filled with Mel's Mix

○ Trowel

Trench planting is a great way to encourage a more extensive root system on tomato plants. Just take care not to damage the stem as you bend the tip upwards and out of the Mel's Mix. Laying the tomato transplant on its side for 24 hours prior to planting encourages the tip of the seedling to automatically turn up, reducing the chance of damage during trench planting.

Process

Step 1: Prepare the tomato plant.

Remove all but the top-most 4 or 5 leaves from the tomato plant's stem.

Step 2: Dig a trench.

In the tomato's grid square, dig a trench 3 to 4 inches deep and about half of the way across the square.

Step 3. Place the plant.

Set the tomato plant horizontally in the trench and curve the tip up gently so its roots and bare stem are down in the trench and its leaves are above the surface. The top of the plant should poke out of the hole in the center of the square. **Note:** If it is a determinate variety that will take up 4 squares, aim to keep the top of the plant poking out at the center of the four squares in which it will grow.

Step 4: Settle in the plant.

Fill the trench in with the Mel's Mix, burying the stem and root mass, and gently pat down the growing medium. Be gentle with the stem. Water it well.

Keeping Track

With all of the "ifs" involved in starting a garden—if the weather was warmer than usual, if the seeds had a low germination rate, if you got started on time, and so on—keeping notes will help you improve your SFG-bed performance each season. There's really no wrong way to keep track of garden happenings. Write in a notebook, open a note-taking app on your phone, or scribble notes on a calendar. You can even write notes directly on your SFG grid plan. Choose a recordkeeping method that will be easy for you to use on a regular basis.

Here are some things you'll want to make note of:

- Dates you started seeds, the source of the seeds, and their germination rate
- Dates you transplanted, the source of the transplants, and notes on how they fared
- Weather conditions for the season, to keep track of how certain varieties performed
- Any pest or disease issues you had and how you handled those
- Your harvest dates, amounts, and other notes

Hold on to your SFG grid plans each season so you remember which plants went in which squares. You'll need this for crop-family rotation, and it'll be nice to have this as a record of how you arranged taller plants, trellises, and other supports.

When it's time to plan next year's garden, pull out your notes from past seasons to make your planting decisions.

Store seeds properly for the longest life and highest germination rates.

Storing and Saving Seeds

The SFG Method is designed to use as few resources as possible from season to season. This includes seeds. One packet of seeds could contain hundreds more than you need to plant your SFG bed. For example, one packet of fennel seeds might contain 200 seeds. You would only need one seed to plant one square of fennel. Now you have 199 seeds to store and share.

Seed storage

A seed is a living organism that requires proper conditions to remain viable. The Planning & Planting Chart on page 244 outlines the potential viability expectancy for various crops' seeds under ideal conditions. Often, these are ideal conditions as determined in a laboratory, not in a normal person's home. Yet just because the chart, or a seed packet, says the seeds are good for three years doesn't mean they won't be good for four or even more. Seeds are both science and mystery in this way.

Because you will invariably have seeds left over after planting, it's up to you to set them up in their preferred conditions. This looks like:

- Relative humidity below 60 percent
- Air temperature that never exceeds 90°F and preferably stays around 40°F
- Out of direct sunlight
- In a sealed container—ensuring there's no moisture in the container or on the seeds before storage
- Away from pests, like mice, that might eat them

A glass jar with a light-fitting lid can hold many seed packets. Refrigerators are humid places, but if the jar remains sealed, moisture will stay out. When you remove the jar from the refrigerator, let it come to room temperature before opening it to avoid condensation on the inside of the container. If you're lucky enough to have a root cellar or cool basement, these are also good locations for seeds kept in a sealed container.

Germination test

If your seeds are old or you're having trouble getting them to germinate, test their viability with a germination test. To do a proper germination test, you'll use a lot of seed. If you don't have a large quantity, test as many as you're comfortable with losing—if these seeds aren't germinating, you've already lost them anyway.

Here's a simple germination test:

Step 1: Count and spread 10 to 20 seeds on a premoistened paper towel. Use one type of seed per paper towel, and label it.

Step 2: Roll up the paper towel like a burrito or fold it in half over the seeds.

Step 3: Place the paper towel into a plastic bag, and put the bag in a spot that's close to the seeds' preferred germination temperature.

Step 4: Every 1 or 2 days, open the bag and paper towel and check the seeds for germination. Be sure the paper towel is still moist. Use a mister or spray bottle to re-wet it if necessary.

Step 5: In 10 days, or at the end of that seed's days-to-germination period, count the number of seeds that germinated, and divide by the number of seeds in your test. Multiply that by 100. This gives you the germination rate of your seeds.

Using your germination test results:

If your germination rate is 70 percent or less, you might be better off purchasing new seed. If you find your seeds are germinating in the test but not in your SFG bed or your seed-starting setup, this is a sign you should adjust your seed-starting conditions. It could also be that you're working with a variety that's difficult to germinate. If that's the case, this paper-towel sprouting method may be the best way for you to start those seeds.

You can plant the seeds that germinated in the test. To do this just cut off that piece of paper towel, and transplant both the sprouted seed and the paper towel.

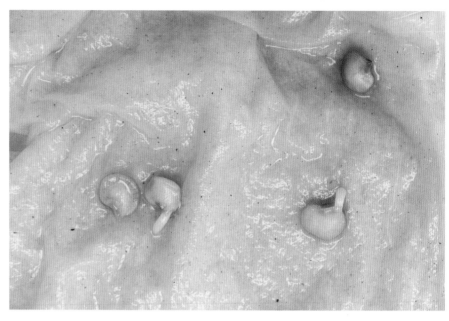

The paper towel germination test.

Seed lists

It's easy to collect seeds as you might collect stamps or coins. Because seeds have a limited life span, it's best to not buy more than you need. Like you keep records of the activity in your SFG bed, you should keep records of your seeds, too. This will help slow you down—but certainly can't stop you—when you get excited about bringing home another packet or three of new seeds.

In whatever format works best for you, keep record of:

- Type of crop
- Variety name
- Year packaged
- Quantity
- Any notes you want to make about the seed or variety

Update this list as you use or give away seeds and add more seeds to your collection.

Saving Seeds

A further step toward producing your own food economically with the SFG Method is saving your own seeds. Some crops have seeds that are easy to save; others are less easy.

If you want to try saving your own seeds, start with the easier plants first. These include:

- Tomatoes
- Peppers
- Beans
- Peas
- Luffa
- Many types of flowers
- Dill
- Cilantro (coriander)

If you're working with a biennial crop, like kale or beets, you'll have to wait two seasons for the plant to set seeds. If you're working with a crop whose flowers you eat, such as broccoli or cabbage, you won't be able to harvest the edible plant portion that season. Likewise with the plants whose seeds you eat, including beans and peas.

You can save seeds from heirloom and open-pollinated crops and know they will be the same variety as their parents, but remember that when you save seed from hybrids, they won't come true. Refer back to Selecting Varieties on page 166 for more about this. It's also important to be aware that there are crops that can easily cross-pollinate, like certain types of winter squash and other members of the cucumber family, even if they are

open-pollinated or heirloom varieties. They make the process more complicated. If you're interested in saving seeds, the list above is your best place to start because these crops don't readily cross pollinate.

Unless you're growing a whole lot of one crop in your SFG bed, you're limited to saving seed from just one or two plants. Only save the seed if you're happy with that plant's performance, because the collected seed contains the same genetic material and will produce a similar plant. You're looking for seeds from plants that are vigorous, taste good, and are free of disease.

In the case of dry beans, hot peppers, dill, and cilantro—the seeds of which are coriander—the seeds you're saving are themselves a crop. Chapter 10 will cover harvesting seeds as a food source.

If you think you'd like to save your own seed, look to the many books and Cooperative Extension resources about this process, as seed saving differs slightly depending on the crop.

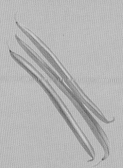

Save Tomato Seeds

Tomato seeds have relatively good germination rates when properly harvested and stored. Seed savers have an extra step in collecting tomato seeds, as the seeds need to ferment to remove their gelatinous coating. This is an easy process.

MATERIALS AND TOOLS

- Fully ripe tomato from a plant that was disease free
- Jar with lid
- Water
- Parchment paper, wax paper, or a coffee filter
- Envelope
- Knife
- Spoon
- Strainer

Saving tomato seeds is a fun and easy project.

Process

Step 1: Scoop out the seeds.

Cut the tomato in half. Scoop out its gelatinous insides that contain the seeds. Put it in a jar covered by a few inches of water.

Step 2: Agitate the seeds.

Twice a day, stir or shake the mixture, and vent the lid. The seeds will sink to the bottom of the jar as they lose their gelatinous coating.

Step 3: Drain the seeds.

In 5 days, pour off the liquid. Rinse the seeds to finish separating them from the gel coating.

Step 4: Dry the seeds.

Spread out the seeds on parchment paper, wax paper, or coffee filters to dry. Do not use newspaper or paper towels or the seeds will stick. Allow the seeds to dry completely for several days.

Step 5: Store the seeds.

Place the seeds in an envelope or other paper packet, labeled with the crop, variety, and date. Store them with your other seeds in a cool, dark, dry place.

Save Dill Seeds

In the case of plants whose seeds are external, including herbs and flowers, seed saving is straightforward. The tricky part here is being sure you wait until the seeds are fully mature before you harvest them. You're probably rotating crops through your SFG bed succession plan during most of the year. Letting these flowering plants stay in their grid space past their prime at the end of your regular growing season will give you time to let them dry and turn brown. Then you can collect the seeds.

MATERIALS AND TOOLS

○ Dill seed head

○ Paper or fine-mesh bag

○ Envelope

Process

Step 1: Collect the seed head.

Cut the dill seed head from the plant on a clear day, after any dew has dried.

Step 2: Let the seeds release.

Put the seed head in a paper or fine-mesh bag to fully dry. The seeds will fall off the seed head and collect in the bottom of the bag. Give the seed head about a week to release its seeds. Shake the bag to knock remaining seeds from the seed head.

Step 3: Store the seeds.

Pour the seeds from the bag into an envelope or other paper packet. Label them with the crop, variety, and date. Keep these with the rest of your seed collection.

With your seeds and plants in place, you get to watch as they grow from something often unrecognizable into nutritious, edible fruits and vegetables. The transformation is fun to witness, and at the end, you get to enjoy food you grew yourself. In the next chapter, you'll learn about how you can help your plants along their journey with watering, mulching, and other regular SFG bed maintenance practices.

9

Maintaining Your Square Foot Garden

With your Square Foot Garden box planned, built, and planted, you can just kick back and wait for the harvest to start rolling in. Well, it's almost that easy. The SFG Method consolidates and simplifies traditional ways of thinking about growing food. While you don't have a bunch of weeding, fertilizing, and other tasks to attend to, there are a few things on your garden-maintenance list. This chapter will cover your maintenance agenda, including dealing with weeds and pests, keeping your SFG bed watered, extending your growing season, and supporting pollinators.

Weeding

One of the most tedious garden chores is weeding. With an in-ground garden or even in a raised bed garden that's filled with native soil, managing the weeds is an ongoing task. Most native soils contain a plethora of weed seeds lying dormant, waiting to be exposed to light and moisture to germinate. When these traditional gardens are tilled or turned, weed seeds are brought up to the surface where they'll soon germinate and grow. Let just one of those weeds go to seed, and it can spread hundreds of weed seeds across the growing space. It's a lot to keep up with.

The Mel's Mix in your SFG, however, does not have all those weed seeds lying in wait. Peat moss and vermiculite are weed free, and if the compost you've used to create your mix is made correctly, there should be few weed seeds to deal with there.

Having to deal with so few weeds is one of the great benefits of growing crops in a SFG bed. However, weeds can occasionally pop up in your SFG. Their seeds can enter a SFG box in a few different ways:

In compost. Sometimes compost can contain weed seeds. Be sure you trust the source of your compost, as weed seeds can be viable in compost that's prepared at too low a temperature, as you learned in chapter 7.

In seeds. In chapter 8, you read about the difference between purchasing seeds from a commercial source, like a seed catalog, and getting them from less-controlled sources, like individuals and seed swaps. The chance of finding weed seeds mixed in with the intended plant seeds is one of the risks you take.

In mulch. Bringing mulch into your SFG bed can bring weed seeds, as well. Straw is a common weed seed culprit. If the straw still has mature seed heads left on the grain stalk, those seeds can end up in your Mel's Mix. You'll find more about mulch later in this chapter.

From above. Weed seeds can be carried into the bed by bird droppings or blow in on the wind. Think about all of the seeds in just one fluffy dandelion head. One plant produces hundreds or thousands of seeds, and invariably some could end up in your garden bed.

From below. Some of the most persistent weeds can creep into a SFG bed from underneath, by their spreading rhizomes. In areas with persistent weeds that spread by rhizomes, a plywood bottom may be called for. Common culprits include Canada thistle, quackgrass, johnsongrass, bermudagrass, and field bindweed.

Weeds can move into a SFG bed by any of the above methods, just as they would move into a traditional in-ground garden. The difference is that when you do find a weed in your SFG bed, there's no need to reach for herbicides or complicated tools. Just grasp the weed at its base, and pull it out. Remove the whole plant—roots and all. Because Mel's Mix is so loose and workable, this should be easy to do. You can use a trowel to loosen the soil, if the weed has really taken root, but that's likely not necessary. The grid planting system also makes it easy to spot weeds even while they're young.

Mulching

Mulching is an easy way to improve your Square Foot Garden. Like an all-weather blanket for your garden bed, mulching can benefit your growing medium and your plants. This growing-medium cover is easy to apply to your SFG bed—just mulch the grid squares that need it, and leave open those that don't.

Benefits of mulching

Mulch acts as an insulating layer between the air and the growing medium. When the sun is beating down, mulch reflects some of the heat. (One study from Michigan State University found soil temperature can be reduced by as much as 18°F midday when a layer of mulch is in place.) When the air gets cold, mulch keeps the soil warmer.

When it rains, mulch prevents the growing medium from splashing back onto the plants, reducing fungal issues.

It also helps to retain soil moisture, meaning you don't have to water as much. In hot, dry climates, mulch is of even more value because it helps reduce moisture evaporation, keeps the growing medium and roots cool and slows Mel's Mix from drying out during drought conditions.

Weeds are generally not a problem in a SFG bed, but if weeds do show up, mulch will help suppress them. Mulch blocks the sunlight weeds need to grow and can prevent weed seeds from dropping onto the soil surface to begin with.

If you're using an organic mulch, as it breaks down, it'll leave organic matter in the soil, further enriching the available nutrients for the next planting season.

Types of mulch

Mulch is, simply, a soil covering. There are many different types of organic—meaning made of natural materials—and synthetic mulches. Here are a few to know:

Straw is an excellent mulch for a Square Foot Garden and is especially valuable in arid regions where a lack of consistent soil moisture is more of a concern.

Straw. Straw is the dried stalks of grain plants such as wheat and oats. It's important to find straw from crops that haven't been treated with pesticides or persistent herbicides. You also want straw that doesn't have seeds in it, because those seeds can sprout and become weeds.

It's important to note the difference between straw and hay. While straw is the plant material leftover after grains have been harvested, hay is various grasses mixed with other plants, such as alfalfa and clover, that is cut from hay fields when it's still green. It often has seeds still attached. It is then dried, baled, and used for animal fodder. Because of those seeds, you would not want to use hay as mulch.

Shredded straw. Available as a ready-to-use mulch in bags from farm and garden stores as well as pet stores, shredded straw is often noted by the packager to be free of noxious weed seeds, thanks to the way it is processed. The shredded material is easy to spread on a garden bed.

Dry autumn leaves. Small leaves (or leaves that have been chopped and shredded into small pieces) make a nutrient-rich mulch.

Pine needles. Also known as pine straw, this light and airy mulch is great for moisture retention and penetration, however pine needles are slow to decompose.

When <u>Not</u> to Mulch

For all of the benefits mulch provides, there are times when mulch isn't necessary or could even work against you. Consider this advice:

- Assemble and install your drip irrigation *before* you put down mulch. You want the irrigation emitters to direct water straight to the plants' root zones rather than requiring it to pass through a maze of mulch materials.

- Short-season crops, such as radishes, don't need mulch because they're in and out of the garden bed so quickly. Mulching won't hurt them, but it also won't provide all the benefits that it does for crops that take longer to grow.

- Don't mulch beds before your crop seeds germinate. Let the seedlings get a few inches tall before mulching their square.

- If you're planting from transplants, mulch can be added after the transplants are in place. Or you can mulch first, then clear it away from the small area where you're going to plant each transplant.

- If the source of your mulch is questionable, don't use it. This is especially important when working with straw, which could have been sprayed with a pesticide or persistent herbicide that could cause problems in your garden.

- Prevent mulch from sitting directly against woody stems, such as on your perennial herbs. Organic mulch will hold moisture against the stem and encourage fungal growth or rot. It's okay to mulch perennial crops in your SFG bed—just be sure to leave a couple of inches of space between the stem and the mulch.

Keep mulch products away from the base of woody plant stems, such as perennial herbs like this thyme.

Square Foot Gardener's Tip

Do not allow your Mel's Mix to dry out completely. Even if you're letting a grid square or the whole bed go fallow for some time, keep it hydrated. Restarting the hydration is more difficult than keeping it watered all along.

Shredded straw mulch is available as a bagged or bailed product. The fine particles are easy to spread in a SFG.

Tilling

By using the SFG Method, you did away with one of the most cumbersome common garden chores: tilling. Tilling, or turning over garden soil, has been practiced first by human power, then by horsepower, and now with tractors and rototillers.

This task is hotly debated, with no-till-gardening and no-till-farming advocates warning against it. Tilling's pros are that it kills small weeds, aerates the soil, and returns spent garden plants to the soil. Tilling is also used to work amendments into the soil. The cons are that it brings new weed seeds to the surface, disturbs soil microbial networks, is time and energy intensive, and requires expensive equipment and fuel.

While the till/no-till debate goes on in the in-ground crop-production world, you can carry on with your SFG bed without having to think twice about tilling. Mel's Mix is naturally aerated, it contains no weed seeds, you don't need to amend it on a large scale, and it doesn't become compacted—partly because you'll never walk on it and partly because its ingredients make it friable.

As for returning spent garden plants to the soil, that's why you compost. The SFG version of "tilling" takes place when you mix compost into each grid square after harvest. You'll appreciate the difference between working a trowel and working a tiller.

Mulches to Avoid

Not all mulches are created equal, and some are just a bad idea for the garden. The mulches in this list are each tempting for their own reasons, but you're better off avoiding them.

- Wood chips aren't great for mulching a SFG bed because they tie up nitrogen in the top layer of soil during their decomposition process. Never mix wood chips in with Mel's Mix because the nitrogen further down in the box could also be tied up and made unavailable to plants. Wood chips are attractive in a garden, but it's best to leave them in the walking paths.

- Shredded newspaper is another mulch that sounds like a good idea because it's a readily available household waste, but paper forms a mat as it gets wet and prevents water from penetrating. You're better off mixing the newspaper into your compost pile.

- Non-organic mulches—meaning mulches that won't break down—are not good choices in the SFG bed. These mulches are attractive, so they may tempt you, but avoid gravel, stone, crushed glass, rubber, and the like. When you place them on top of the Mel's Mix, they'll eventually work their way into the growing medium and impede plant growth and root development.

- Black plastic is often used by gardeners in colder growing regions to warm up the soil earlier in the spring. Farmers may also use it as a summer mulch in their fields, but we don't recommend it for SFG as it can hold too much heat in the soil. Take care when using any kind of plastic mulch, as water and air cannot pass through it, and it's possible for plants to scorch.

Watering

Water is a building block of life for humans, animals, microbes, and plants. Watering your SFG bed is the most intensive work you're asked to do—except it's not *intensive* at all. Because your SFG bed is just a few square feet, you don't have to lug around hoses the way you would with a traditional in-ground garden. Granted, if you have an expansive SFG with many beds, there will be some hose moving and you may even opt to install an automated irrigation system, but for those with a smaller number of beds, the watering process is very straightforward. And Mel's Mix is formulated with a mix of ingredients that hold the moisture your garden needs while also allowing excess water to drain.

How much to water

The ideal moisture level for Mel's Mix is that of a wrung-out sponge. Established crops typically want 1 inch of water per week, which comes out to about 0.6 gallons of water per square foot of garden space per week. This doesn't mean the plants want 1 inch all at once. Sometimes you don't have a choice in how much or how quickly water is delivered, given the weather.

When rain doesn't provide enough irrigation, you're in charge. Most gardeners sort of eyeball how long and how often to water. When the Mel's Mix is dry an inch or two beneath its surface, or when the plants

Watering by hand, from bucket or watering can, is just one method gardeners can use. To know when it's time to water and how much to apply, you need to watch your plants and your Mel's Mix for clues.

Square Foot Gardener's Tip

When watering your SFG bed with a soaker hose or drip irrigation, dig an empty tuna can into the ground under an emitter so its rim is flush with the soil surface of the Mel's Mix. Use a tuna can that is 1 inch deep, so that when the can fills up, you know the bed has received 1 inch of water.

look thirsty, it's time to water. That being said, the Mel's Mix dryness level is the better gauge for water needs because wilted plants can be deceiving. A hot, sunny afternoon can cause plants to naturally droop, even when the growing medium is moist, but they recover after the sun goes down. If your Mel's Mix feels moist, give your plants time to perk up before offering more water. Too much water can drown the roots. But if you use your fingers or a trowel to dig down into the growing medium a few inches and the mix is completely dry, it's time to water. Larger, more mature plants will use water more quickly than seedlings, and SFGs in arid climates require more frequent waterings than those in more humid climates. Because of these and other factors, regularly monitoring the moisture level of your Mel's Mix is essential.

Hand watering

By hand watering your plants, you can give an appropriate amount of water to each crop. Lavender doesn't like to be overwatered, so you know to give it less. On the other hand, new seedlings and seeds that have yet to germinate need frequent, consistent soaking to get started.

You may choose to hand water using a hose with a gentle-flow wand or by using a watering can. Use your watering time as an opportunity to inspect plant health and growth. Observing your garden like this every day or every few days allows you to quickly pick up on changes that need attention.

Square Foot Gardener's Tip

A long-handled nozzle is an ideal hose attachment to reach under the plants' leaf canopy without causing you to bend and reach in awkward ways.

Taking the time to hand water allows you to closely observe your garden and be on the lookout for troubles.

Watering Tips

The SFG Method is designed to be an efficient means of gardening, which includes efficient use of water. This advice will help you water wisely, saving time, money on water bills, and water resources.

- Slow, gentle water flow allows the water to soak in, rather than quickly run through, the Mel's Mix. Spread out watering across two or three days per week. If you're under water-use restrictions, as many places are in dry summer months, plan your watering schedule for your permitted water-use days.

- Wet the Mel's Mix rather than the plant. Deliver water straight to the root zone, where the plants can use it.

- Avoid splashing Mel's Mix on plants when possible. Wet foliage can result in fungal issues. Sometimes wetting the leaves is unavoidable when hand watering. Just do your best.

- Water will evaporate from the Mel's Mix faster in the sun, heat, and wind. Mulching can slow down this process. Water early in the morning when possible. Watering in early evening is the second-best time to water, though this can set up plants to be damp overnight and bring on more fungal concerns or issues with pests like slugs.

Drip irrigation

While hand watering is a good way to get to know your SFG bed, drip irrigation is a more efficient way to deliver water directly to your plants' root zones.

There are several types of drip irrigation systems. All work with the same idea: You run tubing with emitters through each SFG grid square, and those emitters *drip* water directly onto the Mel's Mix.

Drip tape. Seen commonly in market-size gardens, drip tape systems are adaptable enough to be designed for SFG use, as well. Drip tape systems use a header hose—the poly-plastic mainline—along one side of the box. One or two pieces of flat plastic tape run through each row—or column, depending on how you want to look at it—of the grid. One end of the plastic tape attaches to the header hose by a small, plastic adapter. The other end is plugged closed with an end cap. Each piece of drip tape has holes at regularly spaced intervals to emit water. Drip tape with 12-inch spacing is common, meaning you could place one emitter in each grid square.

It's possible to set up high-tech watering systems using drip tape, programming each line of tape to run for a different length of time based on plants' water needs.

Drip tape, header hoses, and fittings are available through garden-supply and specialty-irrigation retailers. The drip tape generally comes in 25-foot and longer lengths, so you may have to purchase a little more than you'll actually need.

Tubing and emitters. The tubing-and-emitter setup is typically seen in landscapes because these can run in straight or curved lines, unlike drip tape, which is meant for straight lines. A thin polyethylene main line snakes through the garden bed with even thinner polyethylene tubes and emitters attached to it. Because they're at the end of flexible tubes, you can place the emitter right at the base of the plant.

This clever Square Foot Gardener is using an irrigation system that follows the grid pattern.

This works well when there's just one or two plants per square. More than that could give you a jumble of tubes and emitters in your SFG bed.

Grid irrigation. Inventive gardeners have built their own drip-irrigation systems into their SFG box grid. Build a grid using PVC pipe with $1/32''$ holes drilled throughout and caps on the ends, and you have an accessory that does double duty as both a grid and watering solution. There are also commercial grid irrigation products, including the Garden Grid system from GardeninMinutes.com.

Soaker hoses. A soaker hose is a porous hose that seeps out water all along its length, allowing the water to be distributed through the soil to all of the plants in the garden, not just ones at the end of an emitter. In larger gardens, soaker hoses are not as efficient as drip tape, but in a SFG bed, with plants placed in close proximity, a soaker hose delivers maximum water to the root zones. Soaker hoses are available at home-improvement and garden-supply stores.

Drip irrigation systems built into your SFG offer a quick and efficient way to water. In this garden, each bed is irrigated separately. Notice the shut off valve on the pipe running up into the bed?

How to Install a Soaker Hose System

This simple soaker hose system will simplify irrigation for any SFG bed. Add a timer to make it even easier for this system to keep your plants watered.

The materials list calls for 20 feet of soaker hose, which will cover a 4-foot-by-4-foot SFG bed. You may need a soaker hose with a different length to span your SFG bed if it's not this classic size.

The materials list also calls for a water-flow reducer. Some soaker hoses come with a reducer, so read the package before you buy. This small attachment is the go-between for your garden hose and soaker hose. Too much water pressure can damage the soaker hose, and the reducer regulates the water pressure.

This system is easiest to install before you put out seeds and transplants.

MATERIALS AND TOOLS

- 20' soaker hose
- Water flow reducer
- 15-20 landscape pins
- Garden hose connected to a water supply

Using a soaker hose to water your SFG is more efficient and saves you time, especially if you have your hose set on a timer.

ASSEMBLY

Step 1. Prepare the bed and hose.

1a. Remove the grid and any mulch from your SFG box. The soaker hose will sit directly on the Mel's Mix.

1b. Attach the soaker hose to the flow reducer and then the garden hose. Remove the end cap from the soaker hose, and run water to flush the hose.

1c. Replace the end cap, and run water into the soaker hose until you see water coming through its pores along its length. Turn off the water.

2a

3

Step 2. Place the soaker hose.

2a. Serpentine the soaker hose throughout the bed. Pass it through each grid square once. If the hose is too stiff to manipulate, let it warm up in the sun.

2b. Cut excess soaker hose from the end, following manufacturer's instructions for cutting and recapping.

Step 3. Secure the soaker hose.

Use the landscape pins to secure the hose to the Mel's Mix.

Step 4. Replace the grid.

Return the grid and mulch to the bed.

The basics of setting up a soaker hose system in a traditional 4-foot-by-4-foot SFG bed. The configuration will change if the dimensions of your bed are different.

Square Foot Gardener's Tip

Soaker hoses and sprinkler hoses are two different items. Be sure you're purchasing a soaker hose, which will deliver water at ground level; not a sprinkler hose, which will shoot a mist into the air.

Overhead sprinklers

Many homeowners have at least one overhead sprinkler in the garage. While an overhead sprinkler can deliver water to your SFG bed, its downsides outweigh its good points.

On the plus side, overhead sprinklers are something most of us already have on-hand, so there's no need for a new investment. Once the sprinkler and hose are set up, the system is hands-off, especially if you set your hose on a timer.

The thing you need to know about overhead sprinklers is that their coverage is hard to control, though some newer models offer more control than older styles. You could end up wasting a lot of water by sprinkling not just your 4-foot-by-4-foot SFG bed but everything around it. The water from the sprinkler lands directly on the plant leaves, and as droplets hit the surface of the bed, the Mel's Mix can splash onto the plant parts. Both of these conditions set up your plants for potential health issues. If possible, save your sprinkler for establishing lawns and cooling off on hot summer days.

Irrigation Options

This chart looks at the pros and cons of watering your SFG bed by hand—using either a hose or a watering can—with a drip-irrigation system, or with overhead sprinklers.

Irrigation features	Hand watering	Drip irrigation	Overhead sprinklers
Control over water to individual plants	X		
Delivers water to root zone	X	X	
Time efficient		X	X
Least splashing onto plant parts		X	
Can be set to a timer		X	X
Invites close plant inspection	X		
Lowest water pressure for delicate seedlings		X	
Best coverage for seed starting	X		

Water sources

Because you'll eat the food that's grown in your SFG bed, the water you add to your SFG bed needs to be potable. If you were to put water containing bacteria or other contaminants on your garden, it's possible those contaminants could be absorbed by the plants—a.k.a. your food.

Municipal water systems are the safest source of water because they're monitored and treated for contaminants. If you have a well that you've had tested, this is also a good source.

One questionable water source is surface water—ponds and streams. You can't control the contaminants that come in contact with water from these sources. Testing the water each time you need to use it would be a cumbersome and expensive step. To avoid possible contamination, save these sources of water for ornamental plants, not food crops.

Another source of water is a rainwater catchment system such as a rain barrel or cistern. Using harvested rainwater to water gardens is becoming more and more popular, especially where and when water usage is restricted. Possible contaminants from asphalt shingles can be a concern, particularly with older roofs. Rain barrels can be made of many different materials and depending on your thoughts on using water from a plastic barrel on food crops, you may opt to use harvested rainwater only on ornamental plants. Wooden rain barrels pose less of a contamination risk, but they may not be as long-lived as plastic models. Do your research before deciding which type of rainwater collection vessel to invest in and whether or not you're comfortable using the harvested rainwater on your SFG.

Here's a multi-purpose grid system made from PVC pipe that not only serves to mark off the squares, but it also acts as an irrigation system.

Pollination

Here's a quick science lesson—pollination is essential to plant reproduction. Pollen from the anther (the male flower part that produces pollen) must come into contact with and stick to the stigma (the female flower part where the pollen is received) for a flower to be fertilized and develop fruit and seeds. The pollination process varies though among different plants.

- Flowers that have both male and female parts are known as "perfect flowers." The majority of flowering plants have perfect flowers. Examples in the vegetable garden include eggplants, tomatoes, beans, and lettuce, among many others.
- Flowers with either male reproductive parts OR female reproductive parts are known as "imperfect flowers."
  - When both male and female imperfect flowers occur together on a single plant, that species of plant is monoecious. Examples of monoecious crops with imperfect flowers are squash, corn, and cucumbers.
  - When male and female imperfect flowers each occur on separate plants, the plants are dioecious. This means there are male plants and there are female plants. Examples of dioecious crops are not common, but they include asparagus, spinach, and kiwis.

Some crops with perfect flowers are self-pollinating, meaning it takes only a breeze or the brush of a hand for the pollen to fall from the anther to the stigma within the same flower. Self-pollinating vegetables include beans and peas.

The nightshade family of vegetable crops (which includes tomatoes, peppers, eggplants, tomatillos, and potatoes) have perfect flowers that require some kind of agitation for pollination to occur. Vibra-tion, such as that from a bumble bee's flight muscles, releases the pollen. Often pollination can happen with a brisk wind. You can help it along by buzzing the stem of the flower with an electric toothbrush, though in most cases this is not necessary unless you're growing your nightshades in a closed greenhouse where there are no pollinators.

Honey bees are just one species of bees that pollinate your SFG.

This eggplant flower is self-pollinating, but a bumble bee is required to vibrate the pollen loose.

Monoecious
Monoecious plants have separate male and female flowers on the same plant.

As mentioned, monoecious plants have male and female reproductive parts in different flowers on the same plant, but only the female flowers will produce fruit. They need the pollen from the male flowers to be moved over to the female flowers in order for pollination to occur. Bees, beetles, and other pollinators are responsible for this job. Pumpkins, cucumbers, and zucchini are obvious examples because if you look carefully, you can see that the female flower has a tiny immature fruit at the base while the male flower does not. If there are no pollinators present in your garden or your monoecious plants have poor fruit set, you can use a paintbrush or cotton swab to gently move the pollen from the male flowers over to the female flowers a few mornings a week (see sidebar on page 209 for another way to hand pollinate these crops).

Dioecious plants have male flowers on one plant and female flowers on another. Only the female plants will produce berries or other fruits. The males are there to provide pollen. This is most commonly found in trees and less commonly in garden vegetable and fruit plants. In the case of asparagus, which is arguably the most common dioecious plant in the vegetable garden, it's often recommended that male plants be planted as they are typically stronger growers because they don't need to dedicate energy to forming fruits or seeds.

Regardless of the type of plant parts or flowers they have, plants that don't create an edible fruit or edible seeds—like cabbage, broccoli, leafy greens, and root vegetables—don't require pollination for crop production, only for seed production. You don't have to concern yourself with their pollination. But crops that *do* create an edible fruit or edible seeds—like squash, pumpkins, peppers, tomatoes, cucumbers, beans, peas, and the like—do require pollination for crop production. This is why encouraging pollinators in your SFG is so important.

Know the pollinators

Bees are usually the first insect thought of as pollinators, and they are the most important pollinators for many plants. There are more than 20,000 species of bees in the world, so it's not necessary to have a honey bee hive to have good pollination. Most bee species do not sting or live in hives like honey bees do. The majority of bee species are quite docile, so there's no need to worry about encouraging bees in your garden as long as you leave them to their work without disturbance. The bees are joined in their pollinating efforts by flies, wasps, butterflies, moths, beetles, ants, and hummingbirds, as well.

While we think of pollinators as visiting flowers to serve our purpose—to transfer pollen from one place to another—they're actually visiting for their purpose, which is to feed on the nectar and collect pollen for their own use. Fertilizing the flower is a bonus.

Different pollinators are interested in different flowers based on the shape of their mouthparts and the shape of the flower. Offering multiple blooming plants gives everyone a chance to feed—and to pollinate.

Dioecious
Dioecious plants have separate male and female flowers that occur on different plants. Plants are either male or female.

Anther
The anther is the part of the stamen where the pollen is produced. It's the male part of the flower structure.

Stigma
The stigma is the sticky bulb that collects pollen for flower fertilization. This is the female part of the flower structure.

You can tell this is a female squash flower by the immature, unfertilized fruit at its base. Male flowers have a straight stem.

Bring on the pollinators

With a garden the size of one SFG bed, you want to do all you can to make it a welcoming place for pollinators. Some flowers bloom for just a day, and some for just a few hours a day. You need the pollinators to be in the right place—your garden—at the right time.

Here are some things you can do to increase your pollinator visitors:

- **Put out the buffet.** You read about the benefits of planting flowers on page 68. Using flowering plants to augment your flowering vegetables is a good strategy to entice pollinator visits.
- **Give pollinators a home.** If you have the space, make your yard a pollinator habitat. Vegetative matter left standing over winter and small brush piles make nesting places. You can even build or purchase a small native bee nesting box to hang in a tree or attach to a fence.
- **Leave the weeds.** In your lawn the dandelions and clover many home-owners want to eliminate actually feed pollinators. Let them grow—within reason—and definitely don't spray them. Herbicides can harm insects as well as plants, not to mention the potential water and soil contamination.
- **Offer a drink.** A shallow bowl or bird-bath can provide water for thirsty polli-nators in hot weather. Put a few sticks in the bowl so they have a place to land. Change out this water regularly so you don't create a mosquito-breeding ground.
- **Avoid insecticides.** Insecticide use in your SFG bed, in your yard, and in your neighborhood will impact your pollinator population. While you can't control what's happening on the other side of

Incorporating flowers in and around your SFG means more pollinators will be present to help pollinate your crops.

your fence, you can make your property as safe as possible for insects. Many insecticides—even those approved for organic food production—are nonspecific, meaning they harm a spectrum of insects, not just pest insects. When a pollinator comes in contact with an insecticide, it can carry that substance back to its colony or its brood and endanger the whole population. While organic insecticides are less harmful in general, they should be used with great care and only according to label instructions. Do not use them on windy days and apply them only early or late in the day when pollinators are not active (see page 218 for more on pest control).

Be Your Own Squash Pollinator

There may be a season when you've planted all your favorite cucurbits and you're seeing very little fruit development.

You've already learned that pumpkin, zucchini, watermelon, cucumbers, and other crops in their family have separate male flowers and female flowers (monoecious). Their pollination depends on a pollinator first picking up pollen from a male flower then depositing that pollen on a female flower.

There are several reasons why you may not see the fruit development that you think you should, including bad weather and too few pollinators. In these cases, you can step in and pollinate your cucurbits yourself. It's actually easy. Wait for a day without rain, and get to work when the flowers open in the morning.

How-to Hand Pollinate Cucurbits

Step 1. Identify the male and female flowers.

The male flowers have a plain stem, and you can see the anther when you peel back the petals. The female flowers have tiny fruit where the stem meets the flower. Look for a male flower that is open and not wilted, and cut it off the plant, leaving the flower stem intact.

Step 2. Remove the petals.

Flower petals act as showy adornments to signal to the pollinators that nectar is inside. Remove these from the male flower you cut to make the task easier.

Step 3. Transfer the pollen.

Find a female flower and then rub the pollen from the stamen of the male flower onto the stigma of the female flower. One male flower can pollinate several female flowers. You can also use a paintbrush or cotton swab to transfer the pollen from the male to the female flowers.

Step 4. Be patient.

Watch as the small fruit on the female stem develops into a mature fruit.

Use the stem and stamen (filament and anther) from a male flower to transfer pollen to 3 to 4 female flowers.

Using season extension methods keeps your SFG producing for weeks longer than usual.

A mini hoop tunnel covered in row cover affords the plants growing beneath it a few extra degrees of frost protection.

Season Extension

The last frost of the spring may be the starting line for growing warm-season crops, but your SFG bed has a whole life to live before that day. Likewise, the first frost of the fall closes out the fresh-tomato harvest, but it by no means signals the end of gardening. Using season-extension techniques, it's possible to grow warm-season crops into colder weather. It's also possible to grow cool-season crops in warmer seasons using these techniques. With the right season-extension methods, you can even harvest year-round in many areas.

You're already familiar with a few season-extension tools. To start, the Mel's Mix in a SFG box naturally warms faster in the springtime than in-ground garden soil, so that's one jump on the season. You've also read about:

- Microclimates (page 31)
- Selecting the appropriate crops and varieties for the season (page 57)
- Starting seeds indoors (page 169)
- Mulching (page 193)

Here are even more ways to keep the crops coming.

Row cover

Row cover is an easy way to give your plants a few degrees of additional heat. These light, reusable, spun-bound fabric sheets allow water and light to permeate to the plants. Row cover comes in various weights, based on the amount of temperature protection it provides. A 2-degree row cover is meant to give you 2°F of protection, so if the low hits 32°F, the air underneath should be at 34°F. The tradeoff is that the greater the protection, the less light is transmitted through the fabric.

Cover your Mini Hoop Tunnel (page 131) or Critter Exclusion Cage (page 125) with row cover or allow the row cover to sit directly on top of the plants. You can also make smaller PVC or metal hoops to support the fabric. In freezing temperatures, row cover can freeze to plant tissue and damage it, so be sure the fabric is suspended above the plants as much as possible, rather than resting on them directly.

Row cover doesn't offer the level of sun-soaked warmth that greenhouse plastic can, but neither does it ask for the constant attention that venting requires. It may be the most low-maintenance way to add warmth to your SFG bed and extend your growing season.

Simple structures made from PVC can be covered with plastic sheeting or row cover when cold weather threatens. These SFG beds are prepared when the need arrives.

Passive-heating structures

Passive heat comes from the sun rather than a wood burner or propane heater. Each of the passive-heating structures here increases the temperature of the soil and the air around the plant while the sun is shining. They don't have insulative properties, so that when the sun leaves, the heat goes with it.

Because the sun can create a lot of heat under these structures, they require regular management. It's nothing for a hooped greenhouse to reach 80°F (or warmer) inside on a sunny 40°F day. Vent these structures by opening the plastic, propping open the lid, or removing them altogether before your plants suffer heat stress.

Cloches. A cloche is a clear structure placed over an individual plant to create a greenhouse effect. You can purchase attractive glass cloches and those with water-filled sides that have more of an insulative effect, or you can make your own by cutting the bottom off of a milk jug. You can't get much more low-tech than a DIY cloche. Cloches let you plant cool-weather crops earlier in the season.

Cold frame. Cold frames are a time-tested way of protecting garden plants from the elements. Essentially a bottomless box with a clear covering, you can build a cold frame to sit on top of your SFG box—or on top of a set of grid squares. The clear top can be constructed using a repurposed window, greenhouse plastic, or clear polycarbonate panels. Construct the box so the top sits at an angle aimed at the southern sky in the northern hemisphere or the northern sky if you're south of the equator.

Serious cold-frame users can get automatic lid openers. Set the temperature, and a simple system triggers the lid to open—no electricity necessary.

Plastic high tunnels are a great wintertime home for Square Foot Gardens, if you happen to have one on your property. Though they are typically only passively heated, they keep the harvests coming even when the snow flies.

Cold frames are a wonderful way to extend your growing season. They can be built right on top of a SFG box.

A greenhouse is the ultimate in season extension. This gardener has multiple elevated SFG in their glass greenhouse to keep the harvests coming year round.

Greenhouse plastic. If you built a Critter Exclusion Cage (page 125) or a Mini Hoop Tunnel (page 131) for your SFG box, you already have the structure you need to make a little greenhouse. Cover it with 4 or 6 mil polyethylene plastic sheeting, which is durable in the elements and allows light to pass through.

Shade cloth

Season extension is not just for cool weather. The concept also means you can grow or start cool crops in warmer weather.

Shade cloth serves a great purpose in the hottest months. It is a fine mesh, typically green, brown, or black in color, that comes in varying densities to block out light—or provide shade—while allowing water to pass through. Your heat- and sun-sensitive vegetables may benefit from 30 percent to 50 percent shade cloth during early and late summer months. Shade cloth is useful for delaying bolting in lettuce and other greens when the weather warms.

Shade cloth can damage plants if laid directly on top of them. Instead, attach the material to a mini PVC or wire hoop tunnel placed across the entire bed, or use a smaller PVC or metal frame to support the fabric over just a few squares.

Shade cloth can help reduce the amount of sunlight reaching your plants, extending their growing time into the heat of summer.

Shade cloth can be used over a single square by propping it up with a piece of wire fencing.

Seasonal Checklists

These checklists outline tasks to do in spring, summer, fall, and winter and are meant for gardeners who experience all four seasons.

Depending on where you live, the celestial and meteorological seasons may not match up with your climatic seasons. In the northern hemisphere, the spring equinox is on March 21 and meteorological spring begins March 1, but your actual springtime weather might have already arrived in February—or maybe not until April. For the purpose of dividing up a year in the garden, these seasons are defined as:

Winter. The coldest months of the year with the shortest length of daylight. Days and nights may be below freezing.

Spring. The transition between the coldest and the hottest parts of the year. Most days are above freezing, but nights may be below freezing. Daylight is lengthening, and plant growth is quickening.

Winter To-Do

	Mulch plants for overwintering.
	Manage season-extension methods.
	Harvest as needed.
	Drain and put away hoses and irrigation.
	Take down and put away trellises and other add-ons.
	If not growing this season, remove grid and store indoors.
	Make repairs to your SFG box and accessories.
	Work on building projects for next year.
	Plan for next year's seasons.
	Mark your calendar for seed-starting time.
	Inventory and order new seeds, Mel's Mix ingredients, and supplies.
	Start cool-season seeds indoors when it's time.

Spring To-Do

	Start warm-season plant seeds indoors according to your plan.
	Direct seed and transplant cool-season and warm-season crops when it's time.
	Manage season-extension methods.
	If you let your SFG box go fallow for the winter, start rehydrating the Mel's Mix a couple of weeks before planting.
	Install trellises and other add-ons to your SFG bed before they're needed.
	Stake or support plants as needed.
	Harvest as needed.
	Remove plants that have finished producing, and add compost to those SFG grid squares.
	Keep up with succession planting as you remove plants.
	Preserve the harvest as needed.
	Give your plants adequate water.
	Test your irrigation system and make any needed repairs.

Summary To-Do

	Start cool-season plant seeds indoors for fall planting when it's time.
	Direct seed and transplant warm-season and cool-season crops according to your plan.
	Give your plants adequate water.
	Protect sensitive plants from direct sunlight as needed.
	Prune plants as needed.
	Stake or support plants as needed.
	Manage shade cloth.
	Harvest as needed.
	Remove plants that have finished producing, and add compost to those SFG grid squares.
	Keep up with succession planting as you remove plants.
	Preserve the harvest as needed.

Summer. The hottest months of the year with the longest length of daylight. Days and nights are all above freezing. This is generally the season with the least amount of precipitation.

Fall To-Do

	Direct seed and transplant cool-season crops according to your plan.
	Give your plants adequate water.
	Protect sensitive plants from frost and manage season-extension methods as needed.
	Harvest as needed.
	Remove plants that have finished producing, and add compost to those SFG grid squares.
	Keep up with succession planting as you remove plants.
	Preserve the harvest as needed.
	Disconnect hoses and irrigation equipment ahead of freezing weather.

Fall. The transition between the hottest and coldest parts of the year. Most days are above freezing. Nights are starting to dip below freezing. Waning daylight means plants are slowing their growth.

Some areas don't have four seasons. If you're gardening in perpetual summertime, your rhythm will be different than folks gardening where summer lasts just two months. Wherever you are, you'll quickly develop your own seasonal checklists, and you can use these as your guide.

Preparing your SFG for spring might involve erecting protective structures like hoop tunnels to get a jump start on early planting.

Keep a careful eye on your plants and regularly inspect for pests. A bit of research would help you discover these radish leaves have been nibbled by flea beetles and that their damage is largely aesthetic so no action needs to be taken. But that's not always the case with pests.

Pest Protection

Using the SFG Method, you are likely to see fewer pest problems than you would in a traditional row garden. This doesn't mean you'll have no pests at all, but because your SFG bed is so manageable, you should have no problem taking care of them quickly. Also, plants growing in the SFG bed are generally robust and healthy, able to fend off mild insect attacks.

Garden pests include insects, birds, and mammals. You read about excluding birds and mammals from your SFG bed in chapter 6. This section will focus on the insect pests.

Know your insects

Because there are so many good bugs out there, it's important that you learn to identify the insects visiting your SFG bed before you decide to destroy them all. Pollinators are insects that you want to be sure to keep around, and just as important are the bugs considered beneficial insects.

Some garden insects are fairly ubiquitous, found in most corners of the world. There are others that are specific to certain regions. All regions and crops have their own lists of marauders and heroes. Make it a point to learn about the insects that visit your garden. Your local Cooperative Extension office, mentioned on page 160, is a great place to find this information if you live in the United States. Along with learning about insects in your area, find out what they eat, what their eggs look like, and the best ways to exclude them from your SFG bed.

Beneficial Insects

Beneficial insects are natural enemies of garden pest insects and can prey upon their adults, larvae, and eggs.

An Insect Sampling

While there's no way this book can list all of the insect pests you might encounter in your SFG, here are three examples of insect pests present in many parts of the world and how they operate:

- **Aphids.** There is a specialized species of aphid for nearly every type of plant. These tiny, soft-bodied, pear-shaped insects vary in color, based on their species. They may or may not have wings, depending on their stage of development and species. Most are around ⅒ inch long, and they all feed on plants by piercing the tissue with their needle-like mouthpart and sucking the sap. They congregate by the dozens or hundreds and may also spread disease. The list of garden plants they feed on is long, from arugula to potatoes to corn.

- **Leafhoppers.** Like aphids, various leafhopper species are active all over the world on all kinds of crops. You may see them on beans, tomatoes, lettuce, carrots, and more. These hopping insects range in size, feed on plant materials, and spread disease. They come in many different colors, but brown and green are the most frequently seen in vegetable gardens.

- **Cabbage looper.** Don't let the name fool you. Cabbage loopers go after all members of the cabbage family (brassicas), not just cabbages. They may also damage all manner of other vegetables and flowers. They over-winter in warm climates and spread throughout more temperate areas as the weather warms each year. In its larval stage, the cabbage looper is a green caterpillar that crawls by arching its back—forming a loop—and propelling its front forward. It's a voracious eater of leaves and stems. As an adult, this moth is active at night, laying hundreds of eggs to begin the cycle again. A similar pest, the imported cabbageworm, also appears as green caterpillars feeding on brassicas, but they do not form a loop when crawling. Cabbage-worm adults are white, day-flying butterflies.

Lucky for gardeners, there's an equally impressive list of beneficial bugs—again too many for a comprehensive list. A few you are likely to encounter include:

- **Ladybugs.** Also called ladybirds or lady beetles, hundreds of species of this beetle exist around the world. Not all ladybugs are red with black spots; they come in a broad range of colors. They'll eat various soft-bodied insects, including aphids and mites.

- **Syrphid flies.** There are more than 6,200 species of syrphid flies in the world and 300 in the U.S. state of California alone. At ⅛ to 1 inch long, adults look like small bees or wasps. The adults are important pollinators while the larvae are meat-eaters that control many different pests. The species that eat aphids can consume 100 to 400 each before they pupate.

- **Braconid wasps.** These insects are like something out of a sci-fi film. Braconid wasps insert their eggs into insect hosts, and when they hatch, the small, maggot-like larvae eat the host. One place these are commonly visible is on tomato and tobacco hornworms. The things that look like grains of rice stuck to a hornworm are actually braconid wasp pupal cases.

Look closely on the left side of this spinach image and you'll see a smartly camouflaged cabbageworm who has munched on the leaves. Hand pick these pests when you spot them or their damage.

Ladybugs are just one of hundreds of beneficial insects that help control pests in the SFG. This one is drinking nectar from a dill flower, but soon enough it will be on the prowl for a source of protein—aphids!

Controlling insect pests

When you spot an insect and identify it as a bad bug, you have many options to help you take care of the problem.

Hand picking. It's a dirty job, but someone has to do it, as they say. Pick off insect pests and their eggs as soon as you notice them so they don't get ahead of you. Toss them in a bowl or small bucket of soapy water (or feed them to your chickens if you have them).

Pruning. If the insect issue is limited to one stem of the plant, you may be able to just snip it off, seal it in a plastic bag, and put it in your trash can.

Properly remove infected plants. When you pull your plants from the SFG bed at the end of the season, do not compost any with insect damage. It's possible the insects laid their eggs in the plant tissue, and you want to get those off your property.

Direct water spray. A sharp stream of water can knock off aphids, in particular, but you risk damaging the infested plant and other plants around it.

Beneficial insects. You read previously about wanting to keep the beneficial insects in your yard. They're here to eat your problem bugs. Let them do their work.

Row cover and insect netting. There are a few types of fabric row cover that can protect your crops from insects. The same row cover material used for season extension is useful to keep insects off your plants. Use the most lightweight row cover available. Insect netting is a newer technology for gardeners. It uses the same idea as row cover—a lightweight, permeable fabric cover—but does not trap heat underneath. It's essential that you secure the covers so insects cannot find their way underneath.

Some crops may need protection all season, while others may only need it until they grow large enough to handle some pest pressure. If you're covering crops that require insect pollination, be sure to uncover them when they flower.

Grow in the off-season. One big benefit to growing crops in the early spring and the fall is that before the insects emerge for the season and after most of them go dormant, there's a noticeable difference in pest populations. If you're struggling with controlling pests, lean into growing in the shoulder seasons.

Insecticides. Insecticides should be seen as a last resort for managing insect pests. These sprays, powders, or dusts—whether natural or synthetic—can be useful in controlling pests. They also have

One simple way to keep insect pests out of your SFG is to build a DIY frame over the beds and cover it with netting or tulle fabric. The same structure can be used to support plastic in the winter or shade cloth in the heat of summer.

their downsides. If you want to use insecticides, there are a few things you should know:

- Many insecticides are not specific to the insect you're targeting, meaning other insects that are exposed to it can also be taken out.
- Some substances must come in contact with the pest in order to kill it. For example, if you see aphid damage on your radishes but the aphids are gone when you're ready to spray, you'll waste your time and money by spraying insecticidal soap or oil, because they only affect the insects they directly contact.
- Some insecticides can only be used in the evening so they don't burn the plant leaves and some only during a dry period so they don't wash away.
- Avoid applying any products to your garden when pollinators are active. Instead apply early in the morning or near sundown.
- Always read the label and take seriously the precautions called for.
- Do not use homemade insecticides. They are not labeled for use on plants and could cause unwanted results.

Cutting Back

When your goal is to help your plants grow and produce, the idea of cutting back growth might sound counterproductive. Sometimes, though, less is more.

The plants you'll grow in your SFG bed have been adapted over hundreds or thousands of years by farmers, gardeners, and plant breeders to become what they are today. Many of them still have the wild traits of their ancestors. While these traits served them well growing in unmanaged conditions, some gardener intervention can coax out more of their productive qualities.

There are several ways to cut back plants to promote growth. You'll use different techniques based on the plant.

Deadheading

Deadheading refers not to a 1960s American jam band but the process of pruning old growth, faded flowers, and seedheads from plants. Relieving the plant of this excess material promotes new growth and reflowering. If you were to leave the waning blooms, the plant would put its energy into making seeds instead.

With scissors or pruners or by pinching with your fingers, cut off stems below spent flower blossoms and above the first set of healthy leaves. You don't want to take off new flower buds, so double check before you trim. Do this throughout the season with the flowers and herbs in your SFG.

Pinching back

Pinching back entails pruning off growth to shape the plant. It both encourages bushier, fuller growth and helps limit the plant size. Pinching back also delays flowering, which keeps the plant productive. This is especially true for herbs. Basil is one plant you'll want to pinch back. Let the plant get 8 to 12 inches tall, then pinch off the top-most growth. The basil will readily branch and produce more leaves for your harvest. Continue pinching the newest growth from the new stems, and the plant will continue branching.

Using your fingertips, scissors, or pruners, pinch or cut the stem off just above leaf nodes to encourage the plant to grow new stems from those nodes. Cut back woody stems, such as rosemary or lavender, by no more than one-third their size.

Deadheading is the removal of spent flowers to encourage more flowers to be produced.

Pinching is an important practice for many plants, including basil, which continues to produce delicious new shoots when regularly pinched back.

If you're growing indeterminate tomatoes in your SFG, you're going to want to regularly remove the suckers to keep the plant more contained.

Suckering

Tomato plants are a good example of a crop that needs some attention lest they return to their wild selves. Determinate tomatoes (see sidebar on page 52) grow stocky and bushy, and there's not much you need to do besides offer physical support in the form of a cage or stake. Indeterminate tomatoes have long vines that need to be directed. Given the chance, the leader stem would produce dozens of secondary stems—called suckers—which would also turn into vines. Soon, your SFG bed would be overrun.

Suckering refers to removing the suckers so the indeterminate tomato plant puts its energy into producing fruit instead. Before beginning, be absolutely sure your tomato variety is indeterminate by checking the seed packet. If you were to sucker a determinate tomato, you'll remove important fruiting branches and over-prune the plant.

Suckering also improves airflow around the tomato plant, which is important for reducing fungal issues, and prevents too much shading, because fruit need sunlight to develop.

Start by identifying the suckers. These branches form in the junction between the leaf stem and the leader stem. If you catch them while they're small, they're easy to remove with your fingers. Larger suckers require harvest shears or pruners. Remove every sucker except the one just below the first flower cluster. That sucker will become your second stem for tomato production. Be careful at the top of the plant—it can be difficult to distinguish between suckers and the main stem in the newest growth. If you have any doubt, come back to it in a couple of days.

Pruning for health

Removing plant materials is a good tool for keeping plants healthy. Pruning increases light and air flow and redirects plants' energy into healthy tissue and fruit production. You can also remove leaves or whole stems that look unhealthy or are infested with insects. Sometimes removing the "problem child" from your SFG bed is all you need to prevent spreading.

When pruning to manage pests or disease, use scissors or pruners to remove the affected part of the plant. Put that plant material into the trash can instead of the compost bin. Don't touch other plants after this. Wash your hands and arms, and clean the pruning tool with a disinfectant. You don't want to accidentally spread the problem yourself.

The size of a SFG bed means you won't have to spend every evening and weekend toiling over maintenance and upkeep. The basic principles and activities covered in this chapter will set you up to breeze through the seasons. In the next chapter, you'll get to reap what you've sown in the harvest and enjoyment of your crops.

Prune off diseased plant parts as soon as you spot them to keep the pathogen from spreading. Be sure to toss diseased foliage in the trash, not in the compost pile.

10

Harvesting Your Square Foot Garden

Here comes the part you've been waiting for. After all of your planning, building, planting, and care, the reward is in the harvest. Thanks to your planning, you have a good idea of what you can expect to harvest and enjoy from your Square Foot Garden throughout the seasons. Because you planted only as much produce as you need, you won't have the food waste you're often faced with when buying too much from the grocery store. Think about all the mushy, unused herbs from the grocery store you've thrown away over the years!

Depending on the seasonal design of your SFG bed, you may enjoy harvesting crops from early spring right up until, and after, the first frost. If you're using the right season-extension methods or live in a temperate climate, you may even harvest all year long.

This chapter covers what you need to know for your Square Foot Garden harvest timing, harvest techniques, crop storage, and basic preservation methods so you can get the most from the food you grow this season and beyond.

Harvest Toolkit

There are just few tools needed for harvesting your crops:

- **Scissors or harvest snips** If using scissors, have a pair just for harvesting. Harvest snips can be found at gardening and home-improvement stores.

- **Pruning or harvest shears** These are a bit heavier duty than scissors or harvest snips. They're useful for harvesting crops with thick stems, such as peppers, eggplants, and winter squash.

- **Sharp serrated knife** A small bread-knife or steak knife will do here.

- **Harvest basket** This can be as simple as a large kitchen bowl—anything to transport your harvest from the SFG bed to kitchen.

Harvest Ready

If you've never grown a zucchini before, you might be nervous to think about the right time to harvest it. Same for lettuce, basil, or watermelon. You'll become confident in harvest timing as you gain experience.

The time it takes from seed to harvest is hard to pinpoint exactly. There are several factors affecting the time it takes for a plant to mature. The list of factors is going to look familiar, as these are similar to the variables that affect how much a plant will produce, which you read on page 49. These include:

- **Variety.** The variety of vegetable, fruit, or herb that you choose will have its own maturation time. Take cabbage. If you chose a mini variety, it could be ready to harvest just two-and-a-half to three months after seeding. If you chose a larger variety, it might take four months until you are eating your cabbage. The seed packet will give the best indicator of the approximate maturity for a particular variety.

- **Length of daylight.** As the length of daylight decreases, photosynthesis slows—meaning plant growth slows. In the spring, daylight is increasing, and in the fall, it's decreasing. The crops you plant in the springtime will grow faster than the same crops you plant in the fall. Your salad radishes might be ready to eat in 3 weeks in the spring but 4 weeks in the fall.

- **Sun exposure.** Going back to photosynthesis, if your SFG receives eight hours of direct sunlight versus your neighbor's that receives only six, plants in your bed have an extra two hours each day to grow into maturity. The amount of sun exposure your bed receives throughout the year may change as the sun's trajectory and the shadows it produces change.

When crops are ready to harvest depends on many different factors, one of which is the age of the plant. But some plants are tricky because they have multiple possible harvest times. This kale, for example, can be harvested anytime from baby stage all the way through full maturity.

- **Temperature.** When the temperature unexpectedly dips into the 50s at night in August, your pepper plants are going to know it. Likewise, when you have an unusually hot day in April, your greens will react. Even tomatoes—famously warm-weather plants—don't love extremely hot weather. They'll stop producing blossoms when it's 85°F or hotter during the day and 72°F or hotter at night. A period of hot or cool weather can cause your plants to mature faster or slower. Every season is different.

- **Water.** Consistent water is a friend to your garden plants. If you forget to water your bed and you're not getting enough rain, plants will not produce as well. If rainstorms bring 2 inches of water every few days for a week, plants again will not produce as well. The SFG Method is designed to counteract water inconsistencies, but even Mel's Mix can only do so much to maintain ideal conditions when you're working with large rain events or no rain at all.

- **Transplant shock.** As seedlings transition from life indoors to life in your SFG bed, their adjustment period will vary by plant family and by planting conditions. Cucurbits, such as cucumbers, melons, and squash, are more likely to suffer from transplant shock than nightshades like eggplants and tomatoes. Plants that are put out with little hardening off or during stifling weather may be set back a little, too.

- **Intended size.** This probably goes without saying, but if you're planning to harvest a crop in its baby stage, it will be ready to harvest sooner than if you were to wait until its mature stage. This goes for baby kale, fresh garlic, and baby zucchini. You can even look at green tomatoes and green peppers as being a "baby" stage—or at least an immature stage—of edible fruiting crops.

The amount of sunlight a SFG receives can impact how quickly the veggies are ready to be harvested. The more sunlight, the faster most plants grow.

Square Foot Gardener's Tip

Let the Harvest Chart on page 258 guide you in your first few seasons of harvest. It includes estimated days to maturity, how to tell when the crop is ready for harvest, how to harvest it, and how to store and preserve it.

How to Harvest

The design of the SFG bed is meant for ease of harvest. With a 4-foot-by-4-foot garden bed, you can harvest from all four sides of each square with minimal reaching and stretching. (Gardeners who've worked among large garden rows know the struggle.) Depending on your SFG plan, you may have planted so that you can harvest a little bit of this and a little bit of that every few days, and it's easy enough to do so in this space.

Plants that produce edible fruits or seeds throughout the season—beans, cucumbers, zucchini, etc.—benefit from regular harvesting. If you leave mature pods or fruit on the plant, there is no reason for the plant to continue flowering, because as far as it's concerned, it's completed its life cycle.

Time of day

Plan your harvest for early in the day. Let the dew dry, and then get to work. Greens and herbs lose moisture as the day goes on. They'll keep longer, have better flavor, and retain a crisp texture better when harvested early in the day.

If the crop has frost on it, wait until the frost melts. The greens will recover if left to defrost on their own as the day warms. If you harvest them while they're frosty or, worse yet, frozen, they'll be unusable.

Make your harvests early in the day, when moisture content is high and the plants are not stressed. This prolongs the shelf life of the harvested produce.

Harvest methods

Different types of crops use different harvest techniques. It wouldn't make sense to cut a leaf of lettuce with heavy-duty harvest shears, just as it'll take you a while to whittle through a pumpkin stem with household scissors.

The most important part of any harvest technique is that you pick the produce without damaging the plant or the crop. Look at a sweet potato with its thick skin, and you might think you could toss it into a harvest bin without a care. Sweet potatoes are actually fragile—especially before curing (see page 229)—and can bruise and spilt with rough handling. If something that looks as stout as a sweet potato can be so easily damaged, imagine what would happen to a delicate tomato. Handle your vegetables as if they're eggs, and be careful not to crack them.

Use a pair of herb snips to harvest individual sprigs of basil and other herbs just above a set of leaves. The stem will then go on to produce a pair of new branches from this point.

Here are the basic crop-harvesting methods:

- **Plucking greens and herbs.** Look at how a mature plant of greens like lettuce, arugula, and Swiss chard grows. It has one central crown or stem with multiple stalks and leaves growing off of it. For mature greens, baby greens you're picking by hand, and tender herbs, you can pluck off individual leaves or shoots with your thumb and forefinger. Hold the plant's central crown or stem with one hand, if needed, and use a snapping motion to separate the greens from the plant.

- **Cutting greens and herbs.** Use scissors or harvest snips to separate a green's stalk and leaf from the stem. Also use these tools to cut herbs. This is a more precise way to harvest than hand-plucking the leaves.

- **Cut-and-come-again baby greens.** The dense seeding of cut-and-come-again crops (36 plants per square) won't allow you to harvest leaf-by-leaf from each plant. Harvest across the square using scissors or a serrated knife. Hold the tops of the leaves with one hand, and cut horizontally through the leaf stems with the other a few inches above the level of the Mel's Mix. Be very careful to leave the growing point intact so the plants will continue growing new leaves and you can make future harvests of baby greens from the same square.

- **Clipping fruit.** You're going to think you can tug your eggplants, okra, watermelons, cucumbers, and peppers off the plant by hand, but these fruit have surprisingly durable stems and are best harvested with snips or shears. Pumpkins and winter squash have obviously tough stems that cannot be pulled by hand. In fact, if you do try to pull one of these off the vine, you're likely to pull the fruit right off its stem—which will significantly reduce its storage life—or to pull the plant off its trellis. Use harvest shears for these thicker stems.

Use a pair of clippers to cut eggplants, peppers, and cucumbers from the plant. This prevents any damage.

Harvest heads of lettuce with a sharp knife by cutting them off at the base, just above the Mel's Mix.

Root crops like this beet are easy to pull from the loose, friable Mel's Mix.

Watermelons should be cut from the vine when a bright yellow spot appears on the bottom of the fruit and the tendril across from the melon's attachment point turns brown and dies.

- **Pulling fruits and pods.** Peas, corn, beans, and strawberries are all pods and fruits that can be carefully pulled from the plant. Twist and pull with one hand while holding the plant with your other hand. Ripe cantaloupe almost doesn't give you a choice but to pull it, as it will slip off the vine into your hand with slight pressure when it's ready.
- **Slicing fruits and stems.** Many low-growing crops are best harvested using a serrated knife. These include head lettuce—when you're taking the whole head, not just a few leaves—cabbage, broccoli, kohlrabi, and fennel. Cut just above the level of the Mel's Mix, careful to keep your knife out of the soil.

- **Digging roots and rhizomes.** It stands to reason that root vegetables and rhizomes have to be dug from the Mel's Mix. Digging is a strong verb here, as you're more likely to be able to just pull the vegetable from the SFG bed, considering Mel's Mix's friability. Root vegetables growing close to the surface, like onions, radishes, and turnips, should be easy enough to pull. Those with deeper roots—garlic, carrots, parsnips, daikon radishes—might need some loosening to get them out. And the ginger, turmeric, and potatoes you hilled could require digging by hand through the Mel's Mix, if not loosening the soil with a trowel.

Harvesting Edible Seeds

Growing seed crops as food is similar to growing seeds to save and plant. Open your kitchen pantry, and you'll find seeds you can grow in your own SFG bed such as coriander (which is cilantro seed), dill seed, fennel seed, dry beans, and dry corn.

Seasonings

In the case of harvesting seed for seasonings, you just let the plant bolt and then go to seed. Let the seeds dry, and then put them in an airtight container for your cooking wants. You'll have to leave the crops in the garden for a longer period than if you were harvesting the fresh herbs to give the plants time to mature.

Staple Foods

You may not think of the beans in your baked beans and the corn-meal in your tamales as seeds, but they are. Dry corn and beans take up a lot of space and time in your SFG bed, but they're not hard to grow. Like your seasonings, be sure these are fully dry—you shouldn't be able to dent them with your fingernail—before storing them in airtight containers.

Let kids get in on the harvesting action too. They're more likely to enjoy homegrown produce if they had a hand in growing and picking it.

After Harvesting

What happens to your produce after you harvest it affects its texture, flavor, and storage life. You've put time and energy into growing this food, and your job is not quite done. Now you have to handle it with care to get it from your SFG bed to your kitchen.

Post-harvest handling

As soon as you harvest, get your produce out of the sun and wind. Heat and dehydration will zap its freshness in front of your eyes.

Immediate refrigeration—for crops that want to be refrigerated—cools them quickly. Don't pack them too densely, because you want to let the cool air get in and around them.

Leafy greens do great when cooled in water. After swishing in a clean bowl of water, remove moisture with a salad spinner, or lay out the rinsed greens on a towel, and gently roll it up to sop up the water. A little moisture in storage is okay, but too much will result in rotting.

Then there are the crops that shouldn't be washed until you're ready to eat them. These include most herbs, tomatoes, strawberries—as if you won't eat them right out of the garden—onions, potatoes, and garlic. Moisture will make them degrade.

As soon as your crops are harvested take them inside where it's cooler. Then store them accordingly.

Storage

Because you're growing the amount of produce you need, you might not have too many vegetables to store. There are times that you'll end up with a bumper crop or that you just can't immediately eat everything you harvest. Proper storage is essential to maintaining the flavor and quality of the food you've grown.

Short-life crops. While some crops will store for weeks or longer under the right conditions, others are best eaten immediately. Broccoli, corn, and asparagus are most delicious soon after picking.

Refrigeration. In the Harvest Chart on page 258, you'll find many crops are stored in plastic bags in the refrigerator. Vegetables transpire—they lose moisture through their leaves and skin—and can become limp and dry. Both the cool temperature of the refrigerator and the enclosed container of the plastic bag help the vegetables slow their transpiration.

Non-refrigerated storage. The cold air and high humidity of the refrigerator is too much for some produce. Unless you're lucky enough to have a root cellar or basement, these crops will do best in a cool pantry or even closet—if that's not too weird—assuming yours doesn't get direct sunlight. Be sure these spaces are rodent-free, or they'll get to your food before you do.

If a cool spot isn't possible, countertop storage is a better option than refrigeration. Non-refrigerated crops are typically either sensitive herbs, such as basil, or crops that require curing, which is covered below.

Tomatoes always do best on a countertop. Refrigeration will turn them pithy, and they will lose their flavor.

Curing. Curing certain vegetables concentrates the sugars and dries out or toughens the skin so the vegetable doesn't lose moisture while in storage. Winter squash, pumpkins, potatoes, sweet potatoes, garlic, and onions need to be cured if you plan to store them. (Acorn squash is the exception in the winter squash group, as it will keep better if stored as is.) The flavor will further develop in the squash, pumpkins, sweet potatoes, and garlic, too, as they cure.

The curing process varies by vegetable—see the Harvest Chart for details—and generally entails keeping the harvested crop in a warm space for a couple of weeks. This space can be as simple as a closet with a forced air register from your furnace in it or a drying rack in the garage.

Tomatoes are one crop that prefers not to be refrigerated. Others include winter squash, pumpkins, and onions.

After harvesting, onions need to be cured to prolong their storage life.

Square Foot Gardener's Tip

If you find your leafy greens wilted in the fridge, don't put them in the compost just yet. Put them in a bowl of ice water, and they're likely to perk up again. The same goes for herbs, carrots, and celery.

At-Home Food Safety

If you were to have a job in restaurant food prep, you'd have to take a class and pass a test about food-safety best practices. Food safety is about preventing pathogen transfer, and it's as important in a home garden and kitchen as it is in a food-service kitchen.

Here are some food-safety tips as they relate produce from your SFG bed:

Wash your hands.

Before you harvest and before you prepare food, wash your hands. You don't want any germs you may be carrying to transfer to the produce.

Wash your tools.

Tools include everything from harvest scissors to your harvest basket to a cutting board. You're again preventing pathogen transfer.

Wash your produce.

A bonus to using the SFG Method for growing your food is that by using vertical growing systems and growing in a light and airy growing medium, your crops are likely to be less dirty. Regardless, even if your garden is organic, you still need to wash what you harvest. Think about what they may have been exposed to outside when you're not watching (bird and insect waste, airborne particulates, etc.).

Thoroughly rinsing produce under running water reduces the microorganisms they may have picked up. Don't use bleach or detergents, though some gardeners add vinegar to the wash water in hopes of removing more debris (just be aware that doing so can alter the taste and texture of certain vegetables). Wash with potable water, and be sure it isn't too cold. Fruits—especially tomatoes and cantaloupe—can suck up water and pathogens if the water temperature is more than 10°F cooler than the fruit's interior. (Think about when you jump into a pool and the cold water makes you gasp for air. This is essentially the same thing.)

Don't harvest if you notice animal activity.

If a bird left its calling card on your tomato, put that tomato in the trash. You can't guarantee that you've fully washed off the contamination, and it's not worth taking the risk.

Refrigerate after slicing.

If you're chopping vegetables in advance to prepare for a meal or only using half a butternut squash for tonight's dinner, put those cut vegetables in the refrigerator as soon as possible.

Discard rotten produce.

If you notice mold or other decay, don't eat it.

Always rinse your garden harvest under running water before enjoying it fresh or preparing it for a meal.

Preserving Your Harvest

Food preservation allows you to enjoy your harvest long after the crops have come in. If you chose to grow a little bit of everything, you might not have an abundance for preservation, but if growing for preservation is your goal all along, you now need to choose a good preservation method. You can preserve a little or a lot, as you have the time and the produce available.

Food preservation essentially suspends your garden produce in time. These methods use temperature, microbes, or a combination of those two to prevent food from spoiling.

Pickling

Pickling is a means to preserve produce using a high level of acidity—typically with vinegar—which is as much about taste and texture as it is about food safety. Pickles' flavor continues to develop over time.

While making pickles using cucumbers is the standard, you don't have to limit yourself. You can find recipes for pickled onions, carrots, okra, green beans (called dilly beans), and more.

There's more than one way to pickle a vegetable:

Quick pickles. Quick pickling (or refrigerator pickling), which involves fresh-packing vegetables with a brine and refrigeration, is a simple way to get that pucker-up pickled flavor. Quick pickles will last for some time in your refrigerator—the exact time varies by recipe—but must stay refrigerated.

Quick pickling gives you more license for creativity than processing pickles. Because you're not putting them through a canner, you aren't locked into following any specific recipe and can add different herbs, seasonings, and vegetables, just watch the water-vinegar ratio. Eat these within 3 months.

Processed pickles. Processed pickles are more along the lines of what you'll buy from the grocery store shelves—but better because you grew the produce yourself. Processed pickles are generally first cooked in brine and then put into canning jars and processed in a canner. This extra step of processing the jars means you can safely store them at room temperature for at least a year.

Relishes and chutneys. A relish is simply a chopped pickled condiment. Chutneys are a sweet-sour type of relish. These can be preserved for a month or so in the refrigerator and for about a year as a processed pickled product.

Refrigerator pickles are a real treat for gardeners!

Three Tips for the Best Cucumber Pickles

Impress your friends and even yourself with your pickles using these tips alongside your favorite quick- or processed-pickle recipe:

- Use pickling-variety cucumbers rather than slicing varieties.

- Slice $\frac{1}{16}$ inch from the blossom end—opposite the stem end—as the blossom end contains an enzyme that may cause softening.

- Soak cucumbers in ice water for 4 to 5 hours before pickling to crisp them up.

Pickling and Fermentation Crocks

Be prepared for your preservation endeavor ahead of time so you aren't surprised, after doing all of your chopping, that you don't have the equipment you need.

With the harvest coming from a SFG bed, you're likely to not have more than a few pounds of vegetables to ferment or pickle at a time. You'll probably do fine with a 1-gallon container, which holds about 5 pounds of fresh vegetables. Avoid copper, iron, and galvanized-metal containers and lead-glazed crocks. Glass and stainless steel are good choices. A food-grade plastic bag can do in a pinch.

Lacto-fermentation

Lacto-fermentation puts microbes and salt to work to break down and preserve foods. This is an age-old preservation technique. The "lacto" in lacto-fermentation refers to lactic acid, which is produced during fermentation by microbes present on the surface of all fruits and vegetables. In the anaerobic environment created in a brine, the microbes convert sugars into lactic acid. This acts as a preservative, prevents harmful microbes from setting in, and imparts the sour flavor of fermented foods.

Sauerkraut, kimchi, and pickles are a few fermented foods familiar to grocery-store shelves. From your garden, you can preserve many different types of vegetables through fermentation. Cucumbers and some root vegetables, in particular, can be fermented with great results.

Essential ingredients. Fermentation is a simple preservation method. You just need your vegetables, seasonings, salt, and water. The salt and water create a brine. Cabbage often releases so much liquid during the salting process that it creates its own brine and doesn't require any water.

Recipes and ratios. Start out your fermentation experiments by following recipes. From there, you'll get a sense of how to create your own flavor combinations. If you're using a recipe, use their brine ratio. If you're experimenting on your own, use 2 tablespoons of salt per 1 quart of water for shredded and chopped vegetables; 3 tablespoons of salt per 1 quart of water for whole or chunky vegetables.

Storing fermented foods. Fermentation itself creates the conditions that allow food to be stored without additional heating or cooling. Because they're full of active cultures, ferments continue to "age"—or ferment—as time goes on. This is true whether they're refrigerated or kept in a pantry. The only way to stop the fermentation process altogether is to can them. The canning process will maintain the flavor but do away with the microbes.

Refrigerated, fermented cucumber pickles may be stored for 4 to 6 months, with surface molds regularly removed. Fermented sauerkraut may be kept in a tightly covered container in the refrigerator for several months.

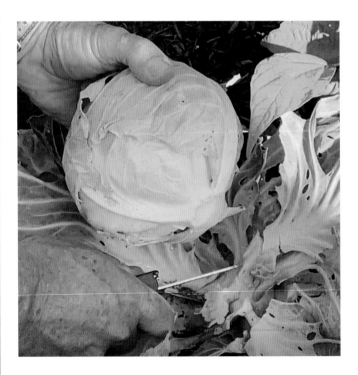

Freshly picked cabbage is a great candidate for fermentation.

Canning

In the late 1800s and early 1900s, canning was regularly practiced to preserve home-grown foods. As refrigeration technology developed and became more available, canning began to drop off in the 1940s. Now canning has regained some popularity, and you can use this preservation method for your SFG-grown produce, too.

Of the preservation methods, canning is the most time consuming. Once the process is finished, though, your canned goods will keep for a year or more without refrigeration—no other time or energy input required.

Depending on what you're canning, you will use one of two methods: pressure canning for low-acid foods or water-bath canning for acidic foods. Either way, the concept is the same. You put food in a jar, screw on a two-piece lid and ring, and heat it to a high enough temperature for a long enough time to kill pathogens and to preserve the taste, texture, and appearance of the ingredients.

The caution that accompanies any canning text is that there's one bacterium that can survive in an anerobic, low acid, moist environment, *Clostridium botulinum*, which causes botulism. This is why it's vital to follow approved canning recipes and take your time with each step in the canning process.

This part of the book is not meant to be a thorough how-to for canning, rather a look at what you can expect from preserving your produce through canning.

Canning recipes. The National Center for Home Food Preservation, some Cooperative Extension services, and canning-jar manufacturers offer recipes that have been tested for acidity and food safety. The recipe passed down to you by your grand mother may or may not pass their muster. You can have it checked by a Cooperative Extension food-safety expert for confirmation.

A recipe will tell you whether you need to cook or heat the foods before they go into the jars, how large to slice or chop, whether to add water, and more. You may read a recipe and wish to make substitutions, but this isn't like a regular cooking recipe.

Canning is the perfect way to preserve the summertime freshness of your SFG garden. Tomatoes and dilly beans are among the easiest candidates for canning.

You can't change it, because doing so can change the acidity of the final product, which brings up the possibility of pathogens like *C. botulinum* in the final product.

You may also question whether you can try canning in the oven or in your instant pressure cooker appliance. It's even possible to find people canning in their dishwashers. The answer to any of those musings is a big "no." Follow only tested, science-based recipes for food safety and quality.

As with all recipes, if you live at a higher altitude, be sure to follow the processing temperature, pressure, and time for your location.

Water-bath canning. Water-bath canning is used for high-acid foods—namely pickles and tomato-based products—because they don't need to be processed at as high of a temperature as low-acid foods. For water-bath canning, you need a canning pot, which will have a wire rack in the bottom that prevents the glass jars from sitting directly on the hot metal bottom. Canners are designed so at least 1 inch of water covers the jars when

the water is at a brisk boil. You'll put the jars in the canner, bring the water to boiling, and start your timer for the amount of time directed in the recipe.

Pressure canning. You'll use pressure canning for pretty much everything that doesn't contain tomatoes or vinegar. Low-acid items must go into a pressure canner—a heavy pot with a lid that can be tightly closed to trap steam—to reach at least 240°F. Other than the difference in how you operate the canning vessel, the idea behind pressure-canning and water-bath canning is the same.

You'll operate the canner using the reading on the pressure dial gauge on top of the lid. For example, if your recipe for canning sliced beets says to process pints for 30 minutes at 10 PSI (pounds of pressure per square inch), you'll wait until the dial shows 10 PSI before you start your timer for 30 minutes.

Canning equipment. Canning requires your vegetables and other ingredients, a pot, jars, lids and rings, and various smaller tools. The canning ingredients and pots are covered above.

Canning jars are a specialized type of glass jar, designed to withstand the heat and pressure of canning. These are more expensive than plain glass jars and are branded with a reputable canning-jar name, such as Kerr, Ball, or Mason. You can reuse canning jars that are free of cracks and chips. Jars come in regular-mouth and wide-mouth styles. You'll find various sizes, from half-pint to half-gallon. Use the size your recipe calls for.

Canning lids have two parts: lids and rings. The most commonly found lids are flat, metal pieces with a seal around the inner rim. You can use these flat lids only once for canning. The rings are, well, metal rings, that secure the lid to the jar. You can reuse the rings until they become rusty.

Harder to find are lids of hard plastic with an additional rubber ring. These are reusable but more challenging to use than the metal lids and might be considered for use after you get the hang of the canning process.

As far as the miscellaneous canning equipment, you can purchase a kit that has everything you need. This will include:

- Jar lifter, which are tong-like tools for putting jars into and taking them out of the canner
- Canning funnel, to help you get your ingredients into the jar rather than all over the counter
- Jar wrench, in case you can't put on or take off a ring by hand
- Bubble remover, which looks like an oddly shaped plastic knife. This tool is multipurpose. You'll use it to remove bubbles from the liquid in the jar as well as to measure the proper headspace between the ingredients and the top of the jar.

After canning. When the jars come out of the canner, you should start to hear the telltale "ping" of the metal lids creating their vacuum seal. Let them sit for 12 to 24 hours to be sure the seal has taken hold, then remove the rings, and store the jars in a room-temperature spot away from light and moisture. Properly sealed jars will have a slight depression at the center of the lid.

Taking the time to gather the correct equipment and follow a trusted recipe ensures your canning success, even if you're a first-timer.

Be sure to follow recipes to the letter when preparing and processing canned goods.

If you find jars that didn't seal upon first inspection, you can reprocess or refrigerate and use them immediately.

As you remove jars from storage for your enjoyment, inspect them again before you open them. You want to be sure the lid seal is still intact. Part of the point of removing the ring before storage is so it won't create a false seal over time. Look for spoilage. If the jar has a broken seal, anything seeping from it, mold or yeast growing on the ingredients, the appearance of gassiness or fermentation, or any off appearance or odor, don't use it. When in doubt, throw it out.

Square Foot Gardener's Tip

Now that you've read this, you may be wondering how anyone ever gets started canning. There is a lot to know. Find someone who's done their share of canning to work with you the first few times. It's more fun to can with others anyway, and of course, always follow published recipes exactly as printed. Also, Cooperative Extension offices everywhere offer hands-on classes and detailed resource guides.

Freezing

If you have the freezer capacity to store bags of frozen homegrown fruits and vegetables, this is a less labor-intensive process than canning. Some vegetables are easier to freeze than others—a little bit of chopping, and they're ready for packaging and freezing. Most require blanching before freezing.

During freezing, the moisture expands and ruptures the food's cells, and vegetables' texture will become less crisp in the freezer. The resulting texture means frozen produce is best used in cooked dishes. It's not a good idea to freeze cabbage, celery, cucumbers, lettuce, or radishes, because they become soggy.

Be sure to clearly label your bags of ready-to-freeze produce before putting it in your freezer.

Frozen vegetables can generally be stored 8 to 12 months at 0°F or colder.

Blanching. Blanching is the process of scalding vegetables in water or steam for a short time, then stopping the cooking process by submerging them in ice water. This step in freezing vegetables cleans the surface of microorganisms, preserves the color, and stops enzymatic action that causes them to break down.

Different vegetables must be blanched for different periods of time. For example, green beans take 3 minutes while large brussels sprouts take 5 minutes. Follow the recommended blanching period so the produce will keep for a long time. You'll find this information at the National Center for Home Food Preservation, in Cooperative Extension publications, and in food-preservation books.

Raw packing. Peppers, onions, strawberries, and herbs are among the few garden gems that don't need to be blanched before freezing. Wash them well, let them dry, chop or slice them as desired, and then package them for the freezer.

Packaging. You've come this far in growing your own food, and you're now taking the time to freeze and preserve it. Don't let an easy-to-overlook detail ruin all your effort—pay attention to your freezer packaging. Proper packaging materials protect foods' flavor, texture, appearance, and nutritive value. Limit containers to half-gallon so foods freeze evenly throughout.

Rigid containers are nice, because they're easily stackable in the freezer. If using plastic containers, look for brands that are freezer safe. Glass containers are precarious, as they can break at freezer temperatures. If you want to use glass, choose wide-mouth jars meant for freezing and canning.

Plant to Preserve

You may be surprised by the quantity of vegetables required to preserve any quantity of food. Before you start dreaming about all the uses for your frozen corn or dehydrated potatoes, read this list of a few commonly preserved items and the quantiles needed of each:

- **Cucumbers:** 1½ to 2 pounds of fresh pickling cucumbers—about 4 inches long—will make 1 quart of canned pickles.

- **Tomatoes:** Boiling water canning pots come in varying sizes; typically holding 9 regular-mouth pint jars, 8 wide-mouth pint jars, or 7 quart jars at once, though some brands may have a different capacity. For reference, to fill 9 pint jars, you'll need about 14 pounds of tomatoes; 7 quart jars takes about 22 pounds of produce.

- **Corn:** Plan for 2½ pounds of corn to make 1 pint frozen.

- **Greens:** You may know that greens—spinach, Swiss chard, collard greens, etc.—cook down a lot. For 1 quart of frozen greens, plan on 2 to 3 pounds fresh.

- **Strawberries:** Half a pound of fresh strawberries can make about 1 pint frozen or 1 pint of strawberry jam.

- **Dehydrated vegetables:** It's hard to estimate this exactly, because every vegetable has its own water content—consider the juiciness of a tomato versus the solid nature of broccoli. On average, 25 pounds of fresh vegetables will dehydrate down to 3 to 6 pounds of dried vegetables.

Blanching is the process of dunking fresh produce in boiling water for a few minutes to lock in the freshness. It's always followed by a dunk in a pot of ice water.

Flexible wrapping, like plastic bags and aluminum foil, are available in different grades. Again, look for wrappings meant for the freezer, which are more durable. Make storage easier by pressing the ingredients flat to freeze. Once they're frozen in this flat shape, stack them or stand them on their sides to fit more bags into the space. If you have a vacuum sealing machine, vacuum sealing the packed bags prior to freezing is helpful for staving off freezer burn.

When putting the packages into the freezer, only add 2 to 3 pounds of unfrozen food per cubic foot of storage space per day. This will ensure the food freezes all the way through quickly.

Blanching

Blanching is the process of heating vegetables just enough to destroy enzymes, but not enough to cook them. It can improve the quality and safety of preserved vegetables.

Many herbs are great candidates for dehydrating and drying.

Dehydrating

By removing the moisture from fruits, vegetables, and herbs, you're removing what pathogens need to survive and multiply, and slowing the enzymatic breakdown of food. You can preserve many garden-grown items by dehydrating them in the oven, microwave, or dehydrator, and—in the case of herbs—by hanging them to dry. Foods chopped into smaller pieces will dry faster, and warm temperatures, low humidity, and air movement also make the dehydration process more efficient.

You'll know your produce is dry when herbs and leafy greens crumble and vegetables and fruits snap when you bend them. Only when they're brittle are they ready

for storage in a sealed container. Packaging them before they're fully dehydrated can cause them to mold and spoil the whole batch.

Dehydration preparation. Washing the produce is the first step in dehydration. Cut out and discard any parts that are damaged. Core or remove fibrous bits.

If you're working with vegetables, fruits, or rhizomes—like ginger and turmeric— these need to be sliced in thin, uniform pieces for even drying.

Some vegetables dehydrate best if they're first blanched. Why would you add moisture by boiling or steaming a vegetable if you intended to dry it out? Blanching before dehydrating does away with the enzymes that would cause the produce to break down in storage, and it softens the tissue so moisture can escape more easily.

Sun drying. The idea of drying your produce in the sun sounds nice, yet this is a dehydration method that requires a lot of care. Herbs may lose their potency when dried in direct sunlight. You have to protect the produce from insects, bring it in at night so dew doesn't collect on it, and bring it in if it's raining. In humid areas, this process takes even longer. A more efficient means of sun drying is to use a solar dehydrator, which is a large and fairly complex item to build.

Food dehydrators. If you're serious about dehydrating your produce, a food dehydrator could save you time. This countertop appliance has lightweight, removable trays, a heating element, and a fan and vents for air circulation.

Temperature settings generally range from 95°F to 160°F, which you can change based on what you're dehydrating. Herbs and leafy greens are more delicate, and they dry at a lower temperature for less time than fruits and vegetables.

Food dehydrators do create a lot of heat, and some models are noisy to operate.

Using an oven. Your oven can act as a dehydrator in a pinch. Ovens are less ideal than dehydrating appliances because—unless you have a convection oven—they don't circulate air, they might not have low-heat settings, and you might need your oven for other purposes while you're dehydrating produce. It takes about twice as long for food to dry in an oven as it would in a dehydrator, but the job will get done.

Using a microwave. You can use a microwave to dry small quantities of produce, though you run the risk of cooking it instead of dehydrating it. You'll have the most success with herbs and leafy greens. Microwave them on a paper towel on high for 2 minutes, check them, and continue for 30 seconds at a time until they're crumbly.

Hanging to dry. Most herbs can be hung to dry. Vegetables—even leafy greens—are too succulent to air dry. This is a simple process. Just tie several herb stems together and hang the bundle in a dry, well-ventilated spot indoors, out of direct sunlight. Let them hang until they're brittle. To dry herbs with seeds—like cilantro,

fennel, and dill—or with delicate flowers that will drop valuable petals, suspend these in a paper bag so the bag catches what falls from the bundle. Chili peppers can also be dried this way, tied up in what is called a ristra, which is Spanish for "string."

With your harvest well underway, you've successfully worked your way through the SFG Method. From the first step, you've taken a whole journey through learning about your growing space and climate to making decisions about what you should grow to discovering how plants produce. Here in the harvest stage, you can look back with satisfaction on your work and get ready to do it again.

In the next chapter—the final chapter—you'll read some common SFG questions and answers that may help you along the way.

Herbs are an easy candidate for air drying. Hang them in small bundles in a warm, dry room.

Food Preservation Guidelines

While each of these food-preservation methods is very different, there are a few guidelines that apply across the board.

- Don't alter the ingredient proportions.

- Use vinegar with the proper acidity level. This means you can't use homemade vinegars.

- Preserve only fresh, firm produce without spoilage or bad spots. This is for flavor as well as food safety.

- Use only canning or pickling salt. Do not use iodized salt, mineral salts, sea salts, kosher salts, flaked salt, or flavored salts.

- Use filtered water or spring water, as these won't contain the chlorine, chloramines, and fluoride that tap water might have. Avoid distilled water.

- Always start with a clean kitchen. You don't want to introduce unwanted bacteria to any food-preservation processes.

- Label every jar and bag. Clearly write the date the food was preserved and what, exactly, is in that jar or bag.

- Rotate your preserved foods so you use the oldest first. Remember, first-in, first-out.

11

Challenges and Solutions

The Square Foot Gardening Method is unique in many ways. It's an efficient, simpler way to grow more in less space, which leads to more enjoyment in the garden. The combination of perfectly formulated Mel's Mix growing medium, carefully planned square-foot-grid planting spaces, and reduced work and resources yields many benefits, as well as some common questions.

This chapter addresses a few of the most common questions asked by SFG users over the decades. What answers you don't find here you may be able to find on the SFG Foundation blog, at SquareFootGardening.org.

Mel's Mix

Is just 6 to 8 inches of Mel's Mix sufficient for growing plants? I thought roots needed deep soil.

A: If you were planting trees or shrubs—deep-rooted perennial plants—in your SFG bed, they would need a greater depth of growing medium to become established. But for most of the garden crops and flowers that you'll want to grow in your SFG bed, 6 to 8 inches is really all they need.

In the SFG bed, you've divided the top growing space into a grid on the surface, but below the surface, there are no barriers. Plants' roots don't grow straight down, rather they use all the space they have around them. While they have just 6 to 8 inches of vertical space directly underneath, the roots will span horizontally, as needed.

One reason plants grow large root systems is to go in search of oxygen, water, and nutrients. By using Mel's Mix and watering the plants' root zones as often as needed, you're setting up the plant roots with all they need to thrive in place.

Can I order Mel's Mix as a bagged mix, or do I have to make my own?

A: Mel's Mix is not sold as an already-bagged product. Chapter 7 in this book offers easy instructions to make your own Mel's Mix with one-part (by volume) each of compost, peat moss, and coarse vermiculite. It is more cost effective for you to source each of those ingredients—and even make your own compost to add to the mix—than it would be to have bagged Mel's Mix shipped to you from far away.

Pests & diseases

I think my herbs have a disease. The oregano has small dark brown-to-black spots on them. Some of the older leaves are covered, and the new leaves don't have any. How can I cure them?

A: The spots do look like a disease, but they're actually bug damage. These spots are caused by four-lined plant bugs. The list of plants these bugs eat is long: your herbs, zinnias, dogwood trees, gooseberry bushes, peppers, and more. Your best defense is observation.

Both the four-lined plant bug nymphs and adults suck the chlorophyll from the leaves, leaving behind these uniformly sized dark, round, sunken spots. These spots are unsightly, but they probably won't kill they plant.

Four-lined plant bugs are small and easily identifiable. The tiny nymphs are red to reddish orange with black wing pads and black stripes or dots, and the adults are greenish yellow with orange-brown heads and four black stripes on the wings.

If you find a few of these pests, dispose of them by hand picking. If you have an infestation, consider using a commercially made insecticidal soap, keeping in mind that the soap only works if it comes in direct contact with the bugs. In the fall, prune off the damaged parts (look for lengthwise slits in the stems) to remove eggs the bugs may have laid. Put those cuttings in the trash rather than in your compost. Next year, consider putting insect netting around these herbs to keep out the four-lined plant bugs.

Just 6 to 8 inches of Mel's Mix is enough for plants to thrive. This newly built bed is filled and ready for the grid.

Four-lined plant bugs and their damage on a sage plant.

Q

Some of the tomatoes I harvested first this year look lumpy and misshapen. What happened?

A: When you find tomatoes that are puckered and bubbly on the blossom end (the end opposite the stem), this is called catface. While no one seems to agree on the exact cause of catfacing, there are a lot of theories about it. They all involve abnormalities while the tomato is developing. Insect damage to tomato blossoms, cold temperatures while the plant is setting fruit, and exposure to certain herbicides are scientists' best guesses. In SFG you avoid using insecticides or herbicides as much as possible, so this is typically not a cause of catfacing in a SFG bed. Large-fruited varieties and certain heirlooms seem to be most likely to develop this issue. Tomatoes with catfacing typically ripen unevenly, but they are safe to eat.

Catfacing on the bottom of a tomato.

Square Foot Garden beds & add-ons

Q

If I already have a 12-inch raised bed but don't want to fill the whole depth with Mel's Mix, what should I fill the bottom with?

A: The best way to fill space in a too-tall raised bed is to start with clean builders sand or topsoil. Put down a 4- or 5-inch layer in the bottom. Top that with landscape fabric, and then put Mel's Mix on top.

You may be tempted to fill the bottom of the bed with a chunkier organic material like wood chips or logs, but this has the potential to tie up nitrogen in your Mel's Mix and make it unusable by plants' roots while the material decomposes. As that wood breaks down over time, the level of all of the growing medium in the bed will get lower. At that point, you'd either have to empty the whole bed and start over with a base of sand or topsoil topped with Mel's Mix, or you'd have to add more and more Mel's Mix throughout the season to bring up the level again.

Q

Can I grow in square buckets instead of a garden bed?

A: The SFG Method works with the notion that plant roots can spread themselves out beyond their designated square. Plants are a little like icebergs—what we see on top of the soil is one amount of the plant, and there's a whole other part underneath. Take tomatoes. An indeterminate tomato—a variety that grows long and tall—can grow roots 2 feet or longer in each direction. When roots bump up against the side of the bucket, they'll be forced to grow downwards in a circular pattern, becoming what's known as root bound, or they'll stop growing altogether. A wide root system helps a plant take up water and nutrients and anchors the plant in the soil for stability against wind, rain, and clumsy gardeners.

A bucket is not an ideal SFG container. If you do try the SFG Method using a bucket, add growing medium to within a few inches of the top, and be sure to drill holes in the bottom for drainage. As with other types of container gardening, you'll need to water more frequently as well.

When growing in elevated Square Foot Garden beds like these or in an on-ground bed, the 6- to 8-inch depth of Mel's Mix means the roots can spread out wide, reaching well beyond their designated square. When growing in a square bucket or other container, the same is not true.

Maintenance

Should I grow cover crops in my SFG bed when grids are empty?

A: Cover crops serve several roles in a garden. Gardeners who are trying to build their soil nutrients, reduce soil compaction and erosion, increase the moisture-holding capacity of their soil, and reduce weeds are encouraged to use cover crops to improve their growing space. Using Mel's Mix and the SFG Method, your garden bed already has the nutrients and moisture-holding capacity it needs, doesn't get compacted, and has few weeds. If you wanted to grow a flowering cover crop—such as buckwheat or phacelia—for its beauty and potential to attract pollinators and other beneficial insects to your space, you could do that. However, there's no need to grow a cover crop for traditional cover-crop purposes of replenishing the soil.

Q

I found moss growing on my Mel's Mix. Am I doing something wrong?

A: Moss wants to grow in soggy, shady areas and can grow in soils—also on wood, rocks, and other materials—where other plants can't. If you're having a wet season and your SFG bed gets significant shade even on sunny days, it's possible for moss to move in. You're probably not doing anything wrong, but you may benefit from moving your SFG bed to a spot with more direct sunlight.

Moss is only growing on the surface of the Mel's Mix. It doesn't have true root systems, so it's easy to remove. Take out the moss, and mix in dry compost to those squares. Get back to planting in those squares as soon as the conditions are right. Moss won't compete for space with healthy plants.

At the end of the growing season, there's no need to plant a cover crop to enrich your soil like there is in a traditional in-ground garden. The Mel's Mix already has everything your plants need. Simply top off the garden with a bit of compost between each round of planting and you'll be ready to grow.

Conclusion

With the close of this book, you are set up for growing more food with less effort in less space than you thought possible using the Square Foot Gardening Method. Using the basic concept that when you give plants the right amount of space, a rich growing medium, and the right amount of moisture, you'll end up with a garden that will make you proud. Whether you're locating your beds on a patio, a yard, or pretty much anywhere else that sees adequate sunlight, you have great gardening success ahead of you.

This book touched on many aspects of not just the SFG Method but of gardening in general. You've taken in a lot of information. Start out slow and steady, and keep in mind the ten SFG principles from chapter 1 along the way. They are:

- Plant in squares.
- Plant densely.
- Be sparing with seeds.
- Rotate crops.
- Grow up.
- Use Mel's Mix, not garden soil.
- Grow shallow.
- Stop using fertilizer.
- Garden where it's most convenient.
- Establish accessible aisles, ideally 3 feet wide.

The whole SFG Method is built on these principles, and you can continue to return to them as you work through your garden's challenges and solutions.

Don't be afraid to return to chapter 2 for a refresh on the eight quick-start steps of the SFG Method. From there, you can refer to the related chapters to take a more in-depth look at the step at hand, from planning to planting and maintenance to harvest. Each time you read this book, a new lightbulb will come on. Each season will be different—as the weather and the crops you plant will be different—and this book will continue to be a valuable resource in simplifying your gardening.

It's our hope that Square Foot Gardening is a pastime you'll grow to love more and more each season.

Questions will continue to arise, several years and more into your SFG journey. Lifelong SFG users still encounter something new from time to time. You're not left on your own—you're part of a whole community of SFG users. Page 286 has information about the Square Foot Gardening Foundation, including the website where you'll find resources that can provide up-to-date answers and support.

Now go dream about the meals you'll cook with your vegetables, the teas you'll drink with your herbs, and the bouquets you'll make with your flowers. The pleasure of each of these things is exponentially greater when they've been created with what you've grown yourself. Your garden is going to be the envy of your block.

References

Planning & Planting Chart

CROP	FAMILY	SEASON	ANNUAL, PERENNIAL, OR BIENNIAL	DIRECT SEED OR TRANSPLANT	DAYS TO GERMINATION	IDEAL GERMINATION CONDITIONS
Arugula	Brassicaceae	Cool	Annual	Direct seed for baby. Either for mature.	5–7	40°F–55°F Seed ¼" deep.
Asparagus	Liliaceae	Cool	Perennial	Transplanting root crowns is preferred.	N/A	70°F–77°F
Basil	Lamiaceae	Warm	Annual	Either	8–14	Seed ⅛"–¼" deep.
Beans (bush or pole)	Fabaceae	Warm	Annual	Direct seed	8–10	70°F–80°F Seed 1" deep.
Beets	Chenopodiaceae	Cool	Annual	Direct seed	5–8	50°F–85°F Seed ¾" deep.
Bitter melon gourd	Cucurbitaceae	Warm	Annual	Either	5–10	77°F–82°F Seed 1" deep. Soak or scarify seeds before planting.
Broccoli	Brassicaceae	Cool	Annual	Transplant	4–7	45°F–85°F Seed ½"–¾" deep.
Broccoli rabe	Brassicaceae	Cool	Annual	Direct seed	4–7	45°F–85°F Seed ¼"–½" deep.
Brussels sprouts	Brassicaceae	Cool	Annual	Either	5–8	45°F–85°F Seed ¼"–½" deep.
Cabbage (head cabbage)	Brassicaceae	Cool	Annual	Either	4–7	45°F–85°F Seed ½"–¾" deep.
Callaloo/ amaranth	Amaranthaceae	Warm	Annual	Either	7–10	70°F–75°F Seed ⅛" deep.
Cantaloupe/ muskmelon	Cucurbitaceae	Warm	Annual	Either	3–10	60°F–95°F The warmer the soil, the faster the germination. Seed ½" deep.
Carrots	Apiaceae	Cool	Annual	Direct seed	7–21	50°F–85°F Seed ½" deep.

WEEKS TO TRANSPLANT	MATURE HEIGHT	# PER SFG SQUARE	SEED VIABILITY (YEARS)	NOTES
4	6" baby 12"+ mature	16 baby 9 mature	5	■ Frost tolerant ■ Use row cover to reduce flea beetle damage.
N/A	5'–9'	1	3 for seeds Crowns should be planted ASAP.	■ Plant crowns 4–6 weeks before last frost. ■ Plant in trenches 5"–8" deep. Cover with 1"–2" Mel's Mix. Cover with more Mel's Mix as the plants grow. Some gardeners build a 12" deep SFG box for asparagus only.
4–6	12"+	1 standard varieties 4 compact varieties	3–5	■ Expect cultivars like lemon, cinnamon, and Thai to grow larger than sweet varieties. ■ Susceptible to downy mildew in humid climates. Look for resistant varieties.
N/A	1'–3' bush 5'–10' pole	9 bush 4 pole	5	■ Can tolerate partial shade but will produce fewer beans.
N/A	12"	9	4	■ Use floating row cover or insect netting to protect from insect pests. ■ Frost tolerant. ■ Beet seedballs may produce 2–6 plants, which should be thinned.
2–3	1'–2' tall with 16' long vine	1 per 3 squares when trellised	2–3	■ Very sensitive to frost. ■ Grow this extra-large vining plant on a trellis.
4–6	2'–3'	1	3–5	■ Can tolerate light shade but maturity will be slower. ■ Use floating row cover or insect netting to protect from insect pests.
N/A	1'–1½'	9	3–5	■ Use floating row cover or insect netting to protect from insect pests.
4–6	2'–3'	1	3–5	■ Frost improves flavor. ■ Brussels sprouts take months to mature. ■ Use floating row cover or insect netting to protect from insect pests.
4–6	1'–2'	1	3–5	■ Tender leaves inside the head can be damaged by heavy freezes. ■ Some shade can be beneficial in warm weather. ■ Use floating row cover or insect netting to protect from insect pests.
N/A	1'–3'	1	4–5	■ Pinch back main stem to encourage branching and bushy growth.
4–6	1'–1½' tall with 3'–12' vines	1	4	■ Trellis or allow the vines to cascade over the side of the SFG box.
N/A	6"+	16	3	■ Tolerates frost and light freezes. ■ Don't allow seeds to dry out. Cover grid square with a piece of cardboard to hold in moisture until germination. ■ Use a top hat for longer varieties.

CROP	FAMILY	SEASON	ANNUAL, PERENNIAL, OR BIENNIAL	DIRECT SEED OR TRANSPLANT	DAYS TO GERMINATION	IDEAL GERMINATION CONDITIONS
Cauliflower	Brassicaceae	Cool	Annual	Either; transplants are generally more successful.	4–7	45°F–85°F Seed ½"–¾" deep.
Celery	Apiaceae	Cool	Annual	Transplant	14–21	70°F–75°F
Chamomile	Asteraceae	Warm	Annual	Either	10–14	55°F–60°F Press seed into surface of the soil and do not cover. Direct seed in fall or just before last frost in spring.
Chives	Amaryllidaceae	Cool	Perennial	Either	7–21	45°F–95°F Seed ¼" deep.
Cilantro/ coriander	Apiaceae	Cool	Annual	Direct seed	7–10	65°F–70°F Seed ¼"–½" deep.
Collard greens	Brassicaceae	Cool	Biennial	Either	4–7	45°F–85°F Seed ¼"–½" deep.
Corn (sweet corn)	Poaceae	Warm	Annual	Direct seed	4–7	65°F–85°F Seed 1" deep.
Cucamelons	Cucurbitaceae	Warm	Annual	Either	10	60°F–70°F Seed 1"–1½" deep.
Cucumbers	Cucurbitaceae	Warm	Annual	Either	3–10	60°F–90°F Seed 1"–1½" deep.
Dill	Apiaceae	Warm	Annual	Direct seed	7–21	65°F–70°F Seed ¼" deep.
Eggplant	Solanaceae	Warm	Annual	Transplant	7–10	60°F–95°F Prefers 85°F or warmer soil. Seed ¼" deep.
Fennel (bulb/ Florence fennel)	Apiaceae	Warm	Typically grown as an annual	Either; prefers direct seeding	7–14	Seed ¼" deep. Soak seeds before planting.
Fennel (herb/ common fennel)	Apiaceae	Warm	Biennial/Tender perennial	Direct seed	7–14	65°F–70°F Seed ½"–¼" deep.
Garlic	Amaryllidaceae	Cool	Annual	Direct seed cloves	N/A	Plant cloves 2" deep with tips up.

WEEKS TO TRANSPLANT	MATURE HEIGHT	# PER SFG SQUARE	SEED VIABILITY (YEARS)	NOTES
4–6	1'–2'	1	3–5	■ Mature heads will not tolerate hard freezes. ■ Some shade can be beneficial in warm weather. ■ Use floating row cover or insect netting to protect from insect pests.
10–12	18"–24"	4	5	■ Difficult crop because of its long growing season. ■ Prefers full sun.
6–8 (transplant when seedlings are 1"–2" tall)	15"–24"	1	4	■ Tolerates light frost. ■ Cut back plants mid-season to encourage new growth. ■ Look for German chamomile, which grows upright, not Roman, which spreads. ■ Flowers not harvested can reseed and become weedy.
6–8	6"–12"	4	3	■ Regular cutting helps keep plants vigorous. ■ Remove plants as they divide and spread. ■ Resistant to pests and diseases.
N/A	12"–18"; 3'–4' when in flower	4	1–4	■ Will bolt in summer heat. ■ Attracts many pollinators when flowering. ■ Cilantro seeds are coriander.
4–6	1½'–3'	1	4	■ Flavor improves when "kissed" by frost. ■ Prefers full sun in spring, but can benefit from light shade during hot weather. ■ Use floating row cover to protect from insect pests.
N/A	4'–6'	4	1–3	■ Plant one 4'×4' SFG box full of corn only for pollination and mutual structural support.
3–4	1'–2' tall with 10' long vines	1	3–6	■ Very sensitive to cold. ■ Grow this vining plant on a trellis or on the edge of the SFG box so it can spill over the side.
3–4	1' tall with 6'+ long vines	1	6	■ Very sensitive to cold. ■ Vining varieties use space more economically. ■ Plant on a trellis, or allow to spill over the side of the box.
N/A	1½'–4'	1	1–4	■ Will bolt in summer heat. ■ Attracts pollinators when flowering.
6–8	2'–6'	1	4	■ Protect from flea beetle damage with row cover.
4–6	up to 6'; generally smaller	1	3–4	■ Will survive a light frost. ■ Grows best during cooler, shorter days. ■ Push Mel's Mix around the bulb to blanch it as it develops.
N/A	3'–5'	1	1–2	■ Flavor intensifies as the plant matures.
N/A	1'–2'	9	1	■ Plant in fall and harvest in summer. ■ Remove flower stalks (scapes) from hardneck varieties in spring.

CROP	FAMILY	SEASON	ANNUAL, PERENNIAL, OR BIENNIAL	DIRECT SEED OR TRANSPLANT	DAYS TO GERMINATION	IDEAL GERMINATION CONDITIONS
Ginger	Zingiberaceae	Warm	Annual	Plant rhizomes	N/A	80°F Plant 2"–4" deep.
Ground cherry	Solanaceae	Warm	Annual	Transplant	7–14	70°F–85°F Seed ¼" deep.
Kale (baby)	Brassicaceae	Cool	Biennial	Direct seed	4–7	45°F–85°F Seed ¼"–½" deep.
Kale (mature leaf)	Brassicaceae	Cool	Biennial	Either	4–7	45°F–85°F Seed ¼"–½" deep.
Kohlrabi	Brassicaceae	Cool	Annual	Direct seed	4–7	45°F–85°F Seed ½" deep.
Komatsuna	Brassicaceae	Cool	Annual	Direct seed	4–7	45°F–85°F Seed ¼"–½" deep.
Lavender	Lamiaceae	Warm	Perennial	Transplant	30–90	65°F–70°F Seed ⅛" deep. Some light needed for germination.
Lemongrass	Poaceae	Warm	Annual; perennial in Zones 9–11.	Transplant	7–14	70°F–75°F Lightly press into Mel's Mix.
Leeks	Amaryllidaceae	Cool	Biennial	Either	5–7	45°F–95°F Peak germination around 77°F. Seed ½" deep.
Lettuce	Asteraceae	Cool	Annual	Transplant mature and head varieties. Direct seed baby leaf types.	2–15	40°F–85°F Seed ⅛" deep.
Luffa	Cucurbitaceae	Warm	Annual	Either	7–14	65°F–70°F Seed 1"–1½" deep. Soak seeds before planting.
Malabar spinach	Basellaceae	Warm	Perennial in frost-free areas	Either, as well as cuttings	14–21	65°F–75°F Scarify to speed germination.
Mizuna	Brassicaceae	Cool	Annual	Direct seed	4–7	40°F–85°F Will germinate at soil temperatures as low as 40°F. Seed ¼"–½" deep.
Mustard greens	Brassicaceae	Cool	Annual	Either	4–7	45°F–85°F Seed ¼"–½" deep.

WEEKS TO TRANSPLANT	MATURE HEIGHT	# PER SFG SQUARE	SEED VIABILITY (YEARS)	NOTES
N/A	2'–3'	4	Plant within a few weeks.	■ Purchase from a reputable seed company. ■ Transplant when temperature is consistently 60°F or above. ■ Plant in a trench, and hill as rhizomes peek out of the soil.
6–7	30"	1 per 2 squares	3–7	■ Similar to tomatillos. ■ Plant may sprawl and need supports.
N/A	6"–12"	4 regular baby-leaf harvest	4	■ Doesn't overwinter as well as mature kale. ■ Use floating row cover or insect netting to protect from insect pests.
4–6	1½'–3'	1	4	■ Flavor improves when "kissed" by frost. ■ May bolt in first warm snap after cold weather. ■ Use floating row cover or insect netting to protect from insect pests.
4–5	1'–1½'	4	4	■ Plants may prematurely bolt during weather extremes.
N/A	8"–12"	16 baby 4 mature	3	■ Somewhat heat tolerant, but prefers mild temperatures. ■ Protect from flea beetles with row cover.
8–10	12"–18"	1	4	■ For best results, purchase transplants or grow from cuttings. ■ Deadheading encourages more blooms. ■ May need winter protection in cold growing zones.
3–4	3'–6'	1 per 2 or more squares	3	■ Can start seeds indoors or grow from cuttings. ■ Will not tolerate frost. ■ Can be potted up and overwintered indoors.
8–10	2'–3'	9	3	■ Mulch heavily for storage over winter in the SFG box. ■ More frost tolerant than their onion cousins.
3–4	6"–12" head and mature leaf 4–6" baby leaf	4 mature 9 baby	2–5	■ Thrives in 60°F–70°F average daily temperatures. ■ Head lettuce is more difficult to grow than leaf lettuce. ■ Transplant at least 1 month before hottest weather.
4–6	2'–3' tall with 15'–30' vines	1	3–5	■ Grow on a trellis.
8–9	2'–3' tall with 3'–6'+ vines	1	4	■ Thrives in temperatures around 00°F. ■ Requires trellising. ■ Transplant 2–3 weeks after last frost date.
N/A	8"	4 mature leaf 9 baby	4	■ Tolerates light frosts. ■ Slow to bolt.
5–6	6"–24"	4	4	■ Tolerates light frost. ■ May bolt quickly in hot weather. ■ Spicy flavor increases with temperature.

CROP	FAMILY	SEASON	ANNUAL, PERENNIAL, OR BIENNIAL	DIRECT SEED OR TRANSPLANT	DAYS TO GERMINATION	IDEAL GERMINATION CONDITIONS
Napa cabbage	Brassicaceae	Cool	Annual	Either	4–7	50°F–80°F Seed ¼"–½" deep.
Okra	Malvaceae	Warm	Annual	Either; prefers direct seeding.	5–10	60°F–105°F Seed 1" deep. Soak seeds before sowing.
Onions (bulb)	Amaryllidaceae	Cool	Biennial	Either, as well as from sets	4–5	45°F–95°F
Oregano	Lamiaceae	Warm	Perennial	Either, as well as cuttings and root divisions.	8–14	Leave seeds uncovered.
Pak choy/ bok choy	Brassicaceae	Cool	Annual	Either	4–7	50°F–80°F Seed ¼"–½" deep.
Parsley	Apiaceae	Cool	Biennial	Either	20–25	40°F–90°F 75°F is optimum. Soak seeds before sowing.
Parsnips	Apiaceae	Cool	Biennial	Direct seed	10–21	50°F–85°F Seed ½" deep.
Peas (shelling)	Fabaceae	Cool	Annual	Direct seed	9–13	40°F–85°F Seed 1"–2" deep. Germinates best at 60°F soil temperature.
Peas (snap)	Fabaceae	Cool	Annual	Direct seed	9–13	See above.
Peas (snow)	Fabaceae	Cool	Annual	Direct seed	9–13	See above.
Peppers (all kinds)	Solanaceae	Warm	Annual	Either	7–21	70°F–95°F Best germination at soil temperatures around 85°F. Seed ¼" deep.
Potatoes	Solanaceae	Cool/Warm	Annual	Plant seed potatoes	14–28	40°F Soil should be at least 40°F.
Pumpkins	Cucurbitaceae	Warm	Annual	Either	5–10	60°F–100°F 95°F is optimal. Seed 1½" deep.
Radishes (daikon)	Brassicaceae	Cool	Annual	Direct seed	3–4	55°F–85°F Seed ½" deep.

WEEKS TO TRANSPLANT	MATURE HEIGHT	# PER SFG SQUARE	SEED VIABILITY (YEARS)	NOTES
4–6	1'–2'	1	4	▪ Transplant just after last frost or in late summer. ▪ Plants may prematurely bolt during weather extremes. ▪ Use floating row cover or insect netting to protect from insect pests.
4–5	3'–7'	1	4–5	▪ Look for spineless varieties to reduce itchiness when handling.
6–8	1'+	9	1	▪ Easiest to grow from sets. ▪ Plant just before last frost date in spring. ▪ If seedlings grow tall and leaves droop before transplanting, trim back to about 3" tall.
6–10	6"–36"	1	1	▪ Different types have different flavor profiles. ▪ Plant in an edge square, or keep pruned. ▪ Remove old, woody stems at the end of winter.
2–4	4"–15"	4 mini varieties 1 large	4	▪ Use floating row cover or insect netting to protect from insect pests.
6–8	6"–12"	4	3	▪ Handle transplants' roots carefully. ▪ Plant moss-curled or flat-leaf varieties, depending on your preference.
N/A	2'–3'	9	1	▪ Let these deep tap roots grow in a top hat or plant shorter-rooted varieties. ▪ Sweeter flavor develops below 40°F. ▪ Keep moist during germination.
N/A	2'–2½' bush 4'–8' climbing	9 bush types 4 climbing types	3	▪ Can tolerate moderate freezes until flowering. ▪ Needs trellising or supports. ▪ May stop producing at temperatures above 85°F. ▪ Look for dwarf bush varieties if you don't want to trellis.
N/A	1½' bush types 7' climbing	9 bush types 4 climbing types	3	▪ See shelling peas, above. ▪ Look for dwarf bush varieties if you don't want to trellis.
N/A	2½' bush 6'–10' climbing	9 bush types 4 climbing types	3	▪ See shelling peas, above. ▪ Look for dwarf bush varieties if you don't want to trellis.
8–10	1'–3'	1	2	▪ Requires full sun. ▪ Nighttime temperatures below 60°F or above 75°F can reduce fruit set in some varieties. ▪ May need supports.
N/A	1½'–3'	1	1	▪ Grow mature (late-season) potatoes in a top hat. Plant seed potatoes in 4" Mel's Mix, and add more as the plant grows. ▪ Cut seed potatoes into 1" pieces with 1–2 eyes, and leave them at room temperature to cure for a few days before planting.
3–4	1½'–3' tall with 5'–15' vines	1 per 2 squares, plus vertical space	6	▪ Very sensitive to frost. ▪ Vines need trellising or space to run off the side of the SFG box. ▪ Look for mini and dwarf varieties.
N/A	up to 18"	9	4	▪ Grow in a top hat. ▪ Roots can grow up to 3' long; look for varieties 1' or smaller. ▪ Heavily mulch and protect greens to overwinter.

CROP	FAMILY	SEASON	ANNUAL, PERENNIAL, OR BIENNIAL	DIRECT SEED OR TRANSPLANT	DAYS TO GERMINATION	IDEAL GERMINATION CONDITIONS
Radishes (salad types)	Brassicaceae	Cool	Annual	Direct seed	3–4	55°F–85°F Seed ½" deep.
Radishes (winter types)	Brassicaceae	Cool	Annual	Direct seed	3–4	55°F–85°F Seed ½" deep.
Recao/ culantro/ Vietnamese coriander	Apiaceae	Warm	Annual	Either	21+	80°F–85°F Barely cover the seeds.
Rosemary	Lamiaceae	Warm	Perennial	Transplant, or root a cutting	14–21+	65°F–70°F Barely cover the seeds.
Rutabaga	Brassicaceae	Cool	Biennial, grown as annual	Direct seed	4–7	45°F–85°F Seed ½" deep.
Sage	Lamiaceae	Warm	Perennial	Either	7–21	65°F–70°F
Scallions/ green onions	Amaryllidaceae	Cool	Annual	Either	4–5	45°F–95°F
Sorrel	Polygonaceae	Cool	Perennial	Either	7–14	60°F Seed ¼" deep or press lightly into Mel's Mix.
Spinach	Chenopodiaceae	Cool	Annual	Either for mature; direct seed for baby	6–10	40°F–75°F Seed ½" deep.
Strawberries	Rosaceae	Warm	Perennial	Transplant bare-root plants	N/A	Plant so the entire root system is covered, with the crown at soil level.
Summer savory	Lamiaceae	Warm	Annual	Either	7–14	65°F–70°F Press seed into Mel's Mix, and do not cover.
Summer squash/ zucchini	Cucurbitaceae	Warm	Annual	Either	5–10	60°F–105°F 95°F is optimum. Seed ½"–1" deep.
Sweet potatoes	Convolvulaceae	Warm	Annual	Transplant slips	N/A	50°F+

WEEKS TO TRANSPLANT	MATURE HEIGHT	# PER SFG SQUARE	SEED VIABILITY (YEARS)	NOTES
N/A	6"–18"	16	4	■ One of the fastest-germinating and -maturing crops. ■ Varieties come in all shapes and colors.
N/A	12"–18"	16	4	■ Winter types include black Spanish and watermelon radish. ■ Longer maturing than salad types.
8	10"–12"	1	2	■ Prefers direct seeding. ■ Requires both shade and warm temperatures. ■ To delay bolting, keep moist and cut off the flower stalk when it appears.
10–12 for transplants 8 for cuttings	2'–5'	1 as annual 1 per 2 squares as perennial	1–4	■ Seeds are difficult to germinate. Purchase transplants or root a cutting. ■ Prune to keep size in check. ■ In colder climates, grow as annual or dig up and bring inside for winter.
N/A	1'–2'	4	3–5	■ Flavor is improved by frost. ■ Sustained temperatures above 80°F can cause cracked and woody roots.
6–8	16"–30"	1	1–3	■ Prune back several times during the season to encourage new, tender growth and delay flowering. ■ Plants become woody after about 3–4 years and should be replaced.
6–8	1'+	16	1	■ Grow from onion seed and harvest before the bulb forms. or grow from specialized scallion seed.
3–4	Up to 3' tall	1	2–3	■ Shade can help prevent bolting in summer heat. ■ After bolting, cut back for another flush of fall/winter growth. ■ Once established, plants can be divided easily.
4	6"–12"	4 mature 9 baby	2	■ Optimal growing temperature is 50°F–60°F; can withstand lows of 15°F–20°F. ■ Quick to bolt with hot and long days. ■ Seed 4–8 weeks before average last frost in spring and 6–8 weeks before average first frost in fall.
N/A	6"–12"	4	Plant ASAP	■ Fruit yield declines after 2–3 years. Replace oldest plants with new ones. ■ Different varieties produce at different times of year. ■ Plants can tolerate frost, but berries must be protected from freezing. ■ Trim runners from plants.
4–6	5"–7"	1	1–4	■ Frost sensitive. ■ Can be moved indoors in winter as potted plant. ■ May need support.
3–4	Bush types 1'–3' tall Vining 4'+	1 plant per 2 or more squares; grow in outer squares	6	■ Very sensitive to frost ■ Most have bush growth habit. Look for vining or compact-bush varieties. ■ Grow this extra-large plant on a trellis, if vining, or on the edge of the bed, if bush variety, so it can spill over the side.
Plant slips with 2–4 leaves	12" tall with 4'–8' long vines	1	N/A	■ Purchase sweet potato slips or root your own. ■ Grow in a top hat. ■ Grow on a trellis or the edge of the bed so vines can spill over the side.

CROP	FAMILY	SEASON	ANNUAL, PERENNIAL, OR BIENNIAL	DIRECT SEED OR TRANSPLANT	DAYS TO GERMINATION	IDEAL GERMINATION CONDITIONS
Swiss chard	Chenopodiaceae	Cool	Annual	Either	5–7	40°F–95°F 85°F is optimal Seed ½"–1" deep.
Tatsoi	Brassicaceae	Cool	Annual	Either	5–15	Soil temperature 49°F–86°F Seed ¼" deep.
Thyme	Lamiaceae	Warm	Perennial	Transplant, plus cuttings and divisions	14–21+	65°F–70°F
Tomatillo	Solanaceae	Warm	Annual	Either	7–10	80°F Seed ½" deep.
Tomatoes	Solanaceae	Warm	Annual	Transplant	6–12	60°F–95°F 75°F–90°F is optimal. Seed ⅛"–¼" deep.
Turmeric	Zingiberaceae	Warm	Annual	Plant rhizomes	N/A	60°F–80°F Plant 2"–4" inches deep.
Turnips	Brassicaceae	Cool	Annual	Direct seed	4–7	45°F–85°F Seed ¼"–½" deep.
Watermelon	Cucurbitaceae	Warm	Annual	Either	3–10	60°F–95°F Germinates quickest at 90°F. Seed ½" deep.
Winter squash	Cucurbitaceae	Warm	Annual	Either	7	60°F–105°F

WEEKS TO TRANSPLANT	MATURE HEIGHT	# PER SFG SQUARE	SEED VIABILITY (YEARS)	NOTES
4	1'–3'	4	4	■ Chard grows from seedballs that produce more than one plant and require thinning. ■ May bolt with prolonged freezing temperatures in spring. ■ Prefers partial sun when it's hot.
4	10"	4 baby greens 1 maturo hoad	3	■ Can handle temperatures down to 15°F. ■ Longer days and warmer temperatures will cause tatsoi to bolt.
8–10	6"–12"	1	3	■ Seeds are difficult to germinate. Start with a transplant, cutting, or division. ■ Cut back in early spring and summer to reduce woody growth. ■ Look for common thyme, not creeping thyme, in different flavor profiles.
6–8	3'–4'	1 per square; prune heavily	6	■ Use a trellis or a cage to keep this sprawling plant upright. ■ Best production with 2 or more plants for cross-pollination.
6–8	10'+ vines for indeterminate varieties; 2'–5' determinate	1 with trellising for indeterminate types; 1 per 4 squares with supports for determinate types	4	■ Tomatoes need at least 8 hours of direct sun. ■ Transplants should have 5–7 leaves before planting. ■ Dwarf varieties may not need supports.
N/A	2'–3'	4	Plant that season	■ Grow in a top hat if hilling. ■ Plant in shallow Mel's Mix, and add more as the plant grows. ■ Transplant when temperature is consistently 60°F or above.
N/A	1'–2'	9 larger turnips 16 smaller turnips and salad varieties	4	■ Light frost improves flavor, but hard freezes will damage roots. ■ Protect from pests with row cover.
2–4	1'–2' tall with 3'–20' vines	1 for bush types or 1 per 2 or more squares, depending on the variety	4	■ Grow on a trellis or allow vines to grow over the side of the SFG box. ■ Protect from pests with row cover early in the season; remove before flowering. ■ Look for mini melon varieties.
3–4	1½'–3' tall with 3'–20' vines	1 for bush types; 1 per 2 or more squares for large types	6	■ Grow on a trellis or allow vines to grow over the side of the SFG box. ■ Protect from pests with row cover early in the season; remove before flowering.

Harvest Readiness Chart

CROP	DAYS TO HARVEST (FROM SEED)	HARVEST INDICATORS
Arugula (baby)	35 for baby; 40–50 mature	• Harvest baby arugula starting at a few inches tall. • Harvest when mature from 6". • Harvest leaves before bolting; eat flowers in salads.
Asparagus	3–4 years from seed; 1 year when planted as crowns	• Spears emerge in early springtime. • Harvest when $\frac{3}{8}$" diameter and 5"–8" tall.
Basil	60–80	• Begin harvesting when the plant is 18" tall. • Harvest before blooming for best flavor.
Beans (bush or pole)	50–70	• Harvest when pods are 4"–6" long and not quite pencil thickness. • If harvesting dry beans, wait until whole pod is brown and beans no longer give.
Beets	50–70	• Harvest when root shoulder pushes up out of the ground and roots reach desired size.
Bitter melon/bitter gourd	40–63	• Harvest when fruit are 4"–8" long and skin is still green, about 15–20 days after fruit set.
Bok choy/pak choy	40–50	• Harvest leaves beginning at a few inches tall. • Harvest whole head when filled out. • Harvest before bolting.
Broccoli	75–95	• Let the whole head form. • Harvest when buds are small and closed. • For broccoli leaves: Harvest 2–4 outer leaves at a time.
Broccoli rabe	40–100	• Harvest before buds open, at 10"–15" tall.
Brussels sprouts	100–200	• Harvest small, dense heads with tightly closed leaves.
Cabbage (head cabbage)	60–90	• Harvest when heads are dense and don't give when you squeeze them.
Callaloo/amaranth	30–55	• Harvest when leaves are hand sized. • When the plant bolts, it will set amaranth seeds, which are also edible.
Cantaloupe/ muskmelon	85–100	• The fruit will slip easily from the vine when it is rotated. • Ripe cantaloupe has a strong scent and a netting pattern on the rind.
Carrots	60–80	• Harvest when roots reach the desired size. Clear soil from the top of the root to see the "shoulder" size, which is a good indicator of the full root size.
Cauliflower	80–110	• Harvest when heads are firm and compact.
Chamomile	60–65	• Harvest when flowers are near full bloom. • Flowers not harvested can reseed and become weedy.

HARVEST PROCESS	STORAGE TIPS	PRESERVATION TIPS
■ For baby arugula, cut individual leaves, or use cut-and-come-again method (see page 59). ■ For mature arugula, cut outer leaves with scissors or a knife so inner leaves continue growing.	✔ Arugula is delicate. Don't wash before storing. ✔ Keep loose in a plastic bag, and store in the refrigerator drawer.	Make pesto and freeze
■ Two years after planting crowns, harvest for up to 2 weeks. The following year, harvest for up to 4 weeks. Then harvest freely. ■ Grip the spear near the base with thumb and forefinger, and cut with harvest shears or bend until it snaps.	✔ Refrigerate in a glass of water—like flowers in a vase—for up to 3 weeks.	Blanch and freeze
■ Harvest early in the day after dew dries. ■ With snips or your fingernails, cut basil just above the leaf buds—the points where new leaves emerge. ■ Harvest up to ⅓ of the plant at a time.	✔ Basil will turn black when exposed to cold refrigerator air. ✔ Keep in a glass of water on the counter for several days.	Dehydrate Make pesto and freeze in ice cube trays.
■ Hold the plant with one hand, and pull down on the pod with the other.	✔ Store fresh beans in a perforated bag in the refrigerator crisper drawer for up to a week. ✔ Store dry beans in a cool, dry place.	Blanch and freeze Pressure can Pickle (dilly beans)
■ Grip the beet greens where they meet the root and pull straight up.	✔ Separate greens and roots. ✔ Keep each in a plastic bag in the refrigerator drawer. ✔ Roots will last for weeks; greens for a few days.	Blanch and freeze greens Pickle roots Ferment roots
■ Cut the fruit stalk from the vine using scissors.	✔ Eat within a few days of harvest. ✔ Wrap in damp paper towels, and refrigerate in a perforated plastic bag or crisper drawer.	Dehydrate Blanch and freeze
■ Harvest the whole head by cutting just above the soil line. ■ Harvest outer leaves over a period of months.	✔ Keep for a week or 2 wrapped in plastic in the refrigerator.	Best eaten fresh
■ Snap off leaves at the base of the plant. ■ Use a knife to slice the broccoli at the base of the head. ■ Harvest side shoots a few weeks later.	✔ Refrigerate immediately. ✔ Store in a plastic bag in the refrigerator drawer for up to 2 weeks.	Blanch and freeze
■ Cut just above where the stem is tough. ■ Leave two full leaves intact to resprout.	✔ Store, unwashed, in a plastic bag in the refrigerator for up to 5 days.	Blanch and freeze
■ Snap off individual heads.	✔ Store in a paper bag in the refrigerator drawer for up to 2 weeks.	Blanch and freeze
■ Cut cabbage with a knife at the base of the head. ■ Remove and compost soiled outer leaves.	✔ Store in the refrigerator drawer for a couple of months. ✔ Wrap in plastic after cutting.	Ferment and refrigerate; blanch and freeze
■ Hand-pick leaves at the stem.	✔ Keep in a perforated plastic bag in the refrigerator.	Blanch and freeze
■ Give it a slight amount of pressure. If you have to cut the vine, the melon is not ripe.	✔ Keep it whole on the kitchen counter for up to 1 week. ✔ Once cut, keep in a sealed container in the refrigerator for a few days.	Purée and freeze
■ Loosen soil, if necessary. ■ Grip tops where they meet the root, and pull straight up.	✔ Separate greens and roots. ✔ Keep each in plastic bags in the refrigerator drawer. ✔ Roots will last for weeks; greens for a few days.	Pickle or ferment roots Blanch and freeze Dehydrate Make pesto with the tops
■ Use a knife to slice the cauliflower at the base of the head.	✔ Store in a perforated plastic bag in the refrigerator drawer for up to 4 weeks.	Blanch and freeze
■ Snip the flower at the stem.	✔ Use right away	Dehydrate

CROP	DAYS TO HARVEST (FROM SEED)	HARVEST INDICATORS
Celery	210	❦ Harvest when the stalks are 8"–12" tall.
Chives	60	❦ Harvest when the greens are 6" or taller. ❦ Flower stalks are tough, but flowers are edible.
Cilantro/coriander	45–80	❦ Harvest when greens are 6" or taller. ❦ Harvest before bolting (flowering) for fresh herbs. ❦ Allow to bolt for coriander seeds.
Collard greens	42	❦ Begin harvesting when leaves are as big as your hand. ❦ Harvest until the plant bolts.
Corn (sweet)	60–100	❦ Ears mature 17–24 days from silk emergence. ❦ Silks will dry and turn brown; husks remain moist and green. ❦ Kernels in the tip of the ear should be plump and juicy.
Cucamelons	70–75	❦ Harvest up to 1" long
Cucumbers	55–65	❦ Harvest pickling cucumbers at 2"–4" long; slicing cucumbers at 6"–8" long.
Dill	40–55	❦ Harvest when greens are 6" or taller. ❦ Allow to bolt for dill seeds or use fresh flower heads for making dill pickles or dilly beans.
Eggplant	90–110	❦ Harvest when fruit skin is glossy.
Fennel (bulb)	50–90	❦ Harvest when bulb reaches desired size.
Fennel (herb/leaf)	50–60	❦ Harvest fresh fennel fronds when stalks reach 12" or taller. ❦ Harvest seeds when dry and brown.
Garlic	250–270 from cloves; may be a shorter growing season in warm climates depending on the type of garlic planted	❦ Harvest in the summer, when the 4 lower leaves die back.
Ginger	5–8 months for baby; 9–12 for mature (from rhizomes)	❦ Harvest all ginger before frost. ❦ Harvest mature ginger when the tops have died back.
Ground cherry	100	❦ Pick when husks are dry and fruit begin to fall from the plant.
Kale	25 for baby; 60+ mature	❦ Harvest when leaves reach desired size.
Kohlrabi	60	❦ Harvest when the bulbous stem reaches desired size.
Komatsuna	20–38 for baby; 35+ mature	❦ Harvest baby leaves when a few inches tall. ❦ Harvest whole plant when upright head forms.

HARVEST PROCESS	STORAGE TIPS	PRESERVATION TIPS
■ To harvest individual stalks: Snap off the stalks at the base of the plant, starting with outside stalks. ■ To harvest the whole head: Cut the entire plant with a knife just above the soil surface.	✔ Store in a plastic bag in the refrigerator drawer.	Blanch and freeze stalks Dehydrate leaves
■ Snip 1"–2" above the soil line.	✔ Store in a plastic bag in the refrigerator drawer for a few days.	Dehydrate Chop, put in ice cube trays with some water, and freeze
■ Snip fresh cilantro 1"–2" above the soil line. ■ For coriander seeds, allow seedpod to dry, then pluck from plant.	✔ Store fresh cilantro in a plastic bag in the refrigerator drawer for a week. ✔ Keep dried coriander seeds in a sealed container.	Make cilantro pesto and freeze
■ Snap off outer leaves by hand. ■ Leave 4 or more inner leaves to continue growth.	✔ Store in a plastic bag in the refrigerator drawer.	Blanch and freeze
■ Hold ear firmly, pull down, and twist off from the stalk.	✔ Best to use immediately. ✔ Store in a paper bag in the refrigerator drawer, if necessary.	Blanch and freeze Pressure can
■ Snip from the vine.	✔ Store in a perforated plastic bag in the refrigerator drawer.	Ferment Quick pickle
■ Snip from the vine.	✔ Store in a perforated plastic bag in the refrigerator drawer.	Ferment Pickle and pressure can Quick pickle and refrigerate
■ Snip 1"–2" above soil surface for greens. ■ Snip whole flower heads from plant for fresh flower use. ■ Pluck seeds from plant when dry and brown.	✔ Store fresh dill in a plastic bag in the refrigerator drawer for a week. ✔ Keep dried seeds in a sealed container.	Make fresh dill pesto and freeze. Dehydrate fresh dill.
■ Snip the stem 1" from the fruit.	✔ Keep on the counter for a few days or in a plastic bag in the refrigerator for up to a week.	Best eaten fresh
■ Use a knife to cut the bulb just above the taproot.	✔ Prune stems to 1"–2" from the bulbs. ✔ Store each in a plastic bag in the crisper drawer; up to 2 weeks for bulbs, 1 week for stems.	Best eaten fresh
■ Snip fresh stalks at the base of the plant. ■ Pluck dry, brown seeds from seed heads.	✔ Best to use fresh fronds right away. ✔ Dried seeds in a sealed container.	Dehydrate fresh fennel
■ Loosen the Mel's Mix around the plant, and pull straight up on the stalk.	✔ For long-term storage, cure garlic until outer layers are brown and papery by hanging the whole plant in a dry place with good airflow. Then, store in a cool, dry area. ✔ For fresh garlic, cut the bulb from the stalk, and keep the bulb in a plastic bag in the refrigerator.	Slice and dehydrate; grind into powder. Shred and freeze in ice cube trays with olive oil. Roast, purée, and freeze in ice cube trays.
■ Loosen the soil around the grid square, and carefully lift the ginger plant from the base of the stalks.	✔ Store unpeeled ginger in a plastic bag in the fridge for 2–3 weeks.	Freeze Mince and dehydrate
■ Pick up ripe fruit from the ground. ■ Pluck by hand with little pressure—if it's ripe, it'll give.	✔ Keep in husks 2–3 months in the refrigerator. Use those with opened or damaged husks within 10 days.	Freeze Make jam or jelly Dehydrate
■ Snip leaves from plant. ■ Harvest baby kale using cut-and-come-again method, or cut individual leaves.	✔ Store in a plastic bag in the refrigerator drawer for 7–10 days.	Blanch and freeze mature kale
■ Cut bulb just above taproot.	✔ Separate greens from bulb and store in plastic bags in the refrigerator drawer.	Blanch and freeze
■ For baby greens, cut individual leaves or use cut-and-come-again method. ■ For mature head, use a knife to cut off the head at soil level.	✔ Store in a plastic bag in the refrigerator drawer.	Blanch and freeze mature greens

CROP	DAYS TO HARVEST (FROM SEED)	HARVEST INDICATORS
Lavender	100–110	❦ Harvest just as the flowers start to open for the strongest scent.
Leeks	70–120	❦ Harvest leeks at 1" or larger diameter. ❦ The top growth should be dark blue-green. ❦ Leeks are cold-tolerant and can be harvested after the first frost or overwintered.
Lemongrass	75–85 for stalks; less for leaves	❦ Harvest leaves any time; stalks at ½" or larger diameter.
Lettuce (head lettuce)	70–80	❦ Harvest when heads reach acceptable size and firmness.
Lettuce (leaf lettuce)	25 for baby; 60 mature	❦ Harvest when leaves are desired size.
Luffa/loofa	150+ for sponges; less for edible squash	❦ For sponges, harvest when the skin feels loose and brittle around the hardened fibers inside, or harvest at the frost and continue drying indoors. ❦ For eating, harvest when small and tender.
Malabar spinach	50	❦ Young leaves have the best flavor. ❦ Flowers and berries are edible.
Mizuna	21 for baby; up to 50 mature	❦ Begin harvesting baby mizuna when leaves are a few inches tall. ❦ Harvest in the morning, after the dew dries but before heat softens the greens.
Mustard greens	45–50	❦ Harvest starting when leaves are 4"–5" long. ❦ Leaves are spicier in hot, dry conditions. ❦ Harvest before bolting.
Napa cabbage	70–90	❦ Heads should feel firm and dense. ❦ Harvest before bolting.
Okra	80–90	❦ Pick when pods are 2"–3" long, about 5 days after flowering. ❦ Plant will stop producing if pods aren't harvested.
Onions (bulb)	100–120	❦ Harvest onions when about half the tops are falling over and dry.
Onions (pearl)	90	❦ Harvest after tops have fallen and dried thoroughly.
Oregano	80–90	❦ Harvest any time, ideally just before the plants flower.
Parsley	90–100	❦ Harvest when stems become a usable size.

HARVEST PROCESS	STORAGE TIPS	PRESERVATION TIPS
■ Use scissors to cut the stems above the leaves. Do not harvest more than ⅓ of the plant at once.	✔ Use right away, or keep in a glass of water like a bouquet.	Dehydrate
■ Gently twist and pull them from the bed, or loosen the soil with a trowel and lift them.	✔ Wrap unwashed leeks in plastic and store for up to 2 weeks in the refrigerator crisper drawer. ✔ Leeks may impart allium flavor on other foods; wrap well.	Dehydrate
■ Harvest leaves by cutting with scissors. ■ Harvest stalks by using a sharp knife to cut as close to the root as possible, or by bending the stalk and twisting. ■ Wear gloves, as leaf edges are sharp.	✔ Use leaves fresh, or dry for later use. ✔ Use stalk fresh, refrigerate it wrapped in plastic for a few days, or freeze up to 6 months.	Dehydrate leaves Freeze stalks
■ Use a knife to cut the stem just above the soil level.	✔ Refrigerate in a plastic bag in the produce drawer. ✔ Most store up to 3 weeks; butterheads keep only a few days.	Best eaten fresh
■ Cut outer leaves with scissors or a knife so inner leaves continue growing. ■ Use cut-and-come-again method for baby lettuce.	✔ Use immediately for the best quality. ✔ To store, wash, spin dry, and refrigerate in a plastic bag in the crisper drawer.	Best eaten fresh
■ Cut from the vine with a couple of inches of stem attached.	✔ Keep dried sponges in a dry location. ✔ Refrigerate small, young luffa for eating in a perforated plastic bag in the crisper drawer.	Dry for sponges
■ Cut with scissors or your fingertips. ■ Harvest 8"–12" of tender tips and leaves at a time.	✔ Refrigerate for up to 4 days wrapped in plastic in the refrigerator door.	Blanch and freeze
■ Harvest the mature plant by cutting the whole plant just above the soil level. ■ For baby greens, snip individual leaves or use the cut-and-come-again method.	✔ Wash, spin or pat dry, bag, and store in the refrigerator drawer. ✔ Mizuna should keep for more than a week—particularly mature leaves.	Blanch and freeze
■ Cut outer leaves and let inner leaves continue developing.	✔ Keep in a plastic bag in the refrigerator drawer.	Blanch and freeze
■ Use a knife to cut off the head at the base. ■ Leave one set of outer leaves.	✔ Napa cabbage will store for weeks wrapped in plastic in the coldest part of your fridge.	Ferment in kimchi or sauerkraut and refrigerate
■ Cut from the main stalk with pruners. ■ Some varieties have fine hairs that cause skin irritation. Wear gloves.	✔ Refrigerate unwashed, dry okra pods in the crisper, loosely wrapped in perforated plastic bags. ✔ Keeps for only 2–3 days.	Pressure can Blanch and freeze Dehydrate Pickle
■ Gently pull bulbs from the soil with the tops attached.	✔ To store onions, cure in a well-ventilated 75°F–90°F area for 2 to 4 weeks, until outer bulb scales are dry and neck is tight. Then store in a cool, dry area. ✔ To eat fresh, refrigerate in a plastic bag. Onions will impart flavor on other foods if not kept in a sealed container.	Best eaten fresh Dice, blanch, and dehydrate
■ Gently pull from soil.	✔ See bulb onions, above.	Pickle
■ Cut stem tips, leaving 4 to 6 pairs of leaves to produce branching shoots. ■ Flowering reduces or stops growth for the season and reduces the flavor.	✔ Keep for a few days in a glass of water, like a bouquet.	Dehydrate Air or oven dry
■ Snip off stalks at least 1"–1¼" above the ■ crown, beginning with outside stalks.	✔ Wash, drip dry, and store in a plastic bag in the refrigerator.	Dehydrate Freeze

CROP	DAYS TO HARVEST (FROM SEED)	HARVEST INDICATORS
Parsnips	100–120	• Harvest when roots are 1" or more diameter, ideally after exposure to several light freezes. • Overwinter with a heavy layer of mulch, and harvest in spring, before bolting.
Peas (shelling)	60–65	• Harvest as soon as peas are slightly larger than the dry seed for sweet, tender, thin-skinned peas.
Peas (snap)	58	• Harvest when pods appear almost filled with peas. • Quality diminishes when peas are over-mature.
Peas (snow)	60	• Harvest when pods reach the length on the seed packet. • Peas inside pods should be barely visible.
Peppers (all kinds)	80–100	• Harvest in their green, immature state or wait until color develops for best flavor.
Potatoes (mature)	90–120 from seed potatoes	• Harvest when plants have dried.
Potatoes (new)	50–60 from seed potatoes	• Harvest 7–8 weeks after planting.
Pumpkins	85–120	• Harvest when they've developed a uniform color and have a hard rind. • Harvest before a hard freeze.
Radishes (daikon)	20–60	• Harvest at any size before bolting.
Radishes (salad types)	20–60	• The top of the radish often emerges from the soil. Harvest at desired size. • Harvest before bolting.
Radishes (winter types)	50	• Allow radishes to grow large. • Harvest before bolting.
Recao/culantro/ Vietnamese coriander	50–60	• Harvest when leaves are the desired size. • Harvest before bolting, or it may reseed.
Rosemary	80–100	• Harvest as needed once tips reach a usable size.
Rutabaga	90	• Harvest when the edible root is 4"–5" in diameter. • Frost improves flavor. • Rutabagas will keep in the ground for weeks.
Sage	75	• Harvest as needed when the plant reaches a usable size.

HARVEST PROCESS	STORAGE TIPS	PRESERVATION TIPS
■ Grip parsnip tops where they meet the root, and pull straight up. ■ Loosen soil with a trowel, if necessary.	✔ Store in coldest part of refrigerator in a plastic bag or unbagged in the crisper drawer for several months.	Blanch and freeze
■ Hold plant with one hand, and pull off the pod with the other.	✔ Shell and cool immediately. ✔ Keep more than a week in a plastic bag in the refrigerator.	Blanch and freeze Pressure can
■ Hold plant with one hand, and pull off the pod with the other.	✔ Cool immediately. ✔ Keep more than a week in a plastic bag in the refrigerator.	Blanch and freeze
■ Hold plant with one hand, and pull off the pod with the other.	✔ Cool immediately. ✔ Keep more than a week in a plastic bag in the refrigerator.	Blanch and freeze
■ Cut from plant using harvest snips. ■ Wear gloves when picking hot peppers, and wash your hands afterward.	✔ Store in a warmer part of the fridge for 1 to 2 weeks.	Dehydrate Pickle Freeze In canning recipes
■ Dig tubers on a dry day. ■ Loosen soil around the plant, taking care not to pierce potatoes in the process. Pull up on the base of the plant. ■ Run your hand through the Mel's Mix to find potatoes that have fallen off.	✔ Cure in a dark, well-ventilated 60°F–65°F area for 10 days. ✔ Gently brush soil off the tubers, but do not wash. ✔ Don't refrigerate for long-term storage.	Pressure can Slice, blanch, and dehydrate
■ Dig your hand to the bottom of the SFG box, and turn the whole potato plant upside down to pick the tubers. ■ If growing in a top hat, you can dig beside the plant and take a few potatoes, but leave the plants in place to produce mature potatoes.	✔ New potatoes are dug before skins have thickened. Keep in a paper bag in the fridge for 1 to 2 weeks. ✔ Remove any green sections before eating.	Pressure can
■ Handle carefully to avoid cuts and bruises. ■ Cut the fruit from the vine with pruning shears. ■ Leave a 3"–4" stem. ■ Do not carry the fruit by the stems.	✔ To store and develop flavor, cure at 80°F to 85°F and a relative humidity of 80% to 85%. ✔ After curing, store in a cool, dry place at 50°F to 55°F—not the fridge. ✔ Rinse, roast, and eat the seeds, as well.	Freeze Pressure can
■ Daikon radishes are long and can snap off. Use a trowel to loosen Mel's Mix before harvesting. ■ Grasp the top of the root, and pull straight up.	✔ Remove greens. ✔ Wash and dry roots. ✔ Keep greens and roots in their own plastic bags in the refrigerator crisper drawer.	Ferment in kimchi Pickle
■ Grasp the greens at the bulb, and pull.	✔ See daikon radish, above.	Ferment
■ Grasp the greens at the bulb, and pull.	✔ See daikon radish, above.	Ferment
■ Cut the whole plant at the base. ■ Harvest individual leaves from the stalk.	✔ Wrap loosely in a damp paper towel, and keep in a plastic bag in the crisper drawer for up to 1 week.	Blend with olive oil and freeze
■ Harvest the top few inches of stems using scissors. ■ Do not remove more than 20% of the plant at a time. ■ Avoid cutting into woody parts unless to shape the plant.	✔ Use fresh, or keep for a few days in a glass of water, like a bouquet.	Dehydrate
■ Rutabagas are large. Use a trowel to loosen Mel's Mix before pulling.	✔ Remove the greens and long, thin taproot before storing in a plastic bag in the crisper drawer. ✔ Rutabagas may sprout after a few weeks in the refrigerator.	Best eaten fresh
■ Cut with scissors at leaf growing points so the plant produces branching side shoots.	✔ Pack loosely in plastic and store in the refrigerator for up to 2 weeks. ✔ Do not wash before storing.	Dehydrate

CROP	DAYS TO HARVEST (FROM SEED)	HARVEST INDICATORS
Scallions/green onions	50	❦ Harvest when they reach a usable size.
Sorrel	60	❦ Harvest from early spring until frost kills the growth. ❦ Young leaves are more tender than older leaves.
Spinach	28+ for baby; up to 55 for mature	❦ Tastes best before the heat of summer. ❦ Harvest baby and mature spinach when leaves are the desired size.
Strawberries	90–100 from transplant	❦ Fruit ripens about 4 weeks after flowering. ❦ Pick when the berry is fully colored.
Summer savory	60	❦ Cut leafy tops when plants start to show buds.
Summer squash/zucchini	50–75	❦ Harvest when fruit are shiny or glossy. ❦ Too-large fruit will have large seeds and be less tender. ❦ Harvest baby fruit at a few inches long.
Sweet potatoes	85–120 from slips	❦ Harvest just before first frost or when leaves turn yellow and the vine starts to die back.
Swiss chard	55–65 days	❦ Harvest when leaves are 3" or taller.
Tatsoi	25 baby; 45 mature	❦ Baby leaves are ready at a few inches. ❦ Wait until full rosette forms to harvest whole head.
Thyme	90–95	❦ Harvest as needed once plant reaches a usable size.
Tomatillo	75–100	❦ Harvest when the fruit is firm and fills the papery husk. ❦ If any drop from the plant before ripening, store in husks at room temperature until fully ripe.
Tomatoes	90–120	❦ Leave fruit on the vine until they've developed their full color and flavor. ❦ Harvest all tomatoes before a frost to continue ripening indoors. ❦ Cherry tomatoes are generally the first of the varieties to ripen.
Turmeric	9–10 months for mature turmeric; sooner for baby (from rhizomes)	❦ Harvest when leaves die back. ❦ Harvest before frost, even if leaves are still green.
Turnips	38–50	❦ Harvest when roots are 2"–4" in diameter; smaller for salad varieties. ❦ Flavor deteriorates in hot weather. ❦ Can hold in SFG bed over winter with mulching.
Watermelon	75–100	❦ Harvest when the tendril closest to the fruit becomes brown and dry. ❦ Watermelons do not ripen after harvest.
Winter squash	60–100	❦ Harvest when the rind is firm and doesn't dent when pressed with a fingernail. ❦ Vines die back and stems become hard when squash are ready.

HARVEST PROCESS	STORAGE TIPS	PRESERVATION TIPS
■ Grasp stem at soil level, and pull straight up. ■ Loosen Mel's Mix with a trowel to avoid breaking the plant, if needed.	✔ Store in plastic bags in the refrigerator crisper for up to a week. ✔ Can impart flavor on other foods in the drawer.	Best eaten fresh
■ Cut individual leaves at the stalk.	✔ Store leaves in a plastic bag in the refrigerator for up to 2 weeks.	Blanch and freeze Dehydrate
■ Pick individual leaves off the stalk. ■ Use the cut-and-come-again method for baby spinach.	✔ Store in a plastic bag with a damp paper towel for up to 5 days.	Blanch and freeze
■ Harvest after the dew dries in the morning. ■ Keep harvested berries out of direct sunlight. ■ Put one hand on the plant, and pull the berry with the other, retaining the cap.	✔ Refrigerate as soon as possible. ✔ Do not wash until just prior to use.	Freeze Make jam
■ Snip a few inches from each stem.	✔ Store in the refrigerator in a plastic bag.	Dehydrate Freeze
■ With a sharp knife, cut the stem at the plant.	✔ Store in a plastic bag in the refrigerator crisper for up to 1 week.	Slice, cube, or shred and freeze Pickle Pressure can
■ Dig on a dry day. ■ Loosen soil around the plant, taking care not to pierce sweet potatoes in the process. Pull up on the base of the vine. ■ Run your hand through the Mel's Mix to find sweet potatoes that have fallen off.	✔ Cure for storage in an 80°F to 90°F space at high humidity for 5 to 10 days. ✔ Once cured, store around 60°F and high humidity for up to a year. ✔ Do not refrigerate; this will cause cold damage.	Pressure can Bake or boil and freeze
■ Cut or snap off leaves at base of the plant. ■ Harvest early or late in the day to avoid wilting.	✔ Keep in a plastic bag in the refrigerator crisper.	Blanch and freeze
■ Trim baby leaves with scissors. ■ Cut the whole head just above the soil line with a sharp knife.	✔ Keep up to 1 week wrapped in a damp towel or in a plastic bag in the refrigerator drawer.	Best eaten fresh
■ Harvest the top few inches of stems using scissors.	✔ Use fresh, or keep for a few days in a glass of water, like a bouquet.	Dehydrate
■ Hold the plant with one hand while plucking the fruit with the other.	✔ Store in the husk in a paper bag in the refrigerator for up to 3 weeks.	Freeze Can
■ Hold the plant with one hand, and pull off the fruit with the other. Or, cut the fruit off the vine. ■ Be careful to not bruise the tomato when handling.	✔ Store at room temperature. ✔ Rest slicing tomatoes on their "shoulders"— stem-end down.	Can Freeze Dehydrate
■ Loosen the soil around the grid square, and carefully lift the turmeric plant from the base of the stalks.	✔ Store, unpeeled, in a plastic bag in the refrigerator for several weeks.	Freeze Mince and dehydrate
■ Grasp greens where they meet the bulb, and pull straight up.	✔ Separate greens and roots. ✔ Keep each in plastic bags in the crisper drawer. ✔ Roots will last for weeks or months; greens for a few days.	Ferment
■ Cut from the vine, leaving 2" of stem on the fruit.	✔ Keep at room temperature for 1 week or in the warmer part of your refrigerator for 2 to 3 weeks.	Best eaten fresh
■ Cut from the vine with pruning shears, leaving a few inches of stem.	✔ Cure at 80°F to 85°F and 80% to 85% humidity for a couple of weeks. ✔ Don't cure acorn squash. ✔ Store at 50% relative humidity, 50°F–55°F for 1 to 6 months, depending on the variety.	Pressure can Freeze

About the Square Foot Gardening Foundation

The Square Foot Gardening Foundation continues Mel Bartholomew's original message of growing more food in less space with less waste. Our mission, "Simplifying Organic Gardening and Nourishing Communities Worldwide," works to increase food security—one square foot at a time—so more families and communities can flourish by learning the empowering life skill of gardening and creating their own sustainable, sufficient, and reliable food source.

We are working, in collaboration with the larger gardening community, to make gardening accessible for everyone no matter their skill level or their unique location in the world.

Your purchase of this book helps the Square Foot Gardening Foundation's grant program support local organizations. The Foundation supports gardening projects and hosts a variety of educational opportunities for anyone wanting to learn the Square Foot Gardening Method.

Make a Difference

Support the Square Foot Gardening Foundation. By donating to the Foundation, you are nourishing brighter futures. Your support is helping alleviate food scarcity by making vegetable gardening easier and smarter with less waste. When growing food is simple, more families can eat, thrive, and be better prepared for the future. Growing one's own food changes lives. Every dollar you give will create real change.

Continue Your SFG Education

To learn more about Square Foot Gardening, check out our website to find a variety of different resources.

Acknowledgments

The Square Foot Gardening Foundation is so grateful to the thousands of dedicated Square Foot Gardeners around the world. Their input helps our SFG Team finc tune this successful gardening method while sticking to its core principles. We are especially grateful to our SFG team; Vanessa Gotthainer, Kateryna Horbach, Sigrid Anderson, Rick Bickling, and Wayne Schirner who all worked so diligently to help present the very latest material for this 4th edition of the *All New Square Foot Gardening* book.

Index